The SYBEX Prompter Series

AUTOCAD
INSTANT
REFERENCE

The SYBEX Prompter Series

We've designed the SYBEX Prompter Series to meet the evolving needs of software users, who want essential information presented in an accessible format. Our best authors have distilled their expertise into compact *Instant Reference* books you can use to look up the precise use of any command—its syntax, available options, and operation. More than just summaries, these books also provide realistic examples and insights into effective usage drawn from our authors' wealth of experience.

The SYBEX Prompter Series also includes these titles:

Lotus 1-2-3 Instant Reference
Greg Harvey and Kay Yarborough Nelson
WordPerfect Instant Reference
Greg Harvey and Kay Yarborough Nelson
WordPerfect 5 Instant Reference
Greg Harvey and Kay Yarborough Nelson
dBASE Instant Reference
Alan Simpson
Turbo BASIC Instant Reference
Douglas Hergert
DOS Instant Reference
Greg Harvey and Kay Yarborough Nelson
HyperTalk Instant Reference
Greg Harvey
WordStar Instant Reference
David J. Clark
Ventura Instant Reference
Matthew Holtz
Hard Disk Instant Reference
Judd Robbins
Excel Instant Reference
William J. Orvis

The SYBEX Prompter™ Series

AUTOCAD® INSTANT REFERENCE

George Omura

San Francisco • Paris • Düsseldorf • London

Acquisitions Editor: Dianne King
Series Editor: James A. Compton
Copy Editor: Deborah Craig
Technical Editor: Kenneth Morgan
Word Processors: Christine Mockel, Robert Myren
Technical Illustrations: Omura Illustration
Screen Graphics: Sonja Schenk
Desktop Publishing Specialist: Charles Cowens
Proofreader: Barbara Steuart
Production Artist: Jeff Giese
Indexer: Ted Laux

Series Book Designer: Ingrid Owen
Cover Design: Thomas Ingalls + Associates
Screen reproductions produced by XenoFont

Library of Congress Card Number: **89-60280**
ISBN **0-89588-548-4**
Manufactured in the United States of America
10 9 8 7 6 5 4 3 2 1

To my son, Arthur

ACKNOWLEDGMENTS

Book projects such as this require a team effort. My thanks and appreciation go to the many people at SYBEX who made the *AutoCAD Instant Reference* possible, particularly the following: Dianne King, who got things started; Jim Compton, who kept me on track; Deborah Craig, who clarified points large and small; and Ken Morgan, who made many valuable suggestions throughout.

At Autodesk, Inc., Patricia Peper was invaluable in furnishing current software.

Table of Contents

INTRODUCTION

This book is designed to be a single source of information that you can use quickly and easily. Suppose you are stymied by a function that does not work as planned or a command that produces unpredicted results, or say you want a quick refresher about a certain procedure. This book will help you quickly solve the problem at hand so that you can get on with your work.

The *AutoCAD Instant Reference* is intended to give you the information you need to get the most from AutoCAD's numerous features—the basic commands as well as the built-in functions that you may not use on a daily basis. It covers all versions up to release 10.

Who Should Use this Book

This book is designed for users who have some familiarity with AutoCAD: those who have a general idea of what they need to know but aren't quite sure how all of AutoCAD's features work. It is for both casual AutoCAD users who need to find basic information fast and experienced users who need to refresh their memory about a command.

If you are new to AutoCAD and want a tutorial format, you can read my *Mastering AutoCAD* (Sybex, 3rd edition 1989), which provides a wealth of tips and techniques useful to both beginning and advanced users. *AutoCAD Instant Reference* is an excellent companion to *Mastering AutoCAD*, offering highly encapsulated descriptions of every AutoCAD command and some of its advanced features.

How This Book Is Organized

The chapters in this book reflect the options on the AutoCAD root menu. Whenever you pick an option from the root menu, a submenu appears containing the relevant commands. Those root menu options are:

> Blocks, Dim, Display, Draw, Edit, Inquiry, Layer, Settings, Plot, Ucs, Utility, 3D, and Ashade

For example, all of the commands that deal with drawing are in the Draw chapter (4) in alphabetical order. All of the editing commands are in the Edit chapter (5) in alphabetical order, and so on. The AutoCAD, Setup, and Asterisks options are described in Appendix A.

A few commands appear in two AutoCAD submenus. When this occurs, the command is presented here in the chapter most relevant to it. For example, the Insert command appears in both the Draw and the Block submenus. However, since Insert is more closely related to blocks, its entry in this book is in the Block chapter (1). Similarly, the 3dface command appears in both the Draw and 3D menus. Since it is a three-dimensional object, however, it is covered in the 3D chapter (12).

Each entry presents the following information:

- The numbered AutoCAD versions in which the command is available
- The dialog or sequence of steps you use to invoke the command and provide AutoCAD with the associated information
- A brief explanation of each of the command's options
- A discussion of the command's usage, including its most common and effective applications, any restrictions on

its uses or interactions with other commands, and any special tips or warnings that may apply

- A list of related entries to consult for further information

Appendix A presents information on starting AutoCAD and getting around in its user interface. Appendix B shows how to install AutoCAD and configure it to your hardware setup. Appendix C shows how to load and use the AutoLISP programs supplied on the support disk that came with your AutoCAD package. Finally, Appendix D presents the commands for customizing AutoCAD, which do not appear on any of the program's menus.

CHAPTER 1
Block Commands

This chapter covers the commands on the Block menu. You use these commands to create and work with *blocks,* groups of drawing entities—lines, arcs, circles, and so on—that AutoCAD treats as single objects. Blocks are useful for organizing and manipulating drawings, and can store information in the form of attributes. You can turn a block into a separate drawing file or vice versa. Used carefully, blocks can be one of your most useful AutoCAD tools.

Attdef

Defines a block attribute

VERSIONS

1.4 and later

SEQUENCE OF STEPS

Command: **Attdef**(↵)

To select Attdef from the system menu: **Blocks | Attdef**

Attribute modes -- Invisible:N Constant:N Verify:N Preset:N Enter (ICVP) to change, RETURN when done:

[*Enter* ***I***, ***C***, ***V***, *or* ***P*** *to toggle option on or off or press ↵ to go to next prompt.*]

Attribute tag: [*Enter attribute name.*]

Attribute prompt: [*Enter prompt to be displayed for attribute input.*]

Default attribute value: <*default value for attribute input.*>

Start point or Align/Center/Fit/Middle/Right/Style: [*Enter coordinates, with the cursor select location of attribute text, or select option to determine orientation or style of attribute text.*]

Height (2.0000.: <*attribute text height*> [*Prompt appears only if current text style height is set to 0. Enter height or* (↵) *to accept default*]

Rotation angle <0>: [*Enter angle of attribute text.*]

OPTIONS

Invisible Makes the attribute invisible when inserted.

Constant Gives the attribute a value that you cannot change.

Verify Allows review of the attribute value after insertion.

Preset Automatically inputs the default attribute value on insertion. Unlike the Constant option, lets you change the input value of a preset attribute by using the Ddatte or Attedit commands.

Inserts a backslash where a blank space is required in an attribute prompt or default value

See **Text** for Attdef options related to location, style, and orientation of attributes.

USAGE

Attdef allows you to create a block attribute. A block containing an attribute will prompt you for information when you insert it into a drawing. This information is stored with the block either as visible or invisible text that you can extract and use in programs other than AutoCAD. To give a block an attribute, define the attribute with Attdef and then create a block making sure you include the attribute as part of the block. Later, when you insert the block (see **Block**), you will be prompted for the attribute values. A block can contain as many attributes as you want.

SEE ALSO

Attedit, Attdisp, Attext, Block, Ddatte, Insert, Text, Select/Point selection

Base

Defines drawing insertion point

VERSIONS

All versions

SEQUENCE OF STEPS

Command: **Base**(↵)

To select Base from the menu system: **Blocks | Base**

Base point <(0.0000,0.0000,0.0000>: [*Enter coordinate or pick a point using the cursor.*]

USAGE

When inserting one drawing into another, use Base to set the drawing's *base point*, a point of reference for insertion. The base point you select will be in relation to the WCS (World Coordinate System). The default base point for all drawings is the WCS origin point at coordinate 0,0,0. To select **Base** from the system menu, pick **Blocks** from the root menu and then **Base** from the Blocks menu.

SEE ALSO

Block, Insert, Select/Point selection

Block

Groups and saves set of objects

VERSIONS

All versions

SEQUENCE OF STEPS

Command: **Block**(↵)

To select Block from the system menu: **Blocks | Block**

Block name (or ?): [*Enter name for block. Enter a question mark to list existing blocks.*]

Insertion base point: [*Enter a coordinate value or pick a point to set the base point of the block.*]

Select objects: [*Pick objects to include in the block.*]

The objects you select will disappear, but you can restore them as individual objects by issuing the Oops command.

USAGE

Block allows you to group a set of drawing objects together to act as a single object. For example, you can draw a chair made up of lines and arcs and then select those entities into a block. You can then insert, copy, scale, stretch, or save the block as an external file. Blocks only exist within the drawing in which they are created. However, you can convert them into drawing files with the Wblock command. Blocks can also contain other blocks. You can include attributes in blocks to allow the input and storage of information; see **Attdef**.

If you attempt to create a block that has the same name as an existing block, you will see the prompt:

Block <*name*> already exists.

Redefine it? <N>

To redefine the existing block, enter **Y** for yes. The Block command will proceed as usual and will replace the existing block with the new one. If the existing block has been inserted into the drawing, the new block will appear in its place. If Regenauto has been turned off, the new block will not apear until you issue a Regen command.

The block's insertion point and orientation in 3D are determined by the UCS (User Coordinate System) active at the time you create the block. Later, when you insert the block, its UCS orientation will be aligned with the UCS active at the time of insertion.

SEE ALSO

Attedit, Attdisp, Attext, Ddatte, Insert, Regen, Reganauto, Select object options, Wblock

Insert

Inserts blocks into drawings

VERSIONS

All versions. Versions 9 and 10 support the insert presets and the Attdia system variable. Versions 2.5 and later support the Attreq system variable.

SEQUENCE OF STEPS

Command: **Insert**(↵)

To select Insert from the menu system: **Blocks | Insert**

Block name (or ?)<*last block inserted*>: [*Enter block or drawing name*]

Insertion point: [*Enter coordinate value, pick a point with cursor, or enter a preset option.*]

X scale factor <1> / Corner / XYZ: [*Enter an X scale factor,* ***C*** *for corner,* ***XYZ*** *to specify the individual X, Y,* *and Z scale factors, or ↵ to accept the default X scale factor of 1.*]

If you press ↵ without entering any value or option, the following prompt appears:

Y scale factor (default=X): [*Enter a Y scale factor or ↵ for the default Y=X scale factor.*]

Once you have entered a scale factor, the last prompt appears:

Rotation angle <0>: [*Enter rotation angle for block or pick point on screen to indicate angle.*]

This last prompt does not appear if you use the Rotate preset option.

OPTIONS

X scale factor	Allows you to scale the block in the X axis. If you enter a value, you will be prompted for the Y scale factor.
Corner	Allows you to enter the X and Y scale factors at once. To scale the block by a factor of 1 in the X axis and 2 in the Y axis, enter **C** at the *X scale factor* prompt and then enter **@1,2**. Entering a coordinate value or picking a point at the *X scale factor* prompt has the same effect.
XYZ	Allows you to give individual X, Y, and Z scale factors. You will be prompted for the factors.

The following options are available at the *Insertion point* prompt. They are called insert *presets* because they allow you to preset the scale and rotation angle of a block before you select an insertion point. Once you select a preset option, the dragged image will conform to the setting used.

Scale	Allows you to enter a single scale factor for the block. This factor governs X, Y, and Z axis scaling. You will not be prompted for a scale factor after you select the insertion point.
Xscale	Same as Scale but sets only X scale factor.
Yscale	Same as Scale but sets only Y scale factor.
Zscale	Same as scale but sets only Z scale factor.
Rotate	Allows you to enter a rotation angle for the block. You are not prompted for a rotation angle after you select the insertion point.
PScale	Same as Scale but used only while positioning the block for insertion. You are later prompted for a scale factor.
PXscale	Same as PScale but affects only X scale factor.
PYscale	Same as PScale but affects only Y scale factor.
PZscale	Same as PScale but affects only Z scale factor.
PRotate	Same as Rotate but used only while positioning the block for insertion. You are later prompted for a rotation factor.

USAGE

Insert enables you to insert blocks contained within the current file or to insert other drawing files. If a block has previously been inserted in your current drawing session, it will be the default block to be inserted. If you can't remember the name of a block, enter a question mark for a list of the blocks in the current file. Coordinate values are in relation to the current UCS. You can also drag the block using the cursor. The block will stretch along the X or Y axis depending on the direction of the cursor.

You can insert a block as its individual entities (rather than as a single object) by preceding its name with an asterisk at the *Block name* prompt. To bring in an external file as its individual entities, insert it in the normal way and then use the Explode command to break it into its individual components. You can also insert a mirror image of a block by entering a negative value at either the *X scale factor* or *Y scale factor* prompt.

If the inserted block or file contains an attribute and the Attreq system variable is set to 1, you will be prompted for the attribute information after you have entered the rotation angle. If the system variable Attdia is set to 1, a dialog box with the attribute prompts appears. The default setting for Attreq is 1. Attdia is normally set to 0.

You can also use Insert to replace or update a block with an external drawing file. For example, suppose you have a block in a currently opened file called Chair1 and you have an external drawing file called Chair2 containing a different chair drawing. You can replace the block Chair1 with the file Chair2 by entering **Chair1=Chair2** at the *Block name* prompt. If both the block and the external file names are the same, Chair1 for example, you can enter **Chair1=**. However, named objects in the current drawing have priority over those in an imported file. If an imported file contains a block with the same name as a block in the current file, the block in the imported file will not replace the current file's block. The same is true for layers, line types, and text styles.

When you attempt to replace blocks containing attributes, the old attributes will remain even though the block has been changed. The only solution is to delete the old block and then insert the new (external) block. See **Attredef.LSP** in Appendix C.

Finally, an external file will be inserted with its World Coordinate System aligned with the current User Coordinate System. A block will be inserted with its UCS orientation aligned with the current UCS.

SEE ALSO

Attdef, Base, Block, Explode, and the Setvar variables Attreq and Attdia

Minsert

Inserts multiple copies of block in array

VERSIONS

2.5 and later

SEQUENCE OF STEPS

Command: **Minsert**(↵)

To insert Minsert from the menu system: **Blocks | Minsert**

The prompts for Minsert are the same as those for the Insert command except for the following:

Rotation Angle <0>: [*Enter array angle*]

Number of rows (---) <1>: [*Enter number of rows in block array.*]

Number of columns (|||) <1>: [*number of columns in block array.*]

If the number of rows or columns is greater than one, you will see one of the following prompts:

Unit cell or distance between rows (---): [*Enter a distance or select distance using cursor.*]

Distance between columns (|||): [*Enter distance or select distance using cursor.*]

If both rows and columns are greater than one, you will get both prompts. A row and column array of the block will appear at the specified angle.

USAGE

Minsert allows you simultaneously to insert a block and create a rectangular array of that block. You can rotate the array by specifying an angle other than 0 at the *Rotation angle* prompt.

The entire array acts like one block. You cannot explode a block or use the asterisk option (see **Insert**) on a block inserted with Minsert.

SEE ALSO

Array, Insert

Wblock

Writes block to file

VERSIONS

All versions

SEQUENCE OF STEPS

Command: **Wblock**(↵)

To issue Wblock from the menu system: **Blocks** | **Wblock**

File name: [*Enter filename.*]

Block name: [*Enter block name or press ↵ to select a set of objects.*]

The block or set of objects will be written to your disk as a drawing file.

USAGE

Wblock writes a block in the current file or a selected part or all of a drawing file to a selected file. If you want the file name to be the same as the block name, enter an equal sign at the *Block name* prompt. If you enter the name of an existing file at the *File name* prompt, you will get the prompt:

A drawing with this name already exists.

Do you want to replace it? <N>

You can replace the file or return to the *Command* prompt to restart Wblock.

To write a portion of the current drawing view to a file, press ↵ without entering anything at the *Block name* prompt. You will get the following two prompts:

Insertion base point: [*Enter a coordinate or pick a point.*]

Select objects: [*Select objects using the standard AutoCAD selection options.*]

The objects you select will be written to your disk as a drawing file. The point you select at the *Insertion base point* prompt becomes the origin of the written file. The current UCS will become the WCS in the written file. When you save a block to disk, the UCS active at the time you create a block becomes the WCS of the written file.

You can write the entire current file to disk, stripping it of all unused blocks, layers, line types, and text styles, by entering an asterisk at the *Block name* prompt. This can reduce a file's size and access time.

SEE ALSO

Object selection, Base

CHAPTER 2

Dimensioning Commands

This chapter presents the commands that allow you to display the real-world dimensions of objects in an AutoCAD drawing. It begins with some general information about dimensioning in AutoCAD and the main dimensioning commands Dim and Dim1. The next section covers the dimension subcommands on the Dim menu. The chapter then discusses the subcommands for linear dimensioning on the Dim/Linear submenu as well as options for some of the more common subcommand prompts. The last section explores the dimension variables found on the Dim Vars submenu.

Dimensioning in AutoCAD

Dimensioning in AutoCAD generally involves the same types of dimensions and the same components of dimension labels used in standard drafting. Figure 2.1 illustrates the four types of dimensions you can show in AutoCAD drawings—linear, angular, diametric, and radial.

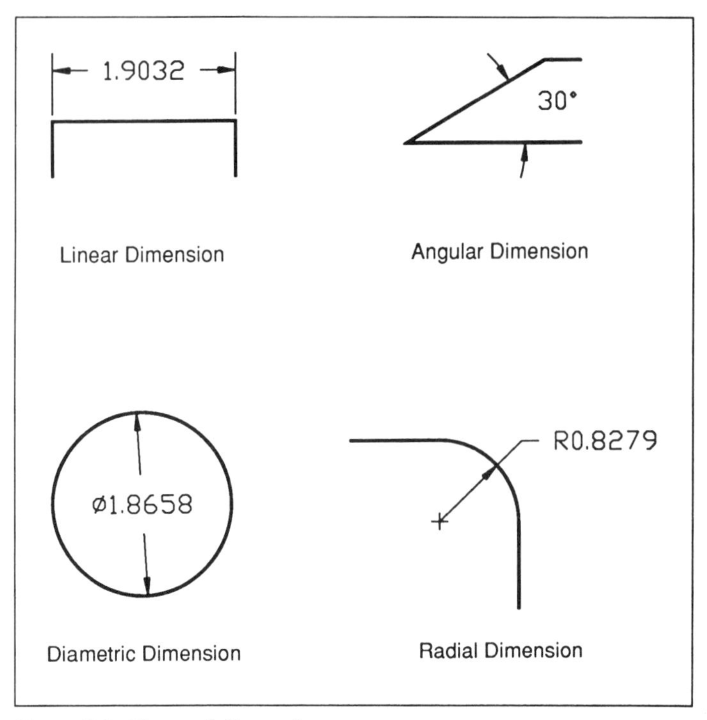

Figure 2.1: Types of dimensions

Dimension labels consist of some or all of the following elements, illustrated in Figure 2.2:

Definition points — The points you pick when you determine the dimension location, plus another point at the center of the dimension text. The definition points for linear dimensions are located at the extension line origin and the intersection of the extension line and the dimension line. The definition points for a circle diameter are the point used to pick the circle and the opposite point of the circle. The definition points for a radius are the points used to pick the circle, plus the center of the circle. The points are located on a layer called Defpoints. Definition points are displayed regardless of whether Defpoints is on, but you must turn Defpoints on to plot them. Definition points are used with *associative* dimensioning; see the next section.

Dimension text — At a minimum, a number indicating the value of the dimension in the specified or default units. May also include tolerance values, alternative units of measure, and descriptive text.

Dimension line — A line or arc with arrowheads or other symbols at each end, drawn at the angle at which the dimension is measured (for example, parallel and linear dimensions). Dimension text may be placed between (within), above, or beside these lines.

Extension lines — Lines drawn from the definition points perpendicular to the dimension line, indicating the end points of the line or arc being measured. Intersections of dimension and extension lines may be marked with arrowheads, tick marks, custom arrowheads, dots, blocks, or nothing. Space permitting, dimension lines are normally drawn between the extension lines.

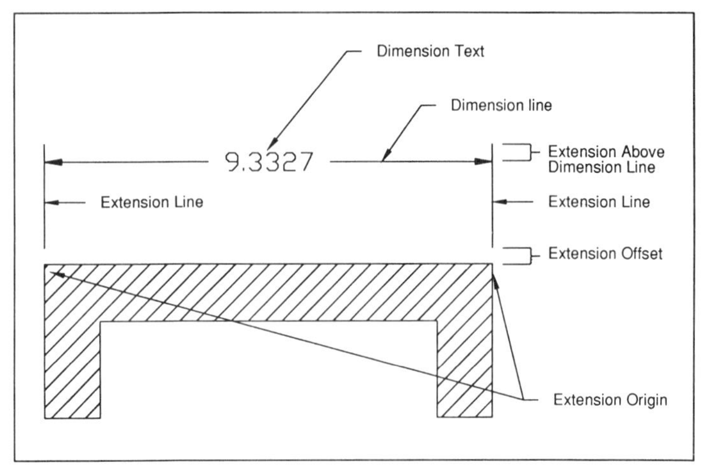

Figure 2.2: Components of dimension labels

Associative Dimensions

Associative dimensions are dimensions that are dynamically connected to *definition points* (in linear dimensions, the same points you pick when you are prompted for the extension line origin). When you move a definition point with the Stretch command, the dimension lines move with the point and the dimension text changes to reflect the new point location. That is, AutoCAD automatically recalculates the dimension value, using the scale factor currently in effect.

Associative dimensions act like single objects. If you pick any part of the dimension at the *Select object* prompt, the whole dimension is selected. You can reduce associative dimensions to their individual components with the Explode command. Once exploded, dimensions are no longer associative.

Associative dimensioning was introduced in version 2.6. You can turn it on or off with the dimensioning variable Dimaso (see **Dim Vars**). The default value is on. When associative dimensioning is turned off, the components of any new dimensions will act like individual drawing entities.

Previously entered associative dimensions will remain intact.

Dimensioning and Drawing Scales

Take care when dimensioning drawings at a scale other than 1:1. If the Dimscale dimension variable (see **Dim Vars**) is not set properly, arrows and text will appear too small. In extreme cases, they may not appear at all. If you enter a dimension and arrows or text do not appear, check the Dimscale setting and make sure it is a value equal to the drawing scale.

Starting the Dimensioning Process

To begin adding dimension labels to a drawing, select **Dim** from the root menu or enter **Dim** or **Dim1** at the *Command* prompt. At this point, the prompt changes to *Dim* and you can enter any of the commands and subcommands presented in this chapter. In fact, these and the transparent commands are the only AutoCAD commands you can enter while in the dimensioning mode.

When you are done entering dimensions under the Dim command, you must issue the **Exit** command or **Ctrl-C** to return to the standard AutoCAD prompt. If you want to enter only a single dimension, use Dim1. This form of the command, introduced in version 2.5, returns you to the *Command* prompt automatically after you enter one dimension.

You can invoke any one of the dimension subcommands by entering its first three letters. For example, you can enter **Dia** instead of **Diameter**.

Options Common to Several DIM Commands

Appending Dimension Text

Appends text to default dimension text

VERSIONS

2.5 and later

SEQUENCE OF STEPS

Dimension text <*default text*>: [*Enter text, placing <> signs where you want default text to appear.*]

USAGE

At the *Dimension text* prompt, you can append text to the default dimension text.

SEE ALSO

Dimpost

Selecting Lines, Arcs, or Circles

Selects line, arc, or circle to be dimensioned

VERSIONS

All versions

SEQUENCE OF STEPS

First extension line origin or RETURN to select: (↵)
Select line, arc, or circle: [*Pick object to be dimensioned.*]

USAGE

At the *First extension line* prompt, you can dimension a line, arc, or circle by picking it instead of picking the dimension extension origin points. If you pick a polyline, only the segment picked within the polyline will be dimensioned. After you select the object, the *Dimension line location* and *Dimension text* prompts appear as usual.

Angular

Dimensions angles between nonparallel lines

VERSIONS

2.0 and later

SEQUENCE OF STEPS

Dim: **Angular**(↵)

To issue Angular from the menu system: **Root|Dim|Angular**

Select first line: [*Pick one of two lines for the angular dimension.*]

Second line: [*Pick the other line for the angular dimension.*]

Enter dimension line arc location: [*Pick a point indicating the location of the dimension line arc.*]

Dimension text <*default dimension*>: [*Press ↵ to accept default angle or enter angle value.*]

Enter text location: [*Pick the location for the beginning of the dimension text.*]

USAGE

Angular adds a dimension label showing the angle between two lines. An arc with dimension arrows at each end is placed between the two lines and the angle value is placed using the current text style.

At the *Dimension text* prompt, you can append text to the default dimension value. See **Common Options/Appending Dimension Text**.

Center

Places cross at arc or circle center

VERSIONS

2.0 and later

SEQUENCE OF STEPS

Dim: **Center**(↵)

To issue Center from the menu system: **Dim|Center**

Select arc or circle: [*Pick arc or circle.*]

USAGE

Center places a cross at the center point of a selected arc or circle. You can choose between a center cross or center lines through the Dimcen dimension variable (see **Dim Vars**). A center cross is a simple cross placed at the center point. Center lines are lines that extend across the entire arc or circle with breaks near the center.

SEE ALSO

Dim Vars/Dimcen

Diameter

Dimensions arc or circle diameter

VERSIONS

1.4 and later

SEQUENCE OF STEPS

Dim: **Diameter**(↵)

To issue Diameter from the menu system: **Dim|Diameter**.

Select arc or circle: <*arc or circle*>

Dimension text <*default dimension*>: [*Press ↵ to accept default dimension text or enter dimension text.*]

If the arc or circle is too small, you will get the following prompt:

Text does not fit.

Enter leader length for text: [*Pick a point representing length of text leader or enter a value.*]

A leader line is drawn from the pick point at the length specified. The direction from the center point to the pick point determines the direction of the leader. A center mark is also placed at the center of the arc or circle.

USAGE

Diameter adds a diameter dimension to arcs and circles. The point at which you pick the arc or circle determines one end of the dimension arrow. If you want the dimension to be horizontal or vertical, use the Quadpoint Osnap override and pick the left or right quadpoint for a horizontal dimension or pick the top and bottom quadpoint for a vertical dimension.

You can append text to the default dimension value. See **Common Options/Appending Dimension Text**.

SEE ALSO

Dim Vars/Dimcen

Dim Vars (Dimension Variables)

Table 2.1 describes variables that control the way AutoCAD draws dimensions. These variables control extension line and text location, tolerance specifications, arrow styles and sizes, and much more.

You can enter these commands at the *Dim* prompt or pick them from the Dim/Dim Vars menu. Since they are actually system variables, you can also set them using the Setvar command (see **Setvar**).

VARIABLE (VERSION)	DESCRIPTION
Dimalt (2.5)	When on, dimension texts for two measurement systems are inserted simultaneously (*alt*ernate). Dimaltf and Dimaltd must also be set appropriately. The alternate dimension is placed within brackets. Angular dimensions are not affected. This variable is commonly used when inches and metric units must be displayed at the same time in a dimension. The default setting is off.
Dimaltd(2.5)	When Dimalt is on, Dimaltd controls the number of decimal places the alternate dimension will have (*alt*ernate *d*ecimal places). The default value is 2.
Dimaltf (2.5)	When Dimalt is on, Dimaltf controls the multiplication factor for the alternate dimension (*alt*ernate *f*actor). The value held by Dimaltf will be multiplied by the standard dimension value to determine the alternate dimension. The default value is 25.4, the number required to display metric units.

Table 2.1: The dimension variables

VARIABLE (VERSION)	DESCRIPTION
Dimapost (2.6)	When Dimalt is on, you can use Dimapost to append text to the alternate dimension (*a*lternate *post*). For example, if Dimapost is given the value "mm," the alternate dimension will appear as *value*mm instead of just *value* The default value is nul. To change a previously set value to nul, enter a period for the Dimapost new value.
Dimaso(2.6)	When on, dimensions will be associative (*asso*ciative). When off, dimensions will consist of separate drawing entities with none of the associative dimension properties. The default is on.
Dimasz(1.4)	Sets the size of dimension arrows or Dimblks (*a*rrow *s*ize. See Dimblk). If set to 0, a tick is drawn in place of an arrow. The default value is .18 units.

Table 2.1: The dimension variables (continued)

VARIABLE (VERSION)	DESCRIPTION
Dimblk(2.5)	You can replace the standard AutoCAD dimension arrow with one of your own design by creating a drawing of your symbol and making it a block. You then give Dimblk the name of your symbol block. This block must be drawn corresponding to a one by one unit area and must be oriented as the right side arrow. The default value is nul.
Dimblk1(10)	With Dimsah set to on, you can replace the standard AutoCAD dimension arrows with two different arrows using Dimblk1 and Dimblk2. Dimblk1 holds the name of the block defining the first dimension arrow while Dimblk2 holds the name of the second dimension arrow block.
Dimblk(2.0)	See Dimblk1.
Dimcen(1.4)	Sets the size of center marks used during the Center, Diameter, and Radius dimension subcommands. A negative value draws center lines instead of the center mark cross, while a 0 value draws nothing. The default value is 0.09 units.
Dimdle(2.5)	With Dimtsz given a value greater than 0, dimension lines can extend past the extension lines by the amount specified in Dimdle (*d*imension *l*ine *e*xtension). This amount is not adjusted by Dimscale. The default value is 0.

Table 2.1: The dimension variables (continued)

VARIABLE (VERSION)	DESCRIPTION
Dimdli(1.4)	Sets the distance at which dimension lines are offset when you use the Baseline or Continue dimension subcommands (*d*imension *l*ine *i*ncrement). The default is 0.38 units.
Dimexe(1.4)	Sets the distance the extension lines are drawn past the dimension lines (*ex*tension line *e*xtension). The default value is 0.18 units.
Dimexo(1.4)	Sets the distance between the beginning of the extension line and the actual point selected at the *Extension line origin* prompt (*ex*tension line *o*ffset). The default value is 0.0625 units.
Dimlfac(2.5)	Sets the global scale factor for dimension values (*l*ength *fac*tor). Linear distances will be multiplied by the value held by Dimlfac. This multiple will be entered as the dimension text. The default value is 1.0. This can be useful when drawings are not drawn to scale.
Dimlim(1.4)	When set to on, dimension text is entered as two values representing a dimension range rather than a single value. The range is determined by the values given to Dimtp (*p*lus tolerance) and Dimtm (*m*inus *t*olerance). The default value is off.

Table 2.1: The dimension variables (continued)

VARIABLE (VERSION)	DESCRIPTION
Dimpost(2.6)	Automatically appends text strings to dimension text. For example, if Dimpost is given the value "inches," dimension text will appear as *value* inches instead of just *value* The default value is nul. To change a previously set value to nul, enter a period for the Dimpost new value. If you use Dimpost in conjunction with appended dimension text (see **Common Options/Appending Dimension Text**), the Dimpost value is included as part of the default dimension text.
Dimrnd(2.5)	Sets the amount to which all dimensions are rounded. For example, if you set Dimrnd to 1, all dimensions will be integer values. The number of decimal places affected depends on the precision value set by the Units command. The default is 0.
Dimsah(10)	When set to on, allows the separate arrow blocks, Dimblk1 and Dimblk2, to replace the standard AutoCAD arrows (separate *a*rrow *h*eads). If Dimtsz is set to a value greater than 0, Dimsah has no effect.

Table 2.1: The dimension variables (continued)

VARIABLE (VERSION)	DESCRIPTION
Dimscale(1.4)	Sets the scale factor for dimension variables that control dimension lines and arrows and text size (unless current text style has a fixed height). If your drawing is not full scale, you should set this variable to reflect the drawing scale. For example, for a drawing whose scale is 1/4" equals 1′, you should set Dimscale to 48. The default value is 1.0.
Dimse1(1.4)	When set to on, the first dimension line extension is not drawn (*s*uppress *e*xtension *1*). The default is off.
Dimse2(1.4)	When set to on, the second dimension line extension is not drawn (*s*uppress *e*xtension 2). The default is off.
Dimsho(2.6)	When set to on, dimension text in associative dimensions will dynamically change to reflect the location of a dimension point as it is being moved (*sho*w dimension). The default is off.
Dimsoxd(10)	When set to on, dimension lines do not appear outside of the extension lines (*s*uppress *o*utside e*x*tension *d*imension lines). If Dimtix is also set to on and the space between the extension lines prohibits the display of a dimension line, no dimension line is drawn. The default is off.

Table 2.1: The dimension variables (continued)

VARIABLE (VERSION)	DESCRIPTION
Dimtad(1.4)	When set to on and Dimtih is off, dimension text in linear dimensions will be placed above the dimension line (*t*ext *a*bove *d*imension line). When off, the dimension line will be split in two and text will be placed in line with the dimension line. The default value is off.
Dimtih(1.4)	When set to on, dimension text placed between extension lines will always be horizontal (*t*ext *i*nside *h*orizontal). When set to off, text will be aligned with the dimension line. The default value is on.
Dimtix(10)	When set to on, dimension text will always be placed between extension lines (*t*ext *i*nside e*x*tension). The default value is off.
Dimtm(1.4)	When Dimtol or Dimlin is on, Dimtm determines the minus tolerance value of the dimension text (*t*olerance *m*inus).
Dimtofl(10)	With Dimtofl on, a dimension line is always drawn between extension lines even when text is drawn outside (*t*ext *o*utside—*f*orced *l*ine). The default is off.

Table 2.1: The dimension variables (continued)

VARIABLE (VERSION)	DESCRIPTION
Dimtoh(1.4)	With Dimtoh on, dimension text placed outside extension lines will always be horizontal (*t*ext *o*utside—*h*orizontal). When set to off, text outside extension lines will be aligned with dimension line. The default is on.
Dimtol(1.4)	With Dimtol on, tolerance values set by Dimtp and Dimtm are appended to the dimension text (*tol*erance). The default is off.
Dimtp(1.4)	When Dimtol or Dimlim is on, Dimtp determines the plus tolerance value of the dimension text (*t*olerance *p*lus).
Dimtsz(2.0)	Sets the size of tick marks drawn in place of the standard AutoCAD arrows (*t*ick *s*ize). When set to 0, the standard arrow is drawn. When greater than 0, tick marks are drawn and take precedence over Dim-blk1 and Dimblk2. The default value is 0.

Table 2.1: The dimension variables (continued)

VARIABLE (VERSION)	DESCRIPTION
Dimtvp(10)	When Dimtad is off, Dimtvp allows you to specify the location of the dimension text in relation to the dimension line (*t*ext *v*ertical *p*osition). A positive value places the text above the dimension line while a negative value places the text below the dimension line. The dimension line will split to accommodate the text unless the Dimtvp value is greater than 1.
Dimtxt(1.4)	Sets the height of dimension text when the current text style height is set to 0. The default value is 0.18.
Dimzin(2.5)	Determines the display of inches when Architectural units are used. Set to 0, zero feet or zero inches will not be displayed. Set to 1, zero feet and zero inches will be displayed. Set to 2, zero inches will not be displayed. Set to 3, zero feet will not be displayed.

Table 2.1: The dimension variables (continued)

Exit

Exits Dim command

VERSIONS

1.4 and later

SEQUENCE OF STEPS

Dim: **Exit**(↵)

Command:

To issue Exit from the menu system: **Dim|Exit**.

USAGE

Once you are done entering dimensions, issue the Exit subcommand to return to the standard *Command* prompt. You can press **Ctrl-C** or type **Exi** in place of **Exit**. If you entered **Dim1** to begin dimensioning, Exit is not needed.

Hometext

Moves dimension text to default position

VERSIONS

2.6 and later

SEQUENCE OF STEPS

Dim: **Hometext**(↵)

To select Hometext from the menu system: **Dim|Next|Hometext**.

Select objects: [*Pick dimensions that need text moved to default position.*]

USAGE

If you have moved the text of a dimension using the Stretch command, you can move it back to its default position with the Hometext subcommand. Hometext works only with associative dimensions that have not been exploded.

SEE ALSO

Dim Vars/Dimaso

Leader

Adds single-line note with leader

VERSIONS

1.4 and later

SEQUENCE OF STEPS

Dim: **Leader**(↵)

To issue Leader from the menu system: **Dim|Leader**.

Leader start: [*Pick point to start leader. This is the point where the arrow will be placed.*]

To point: [*Pick the next point along the leader line.*]

You can continue to pick points as you would when drawing a line. When you are done, press ↵. The next prompt appears:

Dimension text <*default dimension*>: [*Press ↵ to accept the default or enter new dimension text.*]

You can append text to the default dimension value. The default value is usually the last dimension entered. See **Common Options/Appending Dimension Text**.

USAGE

Leader allows you to add notes with arrows to your drawings.

If the distance between the Leader start point and the next point is too short, an arrow will not be placed. The distance between these two points must be at least twice the length of the arrow. Also, if the last line segment of the leader is not horizontal, a horizontal line segment will be added to the end of the last line segment, as illustrated in Figure 2.3.

SEE ALSO

Dim Vars/Dimasz, Dim Vars/Dimscale

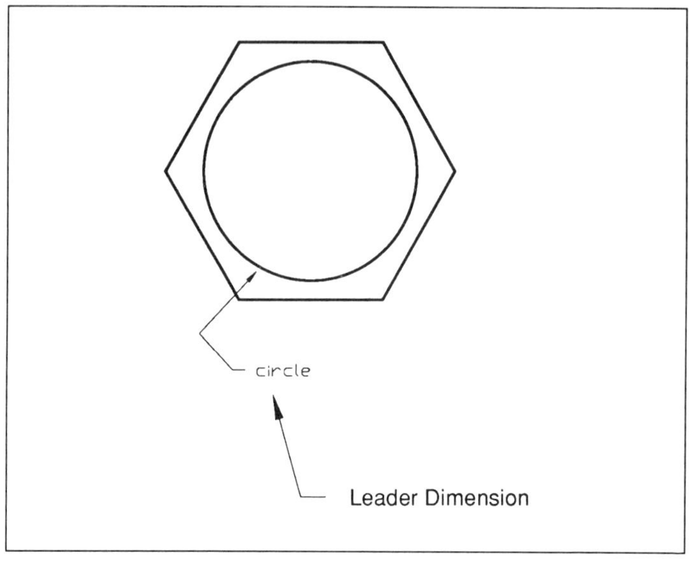

Figure 2.3: A segmented leader

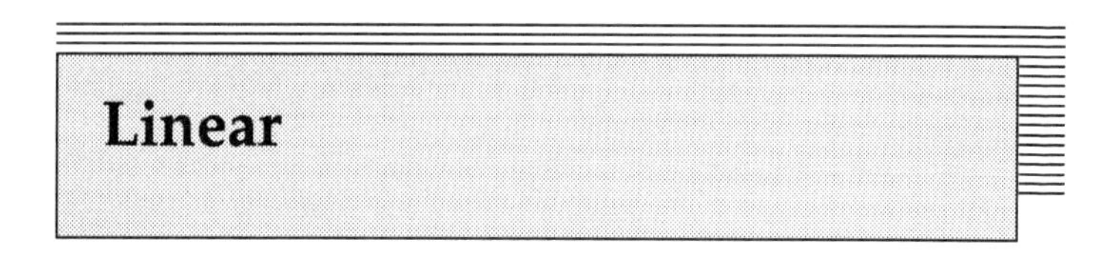

Linear

You can draw linear dimensions with the dimension subcommands grouped in the Linear submenu of the Dim menu.

Aligned

Draws aligned dimension

VERSIONS

2.0 and later

SEQUENCE OF STEPS

Dim: **Aligned**(↵)

To issue Aligned from the menu system:
Dim|Linear|Aligned

First extension line origin or RETURN to select: [*Pick one end of object to be dimensioned.*]

Second extension line origin: [*Pick other end of the object.*]

Dimension line location: [*Pick a point or enter coordinate indicating the location of the dimension line.*]

Dimension text: *<default dimension>*: [*press ↵ to accept the default dimension or enter dimension value.*]

The dimension will appear aligned with the two points you selected at the extension line prompts. If you used the select line, arc, or circle option (see **Common Options**), the dimension is aligned with the object selected.

USAGE

You can align a dimension with two points representing the extension line origins. You can also dimension an object by picking the object rather than its end points. The dimension text appears in the current text style. Figure 2.4 illustrates the difference between aligned and rotated dimensions.

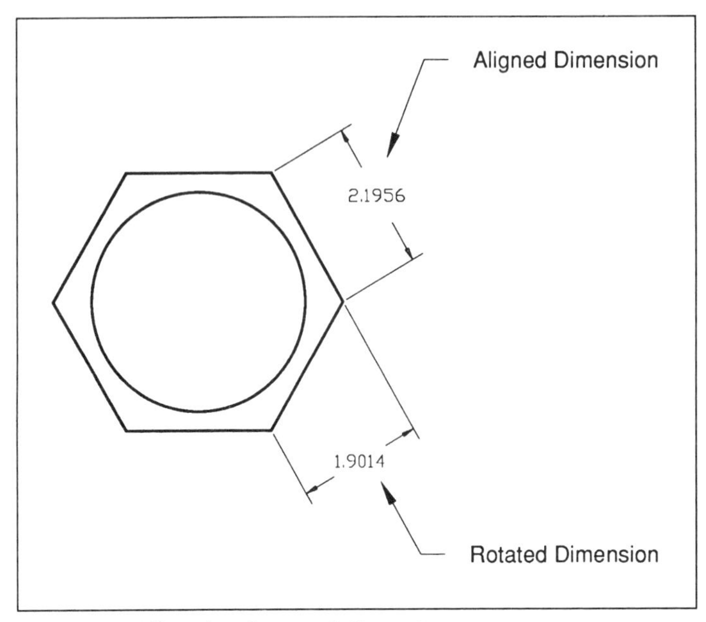

Figure 2.4: Aligned and rotated dimensions

At the *First extension line origin* prompt, you can dimension a line, arc, or circle by picking it instead of picking the extension line origins. See **Common Options/Selecting Lines, Arcs or Circles**.

At the *Dimension text* prompt, you can append text to the default dimension value. See **Common Options/Appending Dimension Text**.

Baseline

Continues a dimension from a common baseline

VERSIONS

1.4 and later

SEQUENCE OF STEPS

Dim: **Baseline**(↵)

To issue Baseline from the menu system:
Dim|Linear|Baseline

Second extension line origin: [*Pick a point indicating the extension line origin for a continuing dimension. The first extension line origin of the last whole dimension entered will be used as the first extension line.*]

Dimension text <*default dimension*>: [*press ↵ to accept the default dimension text or enter new dimension text.*]

USAGE

Baseline continues a dimension string by using the first extension line of the most recently inserted dimension as its first extension line. You are only prompted for the second extension line origin. The dimension is placed above and is parallel to the last dimension. This is useful when you are entering a set of dimensions from a common point or dimension datum.

At the *Dimension text* prompt, you can append text to the default dimension value. See **Common Options/Appending Dimension Text**.

SEE ALSO

Dim Vars/Dimdli

Continue

Adds dimension to dimension string

VERSIONS

1.4 and later

SEQUENCE OF STEPS

Dim: **Continue**(↵)

To issue Continue from the menu system:
Dim|Linear|Continue

Second extension line origin: [*Pick a point indicating the extension line origin for a continuing dimension. The second extension line origin of the last dimension entered will be used as the first extension line.*]

Dimension text <*default dimension*>: [*Press ↵ to accept the default dimension text or enter new dimension text.*]

USAGE

The Continue subcommand continues a dimension string by using the second extension line of the most recently inserted dimension as its first extension line. You are only prompted for the second extension line origin. The dimension is placed inline with and is parallel to the last dimension. This is useful when you are entering a series of dimensions end to end.

At the *Dimension text* prompt, you can append text to the default dimension value. See **Appending Dimension Text**.

SEE ALSO

Dim Vars/Dimdli

Horizontal

Draws horizontal dimension

VERSIONS

1.4 and later

SEQUENCE OF STEPS

Dim: **Horizontal**(↵)

To issue Horizontal from the menu system:
Dim|Linear|Horizontal

First extension line origin or RETURN to select: [*Pick one end of the object to be dimensioned.*]

Second extension line origin: [*Pick other end of the object.*]

Dimension line location: [*Pick a point or enter coordinate indicating the location of the dimension line.*]

Dimension text: <*default dimension*>: [*Press ↵ to accept the default dimensions or enter dimension value.*]

The horizontal dimension will appear.

USAGE

With Horizontal, you can force a dimension to be horizontal regardless of the extension line origins or the orientation of the object picked. You can also dimension an object by picking the object rather that its dimensioning points. The dimension text appears in the current text style.

At the *First extension line origin* prompt, you can dimension a line, arc, or circle by picking it instead of picking the extension line origins. See **Common Options/Selecting Lines, Arcs, or Circles**.

At the *Dimension text* prompt, you can append text to the default dimension value. See **Common Options/Appending Dimension Text**.

Rotated

Dimensions two points at specified angle

VERSIONS

2.0 and later

SEQUENCE OF STEPS

Dim: **Rotated**(↵)

To issue Rotated from the menu system:
Dim|Linear|Rotated

First extension line origin or RETURN to select: [*Pick one end of the object to be dimensioned.*]
Second extension line origin: [*Pick other end of the object.*]

Dimension line location: [*Pick a point or enter coordinate indicating the location of the dimension line.*]
Dimension text: *<default dimension>*: [*Press ↵ to accept the default dimension or enter dimension value.*]

USAGE

With Rotated, you can force a dimension to be measured and placed at a specified angle regardless of the dimensioned object's orientation. The dimension text appears in the current text style. As illustrated in Figure 2.4, a rotated dimension measures a distance at the specified angle; this is a smaller value than the aligned dimension.

At the *First extension line origin* prompt, you can dimension a line, arc, or circle by picking it instead of picking the extension line origins. See **Common Options/Selecting Lines, Arcs, or Circles**.

At the *Dimension text* prompt, you can append text to the default dimension value. See **Common Options/Appending Dimension Text**.

Vertical

Inserts vertical dimension

VERSIONS

1.4 and later

SEQUENCE OF STEPS

Dim: **Vertical**(↵)

To issue Vertical from the menu system:
Dim|Linear|Vertical

First extension line origin or RETURN to select: [*Pick one end of the object to be dimensioned.*]

Second extension line origin: [*Pick other end of the object.*]

Dimension line location: [*Pick a point or enter coordinate indicating location of the dimension line.*]

Dimension text: *<default dimension>*: [*Press ↵ to accept the default dimensions or enter dimension value.*]

USAGE

You can use Vertical to force a dimension to be displayed vertically, regardless of where the extension line origins are placed. The dimension text appears in the current text style. You can issue this subcommand by entering **Ver** instead of the full word **Vertical** at the *Dim* prompt.

At the *First extension line origin* prompt, you can dimension a line, arc, or circle by picking it instead of picking the extension line origins. See **Common Options/Selecting Lines, Arcs, or Circles**.

At the *Dimension text* prompt, you can append text to the default dimension value. See **Common Options/Appending Dimension Text**.

Newtext

Edits associative dimension text

VERSIONS

2.6 and later

SEQUENCE OF STEPS

Dim: **Newtext**(↵)

To issue Newtext from the menu system:
Dim|Next|Newtext

Enter new dimension text: [*Enter text. You can also use the <> signs to append text to the current text.*]

Select objects: [*Pick dimensions to be edited.*]

USAGE

With the associative dimensioning feature, you cannot edit dimension text in the usual way, using the Change command.

Newtext allows you to edit associative dimension text. It also enables you to edit several dimensions at once. You can append text to several existing dimensions at once using the <> signs.

At the *Select object* prompt, select either one or several dimensions. All associative dimensions selected will be changed to the new text.

SEE ALSO

Dimensioning in AutoCAD

Radius

Dimensions arc or circle radius

VERSIONS

2.0 and later

SEQUENCE OF STEPS

Dim: **Radius**(↵)

To issue Radius from the menu: **Dim|Radius**

Select arc or circle: [*Pick arc or radius.*]

Dimension text <*default radius*>: [*Press ↵ to accept default radius or enter text.*]

If the arc or circle is too small, you will get the following prompt:

Text does not fit.

Enter leader length for text: [*Pick a point representing the length of the text leader or enter a value.*]

A leader line is drawn from the selection point at the length specified. The direction from the center point to the pick point determines the direction of the leader. A center mark is also placed at the center of the arc or circle.

USAGE

Radius adds a radius dimension to arcs and circles. The point at which you pick the arc or circle determines one end of the dimension arrow. You can append text to the default dimension value. See **Common Options/Appending Dimension Text**.

SEE ALSO

Dim Vars/Dimcen

Status

Displays current Dimension variable settings

VERSIONS

1.4 and later

SEQUENCE OF STEPS

Dim: **Status**(↵)

To issue Status from the menu system: **Dim|Status**.

[*A text display will show a list of current Dimension variable settings along with brief descriptions.*]

The list will pause and you will see the line:

---Press RETURN for more---

You can press ↵ to continue viewing the list or **Ctrl-C** to abort the command.

USAGE

You can use Status to check the current Dimension variable settings or quickly check the definition of a setting.

SEE ALSO

Dim Vars

Style

Sets current text style

VERSIONS

1.4 and later

SEQUENCE OF STEPS

Dim: **Style**(↵)

To issue Style from the menu system: **Dim|Style**.

New text style <*current style*>: [*Press* ↵ *to accept current style or enter new style name. New style is now the current text style.*]

If you enter the name of a style that does not exist, you will get the message:

No such text style. Use main STYLE command to create it.

USAGE

Style allows you to use a different text style for the dimension text. Once the text style is changed, any subsequent dimensions will contain text in the new style. Existing dimension text is not affected.

SEE ALSO

Style (Chapter 8), Dim Vars/Dimtxt

Undo

Deletes last dimension entry

VERSIONS

2.5 and later

SEQUENCE OF STEPS

Dim: **Undo**(↵)

To issue Undo from the menu system: **Dim|Undo**

USAGE

If you insert a dimension you decide you do not want, you can "undo" it as long as you remain in the dimension mode. If you issue Undo during the Leader command, the last leader line segment drawn will be undone. You can enter **U** in place of **Undo**.

Update

Updates associative dimensions

VERSIONS

2.6 and later

SEQUENCE OF STEPS

Dim: **Update**(↵)

To issue Update from the menu system: **Dim|Next|Update**

Select objects: [*Pick associative dimensions to be updated.*]

USAGE

When you change any of the Dimension variables' settings, new settings only affect dimensions entered after the change.

Update allows you to change old dimensions to the new Dimension variable settings. Update only works on associative dimensions that have not been exploded.

SEE ALSO

Dimensioning in AutoCAD, Dimaso

CHAPTER 3

Display Commands

This chapter covers the commands found in the Display menu. These commands control the way a drawing is displayed as well as the regeneration and redrawing processes. The interaction between the display-control and regeneration commands, which is often significant, is discussed throughout.

Attdisp

Controls attribute display globally

VERSIONS

All versions

SEQUENCE OF STEPS

Command: **Attdisp(↵)**

To issue Attdisp from the menu system: **Display|Attdisp**.

Normal/ON/OFF <Normal>: [*Enter* ***ON***, ***OFF***, *or* ↵ *for your selection.*]

OPTIONS

Normal Attributes set to be invisible are not displayed. All other attributes are displayed.

ON All attributes are displayed, whether set to be invisible or not.

OFF All attributes are made invisible, whether set to be invisible or not.

USAGE

Attdisp allows you to control the display and plotting of all attributes in a drawing. You can force attributes to be displayed, made invisible, or displayed depending on how an attribute's display mode is set. If autoregeneration is on (see **Regenauto**), your drawing will regenerate at the completion of the command and the display of attributes will reflect the option you select. If autoregeneration is off, the attributes will be displayed as they were before you issued Attdisp. The new Attdisp setting will be displayed when you issue Regen.

SEE ALSO

Attdef, Regen, Regenauto, and the Attmode system variable

Dview

Controls views of three-dimensional drawings

VERSIONS

10

SEQUENCE OF STEPS

Command: **Dview(↵)**

To select Dview from the menu system: **Display|Dview**

Select object: [*Pick objects that will help set up your perspective view.*]

CAmera/TArget/Distance/Points/PAn/Zoom/TWist/CLip/Hide/

Off/Undo/<eXit>: [*Select option from menu or enter capitalized letters of the desired option.*]

Depending on the option selected, you will get a series of prompts. Once the option is completed, you are returned to the *Dview* prompt.

OPTIONS

CAmera Allows you to move the camera location in relation to the target location, as if you were moving the camera around while continually aiming it at the target point. When selected, CAmera will prompt you for the vertical and horizontal angles of view. At each prompt, you can either enter a value or use a slide bar (on the right for vertical, on the top for horizontal) to select the view visually. If you enter a value, it will be interpreted in relation to the current UCS (see Figure 3.1).

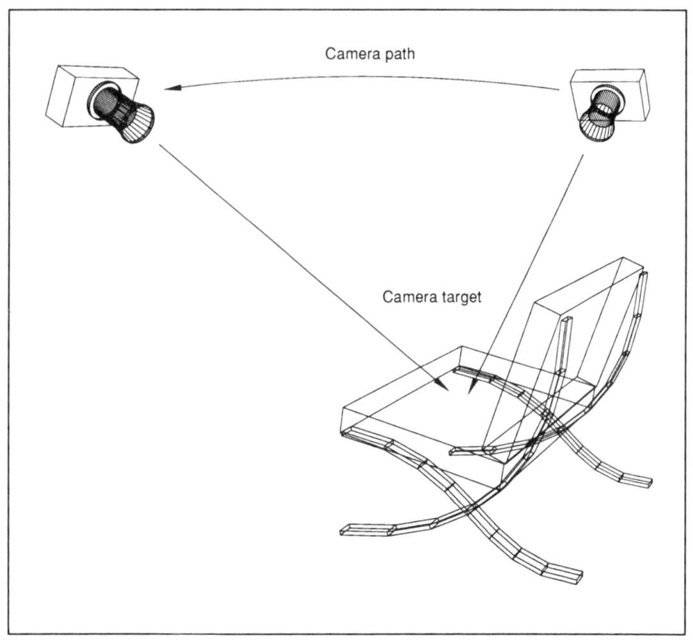

Figure 3.1: The Camera option controls the camera location relative to the target

TArget Allows you to move the target location, as if you were pointing the camera in different directions while keeping the camera location the same. When selected, TArget will prompt you for the vertical and horizontal angles of view. At each prompt, you can either enter a value or use a slide bar (on the right for vertical, at the top for horizontal) to select the view visually (see Figure 3.2).

Distance Turns on the perspective mode and allows you to set the distance from the target to the camera, as if you were moving the camera toward or away from the target point. When selected, Distance prompts you for a new distance. Enter a new distance or move the slide

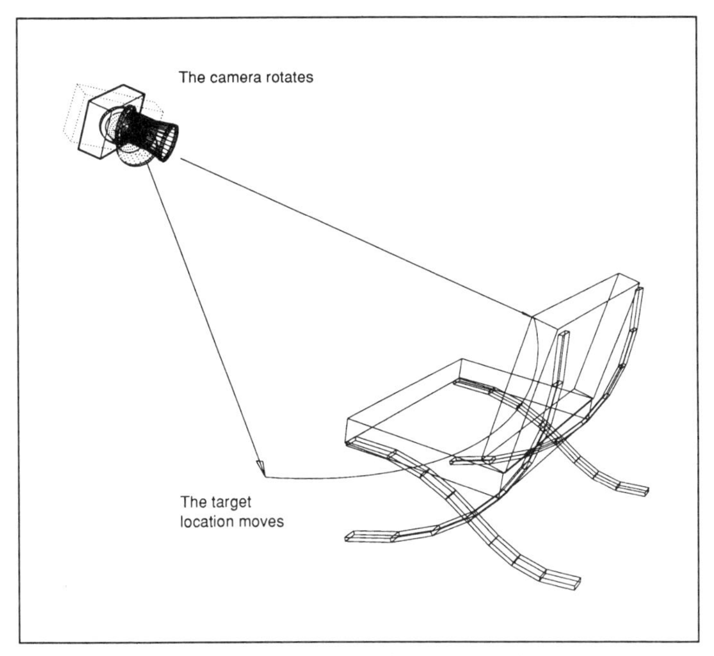

Figure 3.2: The Target option controls the target location relative to the camera.

bar at the top of the screen to drag the three-dimensional image into the desired position (see Figure 3.3).

POints Allows you to set the target and camera points at the same time. The points you pick will be in relation to the current UCS. When chosen, POints prompts you to pick a point indicating where you want to aim your camera and then to pick a point indicating your camera location.

PAn Allows you to move your camera and target point together, as if you were pointing a camera out of the side of a moving car. Since you cannot use the standard Pan command while viewing a drawing in perspective, the

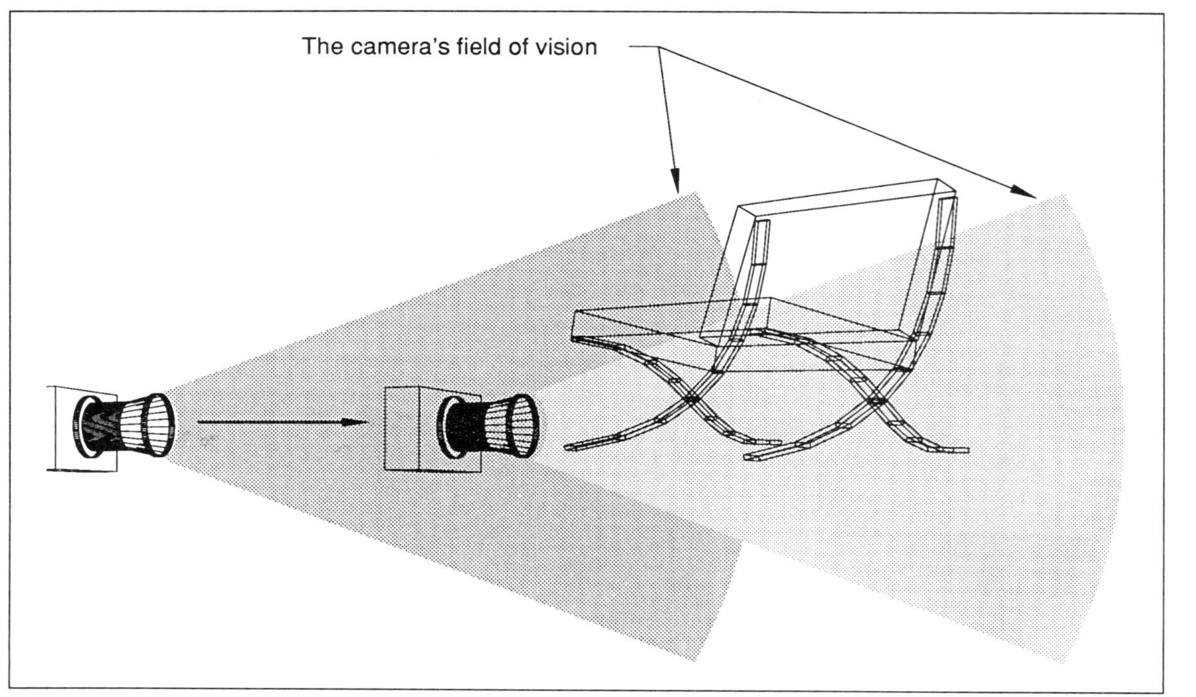

Figure 3.3: The Distance option controls the distance between the camera and the target.

Pan option under the Dview command allows you to perform pans. See **Pan** for more information.

Zoom Allows you to zoom in and out of a view while viewing a drawing in parallel projection. Also enables you to determine a lens focal length when you are viewing a drawing in perspective. Since you cannot use the standard Zoom command while viewing a drawing in perspective, you must use the Zoom option under the Dview command. If your three-dimensional view is a parallel projection, enter a new scale factor or use the slide bar at the top of the screen to visually adjust the scale factor at the *Dview/Zoom* prompt. If your three-dimensional view is a perspective, enter a new lens length value or use the slide bar at the top of the screen to visually determine the new lens length at the *Dview/Zoom* prompt. If you use the slide bar to adjust the focal length, the coordinate readout on the status line will dynamically display the focal length value.

Twist Allows you to rotate the camera about the camera's line of sight, as if you were rotating the camera to skew the view in the camera frame. At the *Dview/Twist* prompt, enter an angle or use the cursor to visually twist the camera view. If you use the cursor, the coordinate readout on the status line will dynamically display the camera twist angle.

CLip Allows you to hide portions of your three-dimensional view. You can use it to remove objects in the foreground that may interfere with a view of a room interior, for example. When selected, CLip displays the following prompt:

Back/Front/<Off>:

Enter **B** to set back clip plane, **F** to set front clip plane, or **O** to turn off clip plane function. If you select **Back**, a prompt allows you to turn the back clip plane on or off, or to set a distance to the clip plane. You can use the slide bar at the top of the screen to visually determine the location of the back clip plane or enter a distance value. A positive value places the clip plane in front of the target point, while a negative number places it behind the target point.

If you select **Front**, a prompt allows you to either set the front clip plane to the camera location, turn the front clip plane on or off, or set a distance to the clip plane. You can use the slide bar at the top of the screen to visually select a front clip plane location. If you want to enter a distance value, a positive value places the clip plane in front of the target point while a negative number places the clip plane behind the target point. The On and Off options are only available if your current view is in parallel projection. The front clip plane is always on when the drawing is in perspective.

If you enter **O** at the *Dview/CLip* prompt, both the front and back clip planes are disabled. If a perspective view is on, the camera location is used as the front clip plane (see Figure 3.4).

Hide Removes hidden lines from the objects displayed, turning a wire-frame view into a planar view.

Off Turns off the perspective mode.

Undo Undoes last Dview option.

eXit Returns you to the AutoCAD *Command* prompt. Any operation you performed while in the *Dview* command prompt will take effect on the entire drawing, not just the selected objects.

USAGE

Dview enables you to see your drawing in perspective. Since the standard Zoom and Pan commands do not work

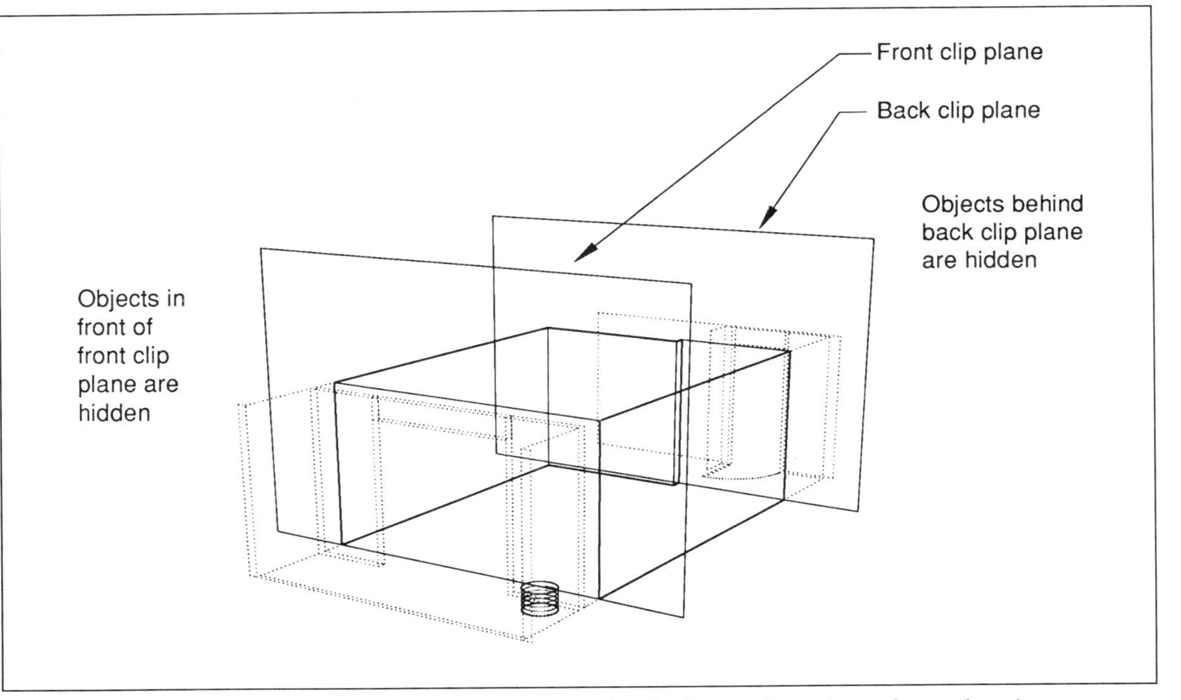

Figure 3.4:* *The Clip option allows you to hide foreground or background portions of your drawing.

on perspective views, Dview allows you to perform zooms and pans.

Dview uses the analogy of a camera to help you determine your view. Most of Dview's options allow you to visually select a view by dragging the objects or the "camera" in the drawing as you move the cursor. Since a large drawing will slow down the drag function, you are prompted to select objects at the beginning of the Dview command. This allows you to limit the number of objects that must be dragged. You should select objects that give the general outline of your drawing and still give enough detail to help you determine the drawing's orientation. If you do not pick any objects, a default three-dimensional image appears that can aid you in selecting a view. You can also define your own default image by making a block of the desired image. The block should be named Dviewblock and it should be 1 unit cubed in size.

SEE ALSO

UCS and Setvar/Backz, /Frontz, /Lenslength, /Target, /Viewctr, /Viewdir, /Viewmode, /Viewsize, and /Viewtwist

Pan

Moves display

VERSIONS

All versions. Transparent capability added in version 2.5.

SEQUENCE OF STEPS

Command: **Pan(↵)**

To enter Pan from the menu system: **Display|Pan** or **Display** pull-down menu|**Pan**

Displacement: [*Pick first point of view displacement.*]

Second point: [*Pick distance and direction of displacement.*]

USAGE

Pan allows you to shift your display to view parts of a drawing that are off the screen. Using the camera analogy of the Dview command, Pan allows you to move the "camera" and the target together, on parallel lines, as if you were pointing a camera outside a moving car. Pan is a transparent command; you can use it while in the middle of another command by preceding it with an apostrophe. You cannot, however, use Pan while viewing a drawing in perspective. Use the Dview command's Pan option for this purpose instead. When chosen, Pan first prompts you for the *Displacement*; that is, the starting point of the panning (or displacement). It then prompts you for a *Second point* of displacement. Finish by picking that point. You can also enter an **X4** value at the *Displacement* prompt, indicating the distance of your pan. Press ↵ at the *Second point* prompt.

SEE ALSO

Dview/Pan, View, Zoom

Plan

Gives plan view of User Coordinate System

VERSIONS

10

SEQUENCE OF STEPS

Command: **Plan(↵)**

To enter Plan from the menu system: **Display|Plan** *or* **Display** pull-down|**Plan view (UCS)** *or* **Plan View (world)**

<Current UCS>/Ucs/World: [*Enter capitalized letter of desired option or press ↵ for the current UCS.*]

OPTIONS

↵ Gives you a plan view of the current UCS. This is the default option. It is automatically issued when you pick **PlanView** (**UCS**) from the Display pull-down menu.

U Gives you a plan view of a previously saved UCS. You are prompted for the name of the UCS you wish to see in plan. Enter a question mark to get a list of saved UCS's.

W Gives you a plan view of the World Coordinate System. This option is automatically issued when you pick **PlanView (world)** from the Display pull-down menu.

USAGE

Plan allows you to view a User Coordinate System in plan, that is, a view perpendicular to the UCS. Such a view allows you to create and manipulate objects in 2D more easily. If you have multiple view ports, Plan only affects the active view port. You can also set the Ucsfollow system variable so that whenever you change to a different UCS, you automatically get a plan view of it.

SEE ALSO

Setvar/Ucsfollow, UCS

Redraw and Redrawall

Refreshes display

VERSIONS

All versions for Redraw. Version 10 for Redrawall.

SEQUENCE OF STEPS

Command: **Redraw(↵)**

or

Command: **Redrawall(↵)**

To enter Redraw or Redrawall from the menu system: **Display|Redraw** *or* **Redrawall** *or* **Display** pull-down|**Redraw** *or* **Redrawall**

USAGE

During the drawing and editing process, an operation may cause an object to partially disappear. Often, the object may have been behind other objects that have been removed. Redraw and Redrawall will refresh the screen and restore such obscured objects. These commands will also clear the screen of blips that may clutter your view. If you have multiple view ports, Redraw will only act on the currently active view port. Redrawall will refresh all view ports on the screen at once. These commands affect only the virtual screen, not the actual drawing database.

SEE ALSO

Regen, Viewres

Regen and Regenall

Updates screen coordinates

VERSIONS

All versions for Regen. Version 10 for Regenall.

SEQUENCE OF STEPS

Command: **Regen(↵)**

To enter Regen from the menu system: **Display|Regen**

or

Command: **Regenall(↵)**

To enter Regenall from the menu system: **Display|Regenall**

USAGE

Regen allows you to update the drawing editor screen in accordance with the most recent changes in the drawing database. An AutoCAD drawing is basically a database of floating-point values that describe the drawing's coordinates and other attributes. This floating-point database is translated into the integer screen coordinates that make up what is called the *virtual screen*, which in turn is used to create the display you see in the drawing editor. (The virtual screen acts like a software version of your display by holding display information in memory where it can be accessed quickly.) This translation occurs whenever you open a file or issue certain global commands, and it appears to you as a drawing regeneration.

If you make a global change in the drawing database and Regenauto is turned on, a regeneration is issued automatically. For example, zooming or panning into an area outside the virtual screen will cause regeneration. Restoring a saved view that protrudes outside the virtual screen will also cause a regeneration. If you have Regenauto turned off, regeneration will not occur automatically, so changes to the drawing database are not immediately reflected in the drawing you see. In case you need to see those changes, Regen will update the display.

When you use multiple view ports, each view port maintains its own virtual screen. For this reason, Regen affects only the active view port. To regenerate all view ports at once, use Regenall.

SEE ALSO

Regenauto, Viewres.

Regenauto

Controls automatic drawing regeneration

VERSIONS

2.5 and later

SEQUENCE OF STEPS

Command: **Regenauto(↵)**

To enter Regenauto from the menu system:
Display|Regenauto

ON/OFF/ *<current status>*: [*Enter* ***ON*** *or* ***OFF****, depending on whether you want Regenauto on or off.*]

OPTIONS

ON The virtual screen (and therefore the display) is automatically regenerated to reflect global changes in the drawing database. Your display will reflect all the most recent drawing changes.

OFF The virtual screen (and therefore the display) is not automatically regenerated to reflect global changes in the drawing database. This can save time when you are editing complex drawings. When a command needs to regenerate the drawing, a prompt allows you to terminate the command or proceed with the regeneration.

USAGE

Drawings are frequently regenerated while being created and edited. These regenerations help maintain an accurate display of the drawing database. As the drawing becomes more complex, however, regeneration can become too time-consuming. Regenauto enables you to turn off automatic regeneration, which is on by default.

SEE ALSO

Viewres, Regen, and Setvar/Regenmode

View

Saves a view for later use

VERSIONS

2.0 and later

SEQUENCE OF STEPS

Command: **View(↵)**

To enter View from the menu system: **Display|View**

?/Delete/Restore/Save/Window: [*Enter capitalized letter of desired option or pick option from the menu.*]

OPTIONS

?	Lists all currently saved views.
Delete	Prompts you for a view name to delete from the drawing database.
Restore	Prompts you for a view name to restore to the screen.
Save	Saves current view. You are prompted for a view name.
Window	Saves a view defined by a window. You are prompted first to enter a view name and then to window the area to be saved as a view.

USAGE

The View command allows you to save views of your drawing that you can recall later. This is useful if you need to shift frequently between different parts of a drawing. Instead of using the Zoom command to zoom in and out of your drawing, you can save views of the areas you need to edit, and then recall them using the Restore option of the View command.

To use View most effectively, keep the saved views within AutoCAD's virtual screen, so that they can be restored at redraw speeds. Otherwise, restoring views may cause regeneration, which can slow down your editing if the drawing is complex. You might also use View to save an overall view of your drawing. Issuing a Zoom/All always causes a regeneration, but as long as a saved view is within the bounds of the virtual screen, restoring it will require only a redraw.

SEE ALSO

Viewres, Regen, Regenauto

Viewres

Controls virtual screen

VERSIONS

2.5 and later

SEQUENCE OF STEPS

Command: **Viewres(↵)**

To enter Viewres from the menu system:
Display|Viewres

Do you want fast zooms? <Y> [*Enter* ***Y*** *or* ***N***.]

Enter circle zoom percent (1-20000) <*current setting*>: [*Enter a value from 1 to 20,000, or press ↵ to accept the default.*]

OPTIONS

Yes If you enter **Y** to the first prompt, AutoCAD sets up a large virtual screen. This is an area roughly equivalent to 32,000 pixels square. Zooms, Pans, and View/Restores that occur within this virtual screen will be performed at redraw speeds.

You are then prompted for a circle zoom percent. This value determines how accurately circles and noncontinuous lines are shown.

No If you enter **N** to the first prompt, AutoCAD will not maintain a large virtual screen and all Zooms, Pans, and View/Restores will cause a regeneration. You are prompted for a circle zoom percent.

USAGE

Viewres controls whether AutoCAD's virtual screen feature is used. It is on by default. Viewres also allows you to control how accurately AutoCAD displays lines, arcs, and circles. A high percent value for circle zoom will display smooth circles and arcs and will accurately show noncontinuous lines. A low value will cause arcs and circles to appear as a series of line segments when viewed up close. Also, noncontinuous lines can appear as continuous. This does not mean that prints or plots of your drawing will be less accurate; only the display is affected.

In addition, the circle zoom percent value affects the speed of redraws and regenerations. A high value will slow them down while a low value will speed them up. Differences in redraw speeds, however, are barely noticeable.

The default value for the circle zoom percent is 100, but at this value, dashed or hidden lines can appear as continuous depending on the Ltscale setting. This can cause a great deal of confusion. A value of 2000 or higher can reduce or eliminate this problem without greatly sacrificing speed.

When you edit a close-up view of circles and arcs, object end points, intersections, and tangents may appear to be inaccurately placed. This is often due to the segmented appearance of arcs and circles and does not necessarily mean the object placement is inaccurate. It may also be hard to distinguish between polygons and circles. Again, these problems can be reduced or eliminated by setting the circle zoom percent to a high value.

The drawing limits will affect the speed of redraws when the virtual screen feature is turned on. If the limits are set to an area much greater than the actual drawing, redraws will be slowed down. For this reason, you should try to keep the drawing limits to the minimum required for your drawing.

To force the virtual screen to contain a specific area, set your limits to the area you want, set the limit-checking feature on, and then issue a Zoom/All command. The virtual screen will conform to the limits of your drawing until another Regen is issued or until you pan or zoom outside of the area set by the limits.

SEE ALSO

Regen, Redraw, Regenauto, Limits

Vpoint

Controls display's 3D viewpoint

VERSIONS

2.1 and later. Rotate was introduced with version 9.

SEQUENCE OF STEPS

Command: **Vpoint(↵)**

To issue Vpoint from the menu system: **Display|Vpoint** *or* **Display** pull-down|**Vpoint3D** *or* (version 9) **Display** pull-down **3DView**

Rotate/<View point> *<current setting>*: [*Enter a coordinate value or enter* ***R*** *for the* ***Rotate*** *option or press ↵ to set the view with the compass and axis tripod.*]

OPTIONS

Rotate	Allows you to specify a view in terms of angles from the XY plane and from the X axis. You are first prompted to *enter angle in X-Y plane from X axis.* Next, you are prompted to *enter angle from X-Y plane.*
View point	Allows you to specify your view point location by entering an X,Y,Z coordinate value.
↵	Allows you to visually select a view by pressing ↵ at the *Vpoint* prompt. You will get the compass and axes tripod.
icon menu	If you pick **3DView** or **Vpoint 3D** from the pull-down menu, an icon menu appears, offering several preset three-dimensional views. You can pick one of these options.

USAGE

Vpoint allows you to select a three-dimensional view of your drawing. There are three methods for selecting a view. You can enter a value in X, Y, and Z coordinates representing your view point. For example, entering –1,–1,1 will give you a view from the lower left of the drawing.

The second method, using the Rotate option, allows you to specify a view point as horizontal and vertical angles in relation to the last point selected. This option prompts you first for the horizontal and then for the vertical angle. At each prompt, enter an angle representing your desired view location. AutoCAD will use the last point entered as the target point for the angle, so use the ID command to establish the view target point before you start Vpoint (see Figure 3.5).

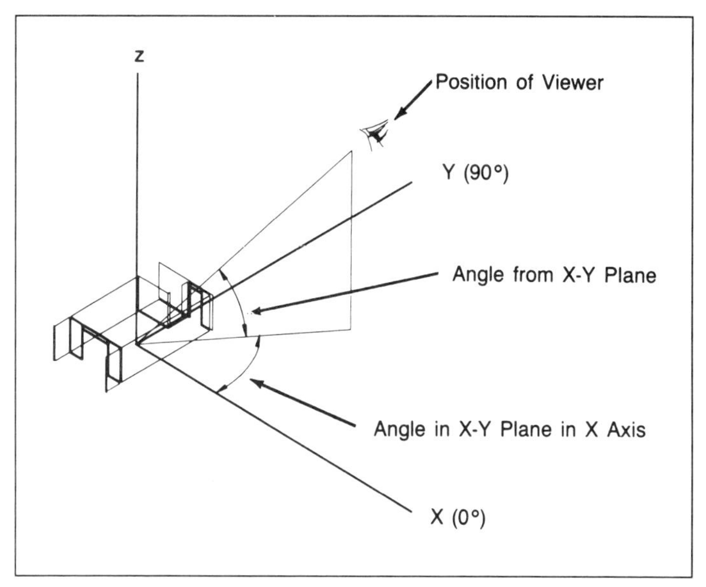

Figure 3.5: The viewpoint angles and what they represent

The third method, pressing ↵ at the *Vpoint* prompt, allows you to visually select a view point using the compass and axes tripod. The tripod rotates as you move your pointing device while the compass shows a cross at your ocation in plan and elevation. To select a view, move your pointing device until the tripod indicates the desired X, Y, and Z axis orientation. Use the compass to help you find your orientation in plan. The cross indicates your location in plan by its orientation to the compass' center. For example, placing the cross in the lower-left quadrant of the compass places your view point below and to the left of your drawing. Your view elevation is indicated by the distance of the cross from the compass' center. The closer to the center the cross is, the higher the elevation. The circle inside the compass indicates a 0 elevation. If the cross falls outside of this circle, your view elevation becomes a minus value and your view will be from below your drawing (see Figure 3.6).

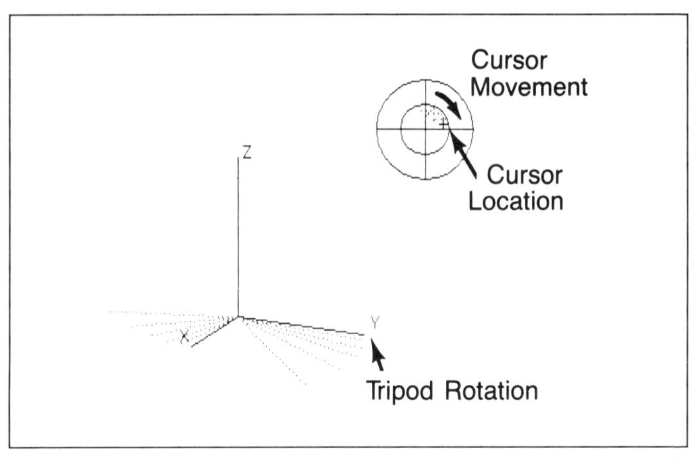

Figure 3.6: How the tripod rotates as you move the cursor around the target's center

SEE ALSO

Dview

Zoom

Enlarges view for close-up editing

VERSIONS

All versions. Dynamic option introduced with version 2.5. Previous option introduced with version 2.1.

SEQUENCE OF STEPS

Command: **Zoom(↵)**

To issue Zoom from the menu system: **Display|Zoom** *or* **Display** pull-down|*option*

All/Center/Dynamic/Extents/Left/Previous/Window/<Scale(X)>: [*Enter desired option.*]

OPTIONS

All Displays area of the drawing defined by its limits or extents, whichever are greater (see **Limits**).

Center Displays view based on a selected point. You are first prompted for a center point and then for a magnification or height. The point you pick at the first prompt becomes the center of your view while the magnification or height value you enter determines the magnification of the view. A value followed by an X is read as a magnification factor; a value alone is read as the desired height in drawing units of the display.

Dynamic Displays the virtual screen and allows you to select a view using a view box. The drawing extents, current view, and the current virtual screen area are indicated as a solid white box, a dotted green box, and red corner marks, respectively. You can pan, enlarge, or shrink the view by moving the view box to a new location, adjusting its size, or both. Whenever the view box moves into an area that will cause a regeneration, an hourglass appears in the lower-left corner of the display (see Figure 3.7).

Extents Displays a view of the entire drawing. The drawing is forced to fit within the display and is forced to the left. The drawing limits (see **Limits**) are ignored.

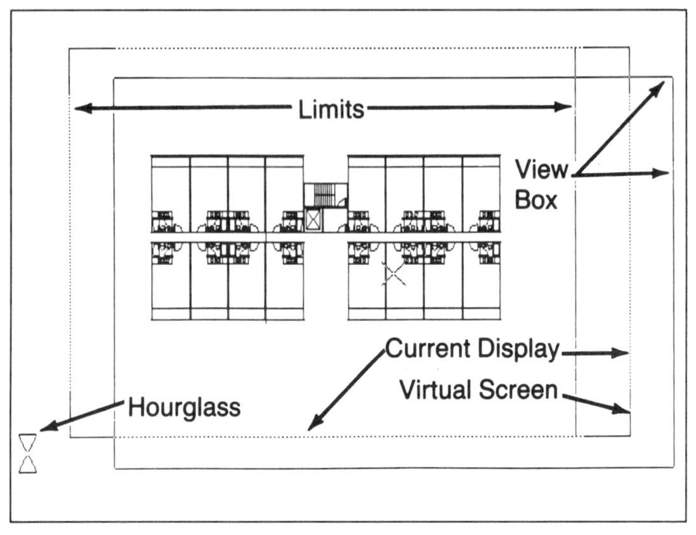

Figure 3.7: The Dynamic Zoom display

Left Similar to the Center option but the point you pick at the prompt will become the lower-left corner of the display.

Previous Displays the last view created by a Zoom, Pan, or View command. AutoCAD will store up to ten previous views (four views for version 9).

Window Enlarges a rectangular area of a drawing based on a defined window.

Scale(X) Expands or shrinks the drawing display. If an X follows the scale factor, it will be in relation to the current view. If no X is used, the scale factor will be in relation to the area defined by the limits of the drawing.

USAGE

Zoom controls the display of your drawing. Zoom/Window is probably the most commonly used Zoom option, allowing you to enlarge an area by "windowing" it. Other options, such as Center, Left, and Scale, allow you to specify a view area greater than the current one. The Previous option allows you to return to the previous view while the Dynamic option gives you a view of your virtual screen, enabling you to dynamically zoom or pan to a part of the drawing not currently available on the screen.

Zoom is a transparent command, which means that you can use it in the middle of another command by preceding it with an apostrophe. You cannot, however, use it while viewing a drawing in perspective. Use the Dview command's Zoom option for this purpose instead.

SEE ALSO

Regen, Redraw, Viewres, Regenauto, Limits

CHAPTER 4

Drawing Commands

The commands covered in this chapter all have to do with creating objects. They can be found in the Draw menu. Some of these commands can also be found in the Draw pull-down menu. You can give all of the objects described a three-dimensional volume by using either the Elev or Change command. You can also assign them layers, colors, and line types.

Since there are more commands in the Draw category than can fit on one menu, the Draw menu is divided into two menus. The first is displayed when you pick **Draw** from the root menu. The second is displayed when you select **Next** from the Draw menu. You can return to the first Draw menu by selecting **Previous**, **Last**, or **Draw** from the Draw/Next menu.

Commands you select from the Draw pull-down menu act differently from those you select from the screen menu. If you select a command from the Draw screen menu, another menu appears, displaying options specific to that command. You can then select options from the menu or enter them through the keyboard. Once the command is completed, you are returned to the *Command* prompt.

If you select a command from the pull-down menu, the command will be issued and will be automatically reissued once it has been completed. To exit a command issued from the Draw pull-down menu, you must either enter **Ctrl-C** or pick another command from either the menu or the pull-down menu.

Many commands prompt you for a point, direction, or length. You can reply to these prompts by either picking a point with your cursor or entering coordinates through the keyboard. See Appendix A for details on entering angles, distances, and points through the keyboard. Also, prompts that ask for direction or length will often display a *rubber-banding line,* which is a temporary line that connects the cursor with the last point entered. As the cursor moves, so does the rubber-banding line. This rubber-banding line helps you visually pick angles and lengths when you are using the cursor.

With the exception of lines, all objects are drawn in the plane of the current User Coordinate System (UCS). Objects that can be drawn in three dimensions are covered in Chapter 12, "Commands for Three-Dimensional Operations."

Arc

Draws arcs

VERSIONS

All versions

SEQUENCE OF STEPS

Command: **Arc**(↵)

To select Arc from the menu system: **Draw** | **Arc** *or* **Draw** pull-down | **Arc**

Center/<Start point>: **C** [*or use mouse to pick start point or arc.*]

If Arc is issued from a menu, the arc menu appears, displaying several preset Arc options. Figure 4.1 illustrates how those options draw arcs.

OPTIONS

Angle Allows you to enter an arc in terms of degrees or current angular units. You are prompted for the *Included angle*. You can enter an angle value or visually select any angle using your cursor.

Center Allows you to enter location of an arc's center point. You get the prompt *Center*. You can enter a coordinate or pick a point with your cursor.

Direction Allows you to enter a tangent direction from the start point of an arc. You are prompted for the *Direction from start point*. You can either enter a relative coordinate or pick a point with your cursor.

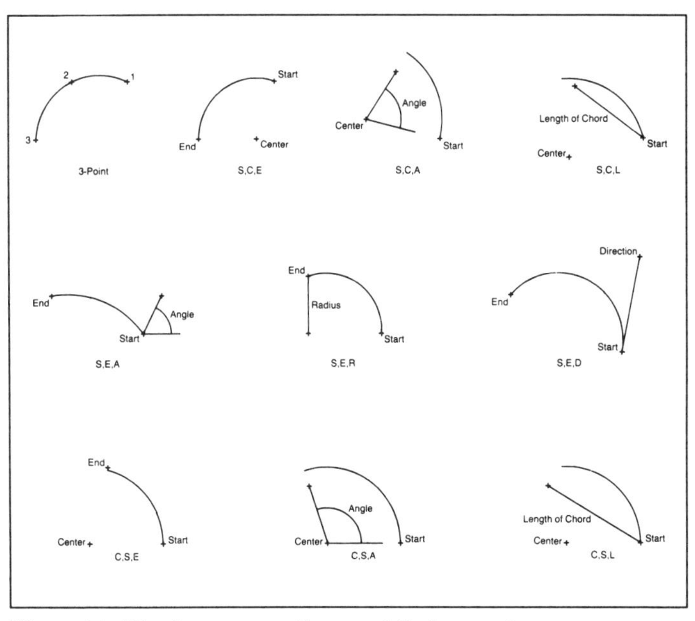

Figure 4.1: The Arc menu options and their meanings

End Allows you to enter the end point of an arc. You are prompted for the *End point*. You can enter a coordinate or pick a point with your cursor.

Length Allows you to enter the length of an arc's chord. You are prompted for the *Length of chord*. You can enter a length or pick a length using your cursor.

Radius Allows you to enter an arc's radius. You are prompted for the *Radius*. You can enter a radius or pick a point defining a radius length.

Start point Allows you to enter the beginning point of an arc.

USAGE

Arc allows you to draw an arc. Its options offer several ways to describe an arc. Perhaps the simplest way to use Arc is to pick three points; the first sets the beginning of the arc, the second sets a point through which the arc passes, and the third sets the end point of the arc. These are the default options for the Arc command. You can enter a different option at any prompt in the Arc prompt sequence.

If you issue a ↵ at the first prompt of the Arc command, AutoCAD will use the last point entered from a line or arc as the first point of the new arc and then prompt you for a new end point. An arc is drawn tangent to the last line or arc drawn.

The Arc screen menu provides several predefined Arc option sequences. For example, S,E,D allows you to select the start point, the end point, and the direction of the arc. See the preceding options to determine the meaning of other menu options. You can access Arc from the Draw pull-down menu.

To draw a three-dimensional cylinder with either one or both ends open, use two 180-degree extruded arcs instead of a circle. A circle extruded into the Z axis will create a cylinder with closed ends so the cylinder appears as a solid. You cannot draw arcs freely in three-dimensional space. You can only create them on the plane of a predefined UCS.

You can convert arcs to polyline arcs with the Pedit command.

SEE ALSO

Change/Thickness, Elev, UCS

Circle

Draws a circle

VERSIONS

All versions

SEQUENCE OF STEPS

Command: **Circle**(↵)

To issue Circle from the menu system: **Draw** | **circle** *or* **Draw** pull-down | **circle**

3P/2P/TTR/<Center point>: [*Enter option or pick point for center of circle.*]

OPTIONS

3P Allows you to define a circle based on three points. Once you select this option, you are prompted for a first, second, and third point. The circle will be drawn to pass through these points.

2P	Allows you to define a circle's diameter based on two points. Once you select this option, you are prompted to select the first and second point on the diameter of a circle. The two points will be the opposite ends of the circle's diameter.
TTR	Allows you to define a circle based on two tangent points and a radius. The tangent points can be on lines, arcs, or circles.
Center	Allows you to enter a center point for the circle.
Diameter/ Radius	Allows you to enter a diameter or radius value.

USAGE

Circle allows you to draw a circle by defining it in any number of ways. As the options indicate, to define a circle you can use two or three points, or use two tangent points and a radius. You can also use the default method, in which you choose a center point and then answer prompts for a diameter or radius. You can also select the **3point** option and then use the Tangent Osnap override to select three objects to which you want the circle to be tangent.

See **Arc** for notes on drawing three-dimensional, open-ended cylinders.

Donut

Draws thick circle

VERSIONS

2.5 and later

SEQUENCE OF STEPS

Command: **Donut** or **Doughnut**(↵)

To issue Donut from the menu system: **Draw | Donut**

Inside diameter <current default>: [*Enter inside diameter of donut.*]

Outside diameter <current default>: [*Enter outside diameter of donut.*]

Center of donut: [*Pick point for center of donut.*]

USAGE

Donut draws a circle (or "donut") whose thickness you specify by entering its inside and outside diameters (see Figure 4.2). You can use this command where a solid dot is required, as in a circuit board layout, by entering **0** at the *Inside diameter* prompt to draw a solid filled circle. The default values for the inside and outside diameter are the most recent diameters entered. Once you issue the Donut command and answer the prompts, you can place as many donuts as you like. Pressing ↵ terminates the command.

Since donuts are actually polylines, you can edit them with the Pedit command.

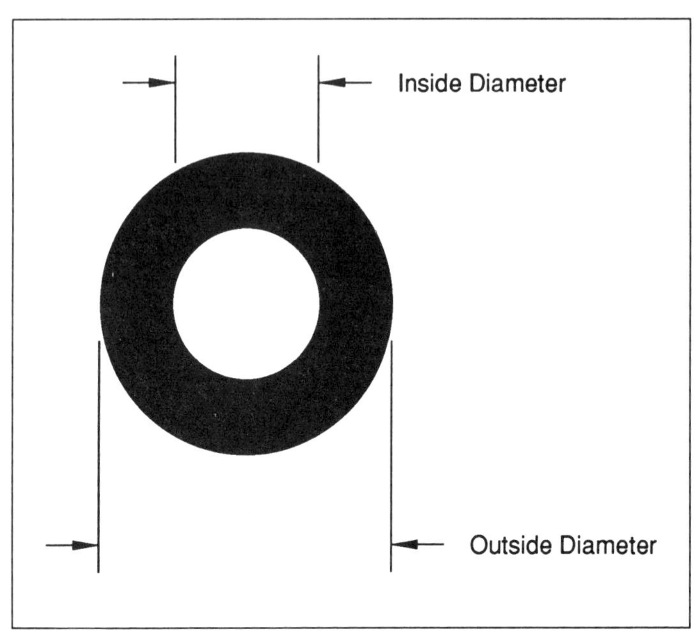

Figure 4.2: Inside and outside diameters of a donut

SEE ALSO

Pedit, Fill

Dtext and Text

Allows text insertion

VERSIONS

2.5 and later for Dtext, all versions for Text

SEQUENCE OF STEPS

Command: **Dtext**(↵) or **Text**(↵)

To issue Dtext or Text from the menu system: **Draw** | **Dtext** *or* **Draw** | **Next** | **Text** *or* **Draw** pull-down | **Dtext**

Start point or Align/Center/Fit/Middle/Right/Style: [*Enter desired options or pick a start point for your text.*]

Height <default height>: [*Enter desired text height or press ↵ to accept the default.*]

Rotation angle <default angle>: [*Enter a rotation angle or press ↵ to accept the default.*]

Text: [*Enter desired text.*]

OPTIONS

Start point Once you pick a point indicating the location of your text, the *Height, Rotation angle,* and *Text* prompts appear. The *Height* prompt only appears if the current text style has its height value set to 0.

Align Forces text to fit between two points. You are prompted to select two points defining the boundary of the text. The text will be scaled to fit within those points.

Center Centers text at the start point. The start point also defines the baseline of the text.

Fit Forces text to fit between two points. You are prompted to select two points defining the boundary of the text. Unlike Align, Fit leaves the text height at the default height and either stretches or compresses the text to fit between the selected points.

Middle Centers text at the start point. The start point also defines a point in the middle of the text height.

Right Right-justifies the text. The start point determines the right side of the text.

Style Allows new text style. The style you enter using this option becomes the new current style.

↵ Issuing a ↵ at the first prompt without an option causes the last line of text entered to highlight. The *Text* prompt will appear, allowing you to continue to add text after that line. The current text style and angle are assumed, as is the justification setting of the last text entered.

USAGE

The Dtext command allows you to enter several lines of text at once. It also displays the text on the drawing area as you type. At the first prompt, you can set the justification of the text to center, middle, right, or the current text style. You can also tell AutoCAD to fit the text between two points using either the Fit or Align options.

Once you select a text location, you are prompted for a text height if the current text style has a height value set to 0. You can enter a height value, visually select a height with your cursor, or press ↵ to accept the default value. If the current text style has a height greater than 0, no height prompt will appear.

Next, you are prompted for the rotation angle of your text. You can enter a value, visually select an angle with your cursor, or accept the default value by pressing ↵. The default is the last text rotation angle entered or 0.

A box will appear showing you the approximate size of the text. As you type, the text appears on your drawing and the box moves along, serving as a cursor. When you press ↵, the box will move down one line and you can enter more text. You can also pick a point to position the next line anywhere on the screen. You can backspace all the way to the beginning line if you need to correct something. If you choose center, middle, or right justification, the effects will not be seen until you finish entering the text.

If you press ↵ at the first prompt without entering an option or selecting a point, the last line of text entered will highlight and the *Text* prompt will appear, allowing you to continue adding text to the last text entered.

The Text command works nearly the same as Dtext; however, it does not display the text on your drawing as you type. The text you enter only appears on the *Command* prompt area. Also, once you press ↵, the text appears on the drawing and you are returned to the *Command* prompt. You cannot enter multiple lines of text unless you press ↵ twice.

In version 10, you can access Dtext from the Draw pull-down menu.

Dtext does not work with Script files.

SEE ALSO

Style, Color, Elev, Change

Ellipse

Draws an ellipse

VERSIONS

2.5 and later

SEQUENCE OF STEPS

Command: **Ellipse**(↵)

To issue Ellipse from the menu system: **Draw | Ellipse**

<Axis endpoint 1>/Center: [*Pick point defining one end of the ellipse or enter* **C** *to enter the center point.*]

If you select the default option by picking a point, the following prompts appear:

Axis endpoint 2: [*Pick a point defining the opposite end of the ellipse.*]

<Other axis distance>/Rotation: [*Pick a point defining the other axis of the ellipse or enter* **R** *to enter a rotation value.*]

OPTIONS

Center	Allows you to pick ellipse center point.
Axis end point	Allows you to enter the end point of one of the ellipse's axes (see Figure 4.3).
Other axis distance	Appears after you have already defined one of the ellipse's axes. Enter the distance from the center of the ellipse to the second axis end point (see Figure 4.3).
Isocircle	If the current Snap mode is set to Isometric, the first prompt includes the Isocircle option. This option will prompt you to select a center for the ellipse and then a diameter or radius. AutoCAD draws an isometric circle based on the points you select and the current Isoplane setting.

Rotation Allows you to enter ellipse rotation value. To understand what this value means, imagine the ellipse to be a two-dimensional projection of a three-dimensional circle rotating about an axis. As the circle rotates, it appears to turn into an ellipse. The more it rotates, the narrower the ellipse. The rotation value determines the rotation angle of this circle. A 0 value will display a full circle while an 80 degree value will display a narrow ellipse. The axis of rotation is defined by the two axis endpoints you select (see Figure 4.4).

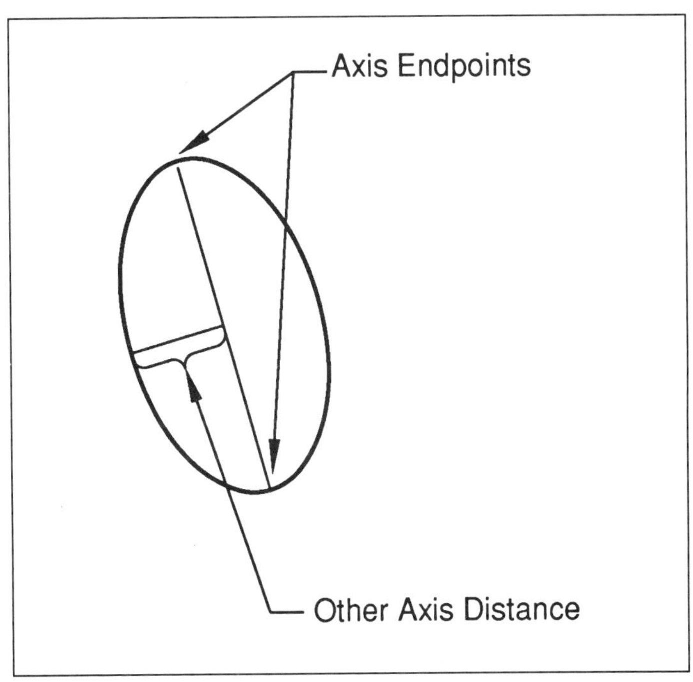

Figure 4.3: Axis end points and Other axis distance

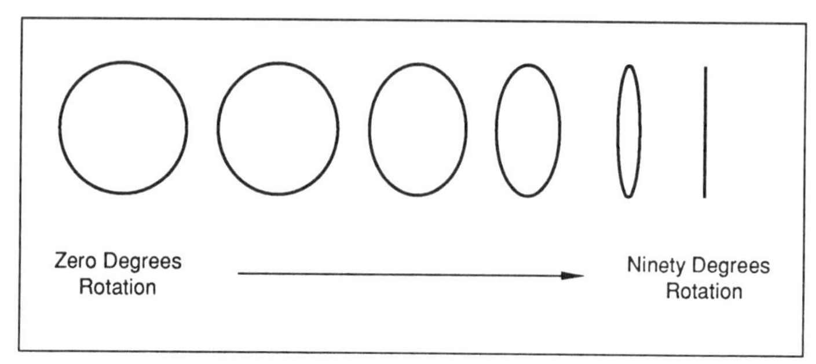

Figure 4.4: A rotated ellipse

USAGE

Ellipse allows you to draw an ellipse by specifying the major and minor axis of the ellipse, or a center point and two axis points, or the center point and radius or diameter of an isometric circle. It also allows you to define a two-dimensional projection of a three-dimensional circle through the Rotation option.

Since an ellipse is actually a polyline, you can edit it using the Pedit command.

SEE ALSO

Snap/Style, Isoplane

Hatch

Draws pattern within defined area

VERSIONS

1.4 and later

SEQUENCE OF STEPS

Command: **Hatch**(↲)

To issue Hatch from the menu system: **Draw** | **Hatch** *or* **Draw** pull-down | **Hatch**

Pattern (? or name/U,style) <default pattern>: [*Enter pattern name or* ***U*** *to create a simple crosshatch pattern.*]

OPTIONS

U Allows you to define a simple hatch pattern. You are prompted for the hatch angle, the spacing between lines, and whether or not you want a crosshatch. If you select crosshatching, it will occur at 90 degrees to the first hatch lines.

? Lists the name of available hatch patterns.

pattern name To use a specific pattern, enter its name at the *Pattern* prompt. You will be prompted for the scale and angle for the pattern. In general, the pattern scale should be the same as the drawing scale.

Besides the preceding options, you can use the following modifiers to control how the pattern is created. To use these modifiers, at the *Pattern* prompt enter the pattern name followed by a comma and the modifier.

N If you use the N option modifier and the objects selected for the hatch pattern are in concentric formation, the hatch pattern will fill each alternate area. For example, if you have four concentric circles and you pick all four circles at the *Select objects* prompt, the hatch pattern will fill in the space between the outer circle and the next circle, skip the space between the second and third circle, and fill the space between the third and fourth circle. The N option is the default.

O If you use the O option modifier, only the outermost area will be filled. In the concentric circle example, only the area between the outermost circle and the next circle will be filled.

I If you use the I option modifier, the entire area within the objects selected will be hatched, regardless of other enclosed areas that may occur within the selected area. This option also forces the hatch pattern to avoid hatching over text.

USAGE

Hatch fills an area defined by lines, arcs, circles, and polylines with either a predefined pattern or a simple hatch pattern. There are 41 predefined patterns, illustrated in Figure 4.5. You can list these patterns by entering **Hatch?** You can also get a graphic display of the patterns by picking **Hatch** from the Draw pull-down menu. You can create your own hatch patterns by using an ASCII text processor to edit the ACAD.PAT file that comes with AutoCAD. This file uses special numeric codes to define the patterns.

Hatch does not work properly if the objects that define the hatch area are not joined end-to-end and are not closed. To ensure a proper hatch pattern, draw a closed polyline enclosing the hatch area. Then, at the *Select objects* prompt, pick the polyline. If you use lines and arcs, be sure the end points of the objects meet exactly end-to-end.

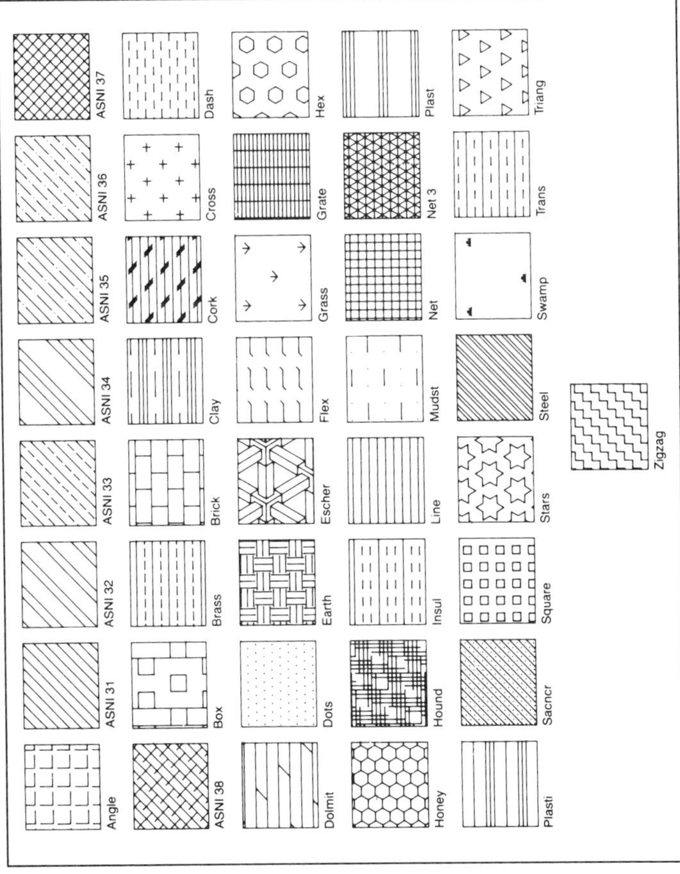

Figure 4.5: The standard hatch patterns

If you need the hatch pattern to begin at a specific point, use the **Rotate** option under the Snap command to set the snap origin to the desired beginning point. Hatch uses the snap origin to determine where to start the hatch pattern.

If for some reason you need to edit a hatch pattern, you can use the Explode command to break a pattern into its component lines.

SEE ALSO

Snap/Rotate, Explode

Line

Draws line or string of lines

VERSIONS

All versions

SEQUENCE OF STEPS

Command: **Line**(↵)

To issue Line from the menu system: **Draw** | **Line** *or* **Draw** pull-down | **Line**

From point: [*Select point to begin the line.*]

To point: [*Select line end point.*]

To point: [*Continue to select points to draw consecutive lines or press ↵ to exit the Line command.*]

OPTIONS

C After drawing at least two consecutive lines, you can enter **C** to close the series of lines.

start from last point You can continue a series of lines from a previously entered line, arc, point, or polyline by pressing ↵ at the *From point* prompt. If the last object drawn is an arc, the line will be drawn at a tangent from the end of the arc. Pressing **U** at the *From point* prompt deletes the last line segment.

USAGE

Line draws simple lines. You can draw a single line or a series of lines end-to-end.

You can convert lines to polylines using the Pedit command.

SEE ALSO

Pedit

Pline

Draws a polyline

VERSIONS

2.5 and later

SEQUENCE OF STEPS

Command: **Pline**(↵)

To issue Pline from the menu system: **Draw** | **Pline** *or* **Draw** pull-down | **Polyline**

From point: [*Pick start point of polyline.*]

Arc/Close/Halfwidth/Length/Undo/Width/<Endpoint of line>: [*Enter desired option or pick next point of pline.*]

OPTIONS

Arc Draws polyline arc. If you choose this option, you can enter either the angle, center, direction, radius, or end point of the arc in addition to the Close, Halfwidth, Undo, and Width options. You can also return to the line drawing mode. See the **Arc** command for the use of the Arc options.

Close Draws line from the current polyline end point back to its beginning, forming a closed polyline.

Halfwidth Allows you to specify half the polyline width at the current point. You are first prompted for the starting half width. The value you enter here indicates half the width of the polyline at the last fixed point. Next, you are prompted for the ending half width. The value you enter here indicates half the width of the polyline at the next point you pick.

Length Allows you to draw a polyline in the same direction as the last line segment drawn. You are prompted for the line segment length. If an arc was drawn last, the direction will be tangent to the end direction of that arc.

Undo Allows you to step backward along the current string of polyline or polyarc segments being drawn.

Width Allows you to determine the width of the polyline in the same way as the *Halfwidth* option, except that you specify the whole width of the polyline. Subsequent polylines will be of this width unless you specify otherwise.

USAGE

Polylines are lines that can take on additional properties such as thickness and curvature. Unlike standard lines, polylines can be grouped together to act as a single object. For example, a box you draw using a polyline will act as one object instead of four discrete lines. If you want to draw two parallel curves or a set of concentric boxes, you can use a polyline for one curve or box and then use the Offset command to make the parallel curve or the concentric box. To give a polyline a smooth curve shape, you must use the Pedit command after you create the polyline.

The Explode command will reduce a polyline to its line and arc components. Polylines with a width value will lose their width once exploded.

SEE ALSO

Pedit to curve a polyline, Offset, Explode

Point

Draws point or dot

VERSIONS

All versions, Pdmode was added in version 2.5

SEQUENCE OF STEPS

Command: **Point**(↵)

To issue Point from the menu system: **Draw** | **Next** | **Point**

Point: [*Enter point location.*]

OPTIONS

You can set the Pdmode system variable to change the appearance of points. Here are the setting values for Pdmode along with brief descriptions of the point the setting will generate. 0 is the default setting. When Pdmode is changed, all existing points are updated to reflect the new setting.

0	A dot
1	Nothing
2	A cross
3	An x
4	A vertical line up from the point of insertion
32	A circle
64	A square

By adding Pdmode variable values, you can generate a point that is a combination of the two variables.

USAGE

You can use Point to place center marks or other marking symbols in a drawing. By combining the different Pdmode variables, you can create 20 different types of points. For example, to combine a cross (2) with a circle (32), set Pdmode to 34 (2 + 32).

At times, you may want to mark a position in a drawing that is not associated with an object. You can draw a point as a marker in a drawing and use the Node Osnap override to select it. For example, you may want to be able to pick the center of a square column using the Osnap overrides. If you place a point at the center of the column, you can use the Node Osnap override to pick the column center.

Polygon

Draws a polygon

VERSIONS

2.5 and later

SEQUENCE OF STEPS

Command: **Polygon**(↵)

To issue Polygon from the menu system:
Draw | Next | Polygon

Number of sides: [*Enter number of sides.*]

Edge/<Center of polygon>: [*Enter **E** to select **Edge** option or pick a point to select the polygon center.*]

If you select the default center of a polygon, the following prompt appears:

Inscribed in circle/Circumscribed about circle (I/C): [*Enter desired option.*]

Radius of circle: [*Enter radius of circle defining polygon size.*]

OPTIONS

Edge Allows you to determine the length of one face of the polygon. You are prompted to select the first and second end point of the edge. AutoCAD then draws a polygon by creating a circular array of the edge you specify.

Inscribed Forces the polygon to fit inside a circle of the specified radius; the end points of each line lie along the circumference.

Circumscribed Forces the polygon to fit outside a circle of the specified radius; the midpoint of each polygon segment lies along the circumference.

Radius of circle Sets the length of the defining radius of the polygon. The radius will be the distance from the center to either an end point or a midpoint, depending on the Inscribed/Circumscribed choice.

USAGE

Polygon allows you to draw a regular polygon of up to 1024 sides. You can specify the outside or inside radius of the polygon or you can define the polygon based on the length of one of its sides. The polygon is actually a polyline which acts like a single object. You can use the Explode command to break the polyline into its component lines.

SEE ALSO

Pline, Pedit

Shape

Inserts predefined shape into drawing

VERSIONS

All versions

SEQUENCE OF STEPS

Command: **Shape**(↵)

To issue Shape from the menu system: **Draw** | **Next** | **Shape**

Shape name (or ?) <default>: [*Enter name of shape or question mark to list available shapes.*]

Start point: [*Pick insertion point.*]

Height <1.0>: [*Enter height value or visually select height using cursor.*]

Rotation angle <0.0>: [*Enter or visually select angle.*]

USAGE

If you have created a group of custom shapes in the form of the AutoCAD .SHX file, you can insert them using the Shape command. You must first load the .SHX file using the Load command. AutoCAD provides a sample .SHX file called PC.SHX. Shapes act like blocks but you cannot break them into their individual drawing components nor can you attach attributes to them. In this respect, they are more like text. In fact, text fonts are created in the same way as shapes. The only difference between the two is the way they are inserted.

Since shapes take up less file space than blocks, you may want to use shapes in drawings that do not require the features offered by blocks.

SEE ALSO

Load

Sketch

Allows "freehand" drawing

VERSIONS

2.0 and later

SEQUENCE OF STEPS

Command: **Sketch**(↵)

To issue Sketch from the menu system: **Draw** | **Next** | **Sketch**

Record increment: [*Enter value representing distance cursor travels before a line is fixed along the sketch path.*]

Pen eXit Quit Record Erase Connect.[*Start your sketch line or enter an option.*]

OPTIONS

Pen — Normally, you would use the pick button on your pointing device to set the pen up or down. You can also press **P** from the keyboard to toggle between the pen-up and pen-down modes. With the pen down, short temporary line segments will be drawn as you move the cursor. With the pen up, no lines are drawn.

eXit — Saves any temporary sketch lines as true lines and then exits the Sketch command.

Quit — Allows you to exit the Sketch command without saving temporary lines.

Record — Allows you to save temporary sketched lines as true lines while in the middle of the Sketch command.

Erase — Allows you to erase temporary sketched lines.

Connect — Allows you to continue from the end of a temporary sketch line.

. *(period)* — Allows you to draw a long line segment while in the Sketch command.

USAGE

Sketch allows you to draw freehand. It actually draws short line segments end-to-end to accomplish this effect. The *Record increment* prompt allows you to set the distance the cursor travels before AutoCAD places a line. The lower the values, the smoother the freehand line. The lines Sketch draws are only temporary lines that show the path of the cursor. You must save the line through the Record and eXit options to make it permanent.

If you need to draw a straight line segment while in the middle of a sketch line, as in the border between countries in a map for example, you can use the period option. To use this option, first set the pen up when you have reached the beginning of the straight line segment. Move the cursor to the other end of the line and then press the period key. A straight line will be drawn from the last fixed point to the current cursor location.

You can set the Sketch command to draw polylines instead of standard lines. Set the Skpoly system variable to 1 by using the Setvar command or by selecting **Skpoly** from the Sketch menu before you start your sketch.

The easiest way to use Sketch is with a digitizer equipped with a stylus. You can trace over other drawings or photographs and refine them later. The stylus gives a natural feel to your tracing.

The *Record increment* value can greatly affect the size of your drawing. If this value is too low, the sketch line segments will look too obvious and your sketched lines will appear "boxy." If the increment is set too high, your drawing file will become quite large and regeneration and redrawing times will increase dramatically. A rule of thumb is to set a *Record increment* value so that at least four line segments are drawn for the smallest 180-degree arc you will draw.

As you begin to sketch a line, your computer may beep and display the message *Please raise the pen*. If this occurs, press **P** to raise the pen. You may have to press **P** twice. When you get the message *Thank you. Lower the pen and continue,* you can press **P** again to proceed with your sketch. This occurs when AutoCAD runs out of RAM in which to store the lines being sketched. It must pause for a moment to set up a temporary file on your disk drive to continue to store the sketch lines. Setting *Record increment* to a low value increases your likelihood of getting this message.

Take care to turn the Snap and Ortho modes off before starting a sketch. Otherwise, the sketch lines will be forced to the snap points or drawn vertically or horizontally. The results of having the Ortho mode on may not be apparent until you zoom in on a sketch line.

If you prefer, you can sketch an object and then use the Pedit/Fit command to smooth the sketch lines.

SEE ALSO

Setvar/Skpoly, Pedit, Pline

Solid

Draws solid filled area

VERSIONS

All versions

SEQUENCE OF STEPS

Command: **Solid**(↵)

To issue Solid from the menu system: **Draw** | **Next** | **Solid**

First point: [*Pick one corner of area to be filled.*]

Second point: [*Pick next adjacent corner of the area.*]

Third point: [*Pick corner diagonal to the last point selected.*]

Fourth point: [*Pick next adjacent corner of the area.*]

You can continue to pick points to define the filled area. The *Third point* and *Fourth point* prompts appear as you continue to pick points.

USAGE

Solid allows you to fill an area solidly. You must determine the area by picking points in a crosswise, or "bow tie" fashion. Solid is best suited to filling in rectilinear areas. Polylines are better for filling in curved areas.

In large drawings that contain many solids, you can reduce regeneration and redrawing times by setting the Fill command to off until you are ready to plot the final drawing. If you leave Fill off when plotting, filled areas will not be filled.

SEE ALSO

Fill, 3Dface, Pline, Trace

Trace

Draws thick line

VERSIONS

All versions

SEQUENCE OF STEPS

Command: **Trace**(↵)

To issue Trace from the menu system: **Draw** | **Next** | **Trace**

Trace width <default width>: [*Enter desired width.*]

From point: [*Pick start point for the trace.*]

To point: [*Pick the next point.*]

As with the Line command, you can continue to pick points to draw a series of connected line segments.

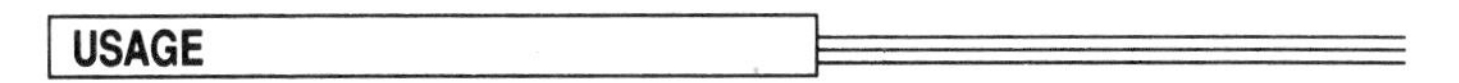

USAGE

You can use Trace where a thick line is desired. Alternatively, you can accomplish the same thing with using the Pline command. If you draw a series of Trace line segments, the corners are automatically joined to form a sharp corner.

SEE ALSO

Fill, Setvar/Tracewid

CHAPTER 5

Editing Commands

This chapter deals with commands that edit existing objects. These commands are found on the main Edit menu. This chapter frequently refers to an "Edit or Modify" pull-down menu, because in version 10 the Edit pull-down menu was renamed Modify. Both versions of this pull-down menu also contain some of the editing commands found in this chapter.

Commands you select from the pull-down menu act differently from those you select from the screen menu. If you select a command from the screen Edit menu, another menu appears, displaying options specific to that command. You can then select options from the menu or enter them through the keyboard. Once the command is completed, you are returned to the *Command* prompt.

If you select a command from the pull-down menu, the command is automatically reissued once it has been completed. To exit a command issued from the Edit pull-down menu, enter **Ctrl-C** or pick another command from the screen or pull-down menu. Also, commands you issue from the pull-down menu use the Si and Auto object-selection options. See the **Select** command in this chapter for details about these selection options.

Some commands prompt you for a point, direction, or length. You can either pick a point with your cursor or enter a coordinate through the keyboard. See Appendix A for details on how to enter angles, distances, and points from the keyboard. Also, prompts that ask for direction or length will often display a *rubber-banding line,* a temporary line that connects the cursor with the last point entered. The rubber-banding line moves with the cursor. This line helps you visually pick angles and lengths when you are using the cursor.

Array

Circular or row and column copies

VERSIONS

All versions

SEQUENCE OF STEPS

Command: **Array**(↵)

To issue Array from the menu system: **Edit | Array**

Select objects: [*Pick objects to array.*]

Rectangular or Polar array (R/P): [*Enter array type.*]

OPTIONS

Rectangular Allows you to copy the selected objects in an array of rows and columns. You are prompted for the number of rows and columns and the distance between rows and columns.

Polar Allows you to copy the selected objects in a circular array. You are prompted first for the center point of the array and then for the number of items in the array. This number should include the original group of objects being arrayed. Next, you are prompted for the

Angle to fill. This is the angle within which the array is to be made. The default is 360 degrees, a full circle. Prefix the number with a minus sign if you want the objects copied in a clockwise direction. Finally, you are asked whether you want to rotate the objects as they area copied. If you press ↵ without entering a value at the *Number of items* prompt, you will be prompted for the angle between items.

C Entering **C** at the *Rectangular* or *Polar* prompt allows you to enter the center point of a polar array. You are then prompted for the angle between items, the number of items or degrees to fill, and are asked whether you want the objects to be rotated as they are copied.

USAGE

Use Array to make multiple copies of an object or group of objects in a row and column matrix. You can also make single row or column copies. In addition, Array allows you to make circular copies of objects in order to form such objects as teeth in a gear or the numbers on a circular clock. Usually, row and column arrays are aligned with the X and Y axes of your drawing. However, you can create an array at any angle by first setting the Snap command's **Rotate** option to the desired angle. Once you do this, rectangular arrays will be rotated by the snap angle (see Figure 5.1).

SEE ALSO

Minsert, Snap/Rotate, Select

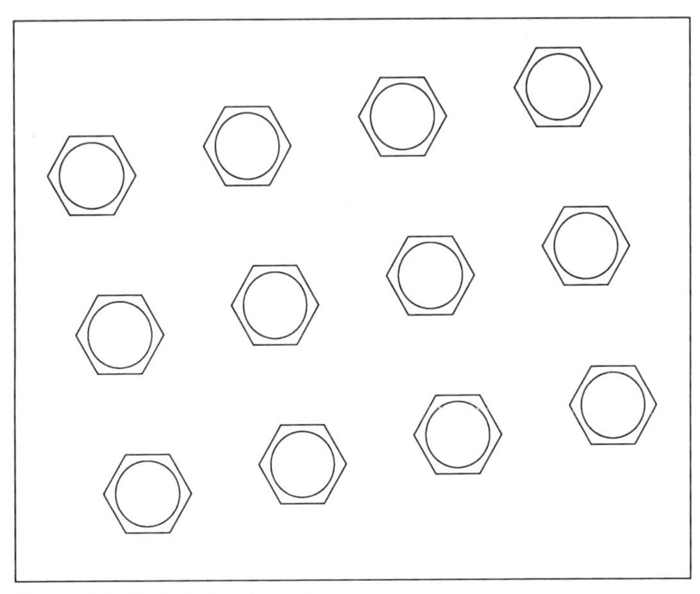

Figure 5.1: Rotated rectangular array

Attedit

Edits attribute values

VERSIONS

All versions

SEQUENCE OF STEPS

Command: **Attedit**(↵)

To issue Attedit from the menu system: **Edit** | **Attedit**

Edit attributes one at a time? <Y>: [*Enter* ***Y*** *for individual or* ***N*** *for global attribute editing.*]

Different prompts appear, depending on how you respond to this prompt. The following prompts always appear:

Block name specification <*>: [*Enter block name to restrict attribute edits to a specific block.*]

Attribute tag specification <*>: [*Enter attribute tag to restrict attribute edits to a specific attribute.*]

Attribute value specification <*>: [*Enter value to restrict attribute edits to a specific attribute value.*]

In most cases, you will next get a prompt asking you to select an attribute. Pick the attributes you want to edit. If you elected to edit the attributes one at a time, an X appears on the first attribute to be edited and you will see the prompt:

Value/Position/Height/Angle/Style/Layer/Color/Next/ <N>:

OPTIONS

Y *(at first prompt)*	Allows you to edit attribute values one at a time. If you press **Y** at the first prompt, you can also change an attribute's position, height, angle, text style, layer, and color.
N *(at first prompt)*	Allows you to globally modify attribute values. If you select this option, you are asked whether you want to edit only visible attributes.
Value	Allows you to change value of the currently marked attribute(s).
Position	Allows you to move an attribute.

Height	Allows you to change height of attribute text.
Angle	Allows you to change attribute angle.
Style	Allows you to change attribute text style.
Layer	Allows you to change layer attribute is on.
Color	Allows you to change attribute color. Colors are specified by numeric code or by name. See **Color**.

USAGE

Attedit allows you to change attribute values after you have inserted them in a drawing. You can edit attributes individually or globally.

If you choose to edit the attributes individually and have answered the prompts, you are prompted to select attributes. After you have made your selection, an X will mark the first attribute to edit. You can then change the value, position, height, angle, style, layer, or color of the marked attribute. The default option, Next, will move the marking X to the next attribute.

If you choose to change an attribute value by entering **V** at the *Value/Position/Height* prompt, you can then change or replace the attribute value. If you choose **Replace**, the default option, you are prompted for a new attribute value. Once entered, the new attribute value replaces the previous one and you return to the *Value/Position/Height* prompt and can further modify the attribute. If you choose **Change**, you are prompted for a specific string of characters to change and for a new string to replace the old. This allows you to change portions of an attribute's value without entering the entire attribute value.

If you choose to globally edit attributes by entering **N** at the *Edit attributes one at a time* prompt, you are asked whether you want to edit only visible attributes. If you enter **Y**, the default, you are prompted to select attributes to edit after answering the attribute specification prompts. You can then visually pick the attributes that you wish to edit. Once you pick the attributes, you are prompted for the string to change and then for the replacement string. Once you have answered the prompts, AutoCAD changes all the selected attributes. If you enter **N** at the *Visible attribute* prompt, you won't be prompted to select attributes. Instead, AutoCAD assumes you want to edit all the drawing attributes, whether or not they are visible. The *Select attribute* prompt is skipped and you are sent directly to the *Change string* prompt.

When answering the attribute specification prompts, you can use wildcard characters (question mark and asterisk) to "filter" a group of attribute blocks, tags, or values.

To restrict attribute edits to attributes with a null value, enter a backslash (\) at the attribute specification prompt.

SEE ALSO

Ddatte, Select

Break

Places break in an object

VERSIONS

2.0 and later

SEQUENCE OF STEPS

Command: **Break**(↵)

To issue Break from the menu system: **Edit** | **Break** *or* **Edit** *or* **Modify** pull-down | **Break**

Select object: [*Pick a single object to be broken.*]

Second point (or F for first point): [*Pick second point of break or enter **F** to specify first and second points.*]

USAGE

Break will erase a line, trace, circle, arc, or a two-dimensional polyline between two points. If you pick the object using the cursor, the "pick" point becomes the first point of the break. You are then prompted to pick a second point or to enter **F** to specify a different first break point. If you selected the object using a window, crossing window, or a **Last** or **Previous** option, you are automatically prompted for a first and second point. Break does not work on blocks, solids, text, shapes, three-dimensional faces, or three-dimensional polylines.

You can only perform breaks on objects that lie in a plane parallel to the current UCS. Also, if you are not viewing the current UCS in plan, you may get an erroneous result. It is best to use the Plan command to view the current UCS in plan before using Break.

When breaking circles, take care as to the break point selection sequence. If you pick the break points in a counterclockwise direction along a circle, the break occurs between the two points. If you select the points in a clockwise direction, the segment between the two points will remain while the rest of the circle will disappear.

In versions of AutoCAD earlier than version 9, ellipses break in an erratic manner. If you have problems breaking an ellipse, try making small breaks near the desired break points and then erasing the segment between them.

SEE ALSO

Trim, Change, UCS

Chamfer

Joins nonparallel lines

VERSIONS

2.5 and later

SEQUENCE OF STEPS

Command: **Chamfer**(↵)

To issue Chamfer from the menu system: **Edit | Chamfer**

Polyline/Distance/<select first line>: [*Pick first line.*]

Select second line: [*Pick second line.*]

OPTIONS

Polyline Allows you to chamfer all line segments within a polyline. When you use this option, you are prompted to select a two-dimensional polyline. All of the joining polyline segments will then be chamfered.

Distance Allows you to specify the size of the chamfer. When you use this option, you are prompted for the first and second chamfer distance. These are the distances from the intersection point of the lines to the beginning of the chamfer.

USAGE

Chamfer joins two nonparallel lines with an intermediate line. It also adds intermediate lines between the line segments of a two-dimensional polyline. You can set the size of the intermediate line with the Distance option.

You can only perform chamfers on objects that lie in a plane parallel to the current User Coordinate System (UCS). Also, if you are not viewing the current UCS in plan, you may get an erroneous result. It is best to use the Plan command to view the current UCS in plan, and then use the Chamfer command.

SEE ALSO

Fillet

Change

Changes property of an object

VERSIONS

All versions; Thickness and Elevation options added in version 2.1

SEQUENCE OF STEPS

Command: **Change**(↵)

To issue Change from the menu system: **Edit** | **Change**

Select objects: [*Select objects to be changed.*]

Properties/<change point>: [*If object is a line, you can pick new line end point. Otherwise, enter* ***P*** *to change the property of the selected object(s).*]

If you select the **Properties** option:

Change what property (Color/Elev/LAyer/LType/Thickness) ? [*Enter desired option.*]

OPTIONS

Properties	Allows you to change the color, elevation, layer, line type, or thickness of an object.
Color	Prompts you for new color of selected objects.
Elevation	Prompts you for new elevation in the object's Z axis.
LAyer	Prompts you for new layer.
LType	Prompts you for new line type.
Thickness	Prompts you for new thickness in the object's Z axis.

USAGE

Change can alter several properties of an object, including all the properties of lines. You can move line end points simply by selecting a point at the first prompt in the Change command. If you select several lines to be changed, all of the end points closest to the point picked will move to the new point. If the Ortho mode is on, the lines will become parallel and their end points will be aligned with the selected point.

You can change the color, layer, or line type of arcs, circles, and polylines. You can also change the rotation angle or layer assignment of a block.

Two options allow you to create three-dimensional objects by changing their Z axis properties. The Thickness option will extrude a two-dimensional line, arc, circle, or polyline into the Z axis. The Elevation option will change an object's base location in the Z axis. Thickness will not affect blocks, however.

When using Change to edit text, you can alter text style, height, rotation angle, or the text itself.

Change will not perform the Elevation option on objects that are not in a plane parallel to the current UCS.

Changing an object's color means that the object will no longer have the color of the layer on which it resides. This can cause some confusion in complex drawings. If you want to make an object the same color as its layer, enter **Bylayer** at the *Color* prompt.

SEE ALSO

Color, Elev, Chprop, UCS, Select

Chprop

Changes properties of objects

VERSIONS

10

SEQUENCE OF STEPS

Command: **Chprop**(↵)

To issue Chprop from the menu system: **Edit** | **Chprop** *or* (Version 10) **Modify** pull-down | **Properties**

Select objects: [*Select objects whose properties you wish to modify.*]

Change what property (Color/LAyer/LType/Thickness) ? <*option*>

OPTIONS

Color Prompts you for new color of selected objects.

LAyer Prompts you for new layer.

LType Prompts you for new line type.

Thickness Prompts you for new thickness in the object's Z axis.

USAGE

Chprop works as does the Change/Properties command, except it allows you to change the properties of all object types regardless of their three-dimensional orientation. Also, the Elevation option is not offered. You can use the Move command in place of the Elevation option.

SEE ALSO

Change, UCS, Elev, Color, Select

Copy

Copies objects

VERSIONS

All versions

SEQUENCE OF STEPS

Command: **Copy**(↵)

To issue Copy from the menu system: **Edit** | **Copy** *or* **Edit** or **Modify** pull-down

Select objects: [*Select objects to be copied.*]

<Base point or displacement>/Multiple [*Pick reference or "base" point for copy or enter **M** for multiple copies.*]

Second point of displacement: [*Pick copy distance and direction in relation to base point or enter displacement value.*]

OPTIONS

Multiple Make several copies of the selected objects.

USAGE

Copy allows you to copy a single object or a set of objects. The standard selection options are available. The points you pick for the base and second point determine the distance and direction of the copy. If you select the **Multiple** option, you are prompted for a base point and the *Second point* prompt appears repeatedly after you pick a second point.

This lets you make several copies of the selected object or group of objects. A ↵ returns you to the *Command* prompt.

AutoCAD assumes that you want to make copies within the current UCS. However, you can make copies in three-dimensional space by entering X,Y,Z coordinates or by using the Osnap overrides to pick objects in three-dimensional space.

When selecting the base and second point of displacement, you can use existing objects as reference points.

If you press ↵ at the *Second point* prompt without entering a point value, the selected objects may be copied to an area off of your current drawing. To recover from this error, use the U or Undo command.

SEE ALSO

Array, Multiple, Select/Si, Select/Auto

Ddatte

Edits attributes through dialog box

VERSIONS

9 and 10

SEQUENCE OF STEPS

Command: **Ddatte**(↵)

To issue Ddatte from the menu system: **Edit | Ddatte**

Select block: [*Pick block containing attribute(s) to edit.*]

USAGE

Use Ddatte to make a quick change to the attribute values of a single block. Ddatte allows you to see and edit all of the attributes in a block at once by displaying them in a dialog box. Once the dialog box appears, you highlight the attribute you want to edit and begin typing. Your entry will replace the attribute's previous value. Once you are done, you can pick **OK** to execute the change or **Cancel** to cancel your edit.

If you need to edit or browse several attributes, you can use Ddatte in conjunction with the Multiple command. Precede Ddatte with the word "Multiple" at the *Command* prompt. Then, every time you finish editing one block, AutoCAD will prompt you to select a block rather than return to the *Command* prompt. To exit the Ddatte command, enter **Ctrl-C**.

SEE ALSO

Attedit, Multiple, Attdef

Divide

Provides equally spaced division marks

VERSIONS

2.5 and later

SEQUENCE OF STEPS

Command: **Divide**(↵)

To issue Divide from the menu system: **Edit | Divide**

Select object to divide: [*Pick single object.*]

<Number of segments>/Block: [*Enter number of segments to mark or name of block to use for marking.*]

OPTIONS

Block Allows you to use existing block as a marking device. When you use this option, you are prompted for a *Block name to insert* and are asked whether you want to align the block with the object.

USAGE

Divide marks an object into equal divisions. You specify the number of divisions and AutoCAD determines the appropriate distance for each division and marks the object into equal parts.

Divide uses a point as a marker by default. Often, a point is difficult to see when placed over a line or arc. You can set the Pdmode system variable to change the appearance of the points and make them more visible, or you can use a block in place of the point by selecting the **Block** option. You will be prompted for the block name and asked whether you wish to align the block with the object. If you respond **Y** to the *Align block with object* prompt, the block will be aligned either along the axis of a line or tangentially to a selected polyline, circle, or arc. The Block option is useful if you need to draw a series of objects equally spaced along a curved path.

SEE ALSO

Point, Block, Measure, Setvar/Pmode

Erase

Erases objects

VERSIONS

All versions

SEQUENCE OF STEPS

Command: **Erase**(↵)

To issue Erase from the menu system: **Edit** | **Erase** *or* **Edit** *or* **Modify** pull-down | **Erase**

Select objects: [*Select objects to be erased.*]

USAGE

Erase erases one or several objects from the drawing. You can use the standard selection options.

When you are erasing overlapping objects, an overlapped object will often appear to have been broken or erased. Redrawing restores the overlapped object.

SEE ALSO

Multiple, Oops, Select/Si, Select/Auto

Explode

Reduces compound objects into components

VERSIONS

2.5 and later

SEQUENCE OF STEPS

Command: **Explode**(↵)

To issue Explode from the menu system: **Edit | Explode**

Select block reference, polyline, dimension, or mesh:
[*Pick object to be exploded.*]

USAGE

Explode reduces a block, polyline, associative dimension, or three-dimensional mesh to its component objects. It "unblocks" a block or "unplines" a polyline. If a block is nested, Explode will only "unblock" the outermost block. Wide polylines will lose their width properties.

Blocks inserted with Minsert and blocks with unequal X, Y, or Z insertion scale factors cannot be exploded.

SEE ALSO

Undo

Extend

Extends object to meet another object

VERSIONS

2.5 and later

SEQUENCE OF STEPS

Command: **Extend**(↵)

To issue Extend from the menu system: **Edit** | **Extend** *or* **Edit** *or* **Modify** pull-down | **Extend**

Select boundary edge(s)... [*Pick one or more objects to which to extend other objects.*] (↵)

Select objects: [*Pick objects to extend one at a time.*]

USAGE

Extend lengthens an object to meet another object. For example, you can make a line touch another nonparallel line or arc or make an arc touch a line. At the *Select boundary* prompt, you can pick several objects that are to be extended to. Once you've selected these boundary objects, press ↵ and the *Select object* prompt will appear, allowing you to pick the objects to extend. You cannot extend objects within blocks or use blocks as boundary edges. Also, boundary edges must be in the path of the objects to be extended.

You can only extend objects that lie in a plane parallel to the current User Coordinate System (UCS). Also, if you are not viewing the current UCS in plan, you may get an erroneous result. It is best to use the Plan command to view the current UCS in plan, and then proceed with the Extend command.

At times, objects will not extend properly even when all conditions are met. If this problem occurs, try changing your view using the Zoom or Pan command, and then reissue the Extend command.

SEE ALSO

Change, Trim

Fillet

Joins two lines or arcs with an arc

VERSIONS

All versions

SEQUENCE OF STEPS

Command: **Fillet**(↵)

To issue Fillet from the menu system: **Edit** | **Next** | **Fillet** *or* (Version 10 only) **Modify** pull-down | **Fillet**

Polyline/Radius/<select first line>: [*Pick first line.*]

Select second line: [*Pick second line.*]

OPTIONS

Polyline Allows you to fillet all line segments within a polyline. When you use this option, you are prompted to select a two-dimensional polyline. All joining polyline segments will then be filleted.

Radius Allows you to specify radius of the fillet arc.

USAGE

Fillet joints two nonparallel lines, a line and an arc, or segments of a polyline with an intermediate arc, whose size you specify with the **Radius** option. The end points closest to the intersection are joined. If the lines (or line and arc) already intersect, Fillet substitutes the specified arc for the existing corner. To connect two nonparallel lines with a corner rather than an arc, set the radius to 0.

If you are not viewing the current UCS in plan, you may get an erroneous result from Fillet. It is best to use the Plan command to view the current UCS in plan before issuing the Fillet command.

SEE ALSO

Chamfer

Measure

Adds division marks at specified intervals

VERSIONS

2.5 and later

SEQUENCE OF STEPS

Command: **Measure**(↵)

To issue Measure from the menu system: **Edit** | **Next** | **Measure**

Select object to measure: [*Pick a single object.*]

<Segment length>/Block: [*Enter length of segments to mark or name of block to use for marking.*]

OPTIONS

Block Allows you to use existing, user-defined block as a marking device. When you use this option, you are prompted for a block name and are asked whether you want to align the block with the object.

USAGE

Measure marks an object into equal divisions of a specified length. This is like using dividers to mark specified equal lengths on a drawn line or arc. The end of the object closest to the pick point is the end at which the measurement begins.

Measure uses a point as a marker by default. Often, a point is difficult to see when placed over a line or arc. You can set the Pdmode system variable to make the points more visible, or you can use any other symbol that you've created as a block in place of the point by selecting the **Block** option. You will be prompted for the block name and asked whether to align the block with the object. If you respond **Y** to the alignment prompt, the block will be aligned along the axis of a line or it will be aligned with a tangent to a circle, arc, or curved polyline. If you respond **N**, the block will be inserted at its normal orientation regardless of the orientation of the object being measured.

The Block option is useful if you need to draw a series of objects a specified distance apart along a curved path.

SEE ALSO

Point, Block, Divide

Mirror

Creates mirror image of object(s)

VERSIONS

2.5 and later

SEQUENCE OF STEPS

Command: **Mirror**(↵)

To issue Mirror from the menu system: **Edit** | **Next** | **Mirror** *or* (Version 10 only) **Modify** pull-down | **Mirror**

Select objects: [*Pick objects to be mirrored.*]

First point of mirror line: [*Pick one end of mirror axis.*]

Second point: [*Pick other end of mirror axis.*]

Delete old objects? <N> [*Enter **Y** to delete originally selected objects or **N** to keep them.*]

USAGE

Mirror makes a mirror-image copy of an object or a group of objects. The mirror axis is determined by two points you provide.

Normally, text and attributes will be mirrored so they read backwards. To prevent mirrored text while using the Mirror command, set the Mirrtext system variable to 0.

Mirroring occurs in a plane parallel to the current UCS.

SEE ALSO

Select, Setvar/Mirrtext

Move

Moves an object

VERSIONS

All versions

SEQUENCE OF STEPS

Command: **Move**(↵)

To issue Move from the menu system: **Edit** | **Next** | **Move** *or* **Edit** or **Modify** pull-down | **Move**

Select objects: [*Select objects to be moved.*]

Base point or displacement: [*Pick reference or "base" point for move.*]

Second point of displacement: [*Pick move distance and direction in relation to base point or enter displacement value.*]

USAGE

Move allows you to move a single object or a set of objects. The standard selection options are available. The points you pick for the base and second point determine the distance and direction of the move.

AutoCAD assumes you want to move objects within the current UCS. However, you can move objects in three-dimensional space by entering X,Y,Z coordinates or by using the Osnap overrides to pick objects in three-dimensional space.

If you press ↵ at the *Second point* prompt without entering a point value, the objects selected may be moved to a position completely off your drawing area. You can use the U or Undo command to recover from this error.

SEE ALSO

Select

Offset

Creates parallel copy

VERSIONS

2.5 and later

SEQUENCE OF STEPS

Command: **Offset**(↵)

To issue Offset from the menu system: **Edit** | **Next** | **Offset**

Offset distance or Through <default distance>: [*Enter a distance value to specify a constant offset distance or* ***Through*** *to specify an offset distance after each object selection is made.*]

Select object to offset: [*Pick one object.*]

Side to offset: [*Pick on which side you want the offset to appear.*]

OPTIONS

Through Allows you to enter a point through which the offset object will pass *after* you have selected the object to offset. You will be prompted for a distance after each object is selected.

USAGE

Offset creates an object parallel to and at a specified distance from the original. If you enter a value at the *Distance* prompt, all of the offsets performed in the current command will be at that distance. Entering **T** at this prompt allows you to specify a different offset distance for each object selected.

Very complex polylines may offset incorrectly or not at all. This usually means that there is insufficient memory to process the offset.

You can only perform offsets on objects that lie in a plane parallel to the current UCS. Also, if you are not viewing the current UCS in plan, you may get an erroneous result.

SEE ALSO

Copy

Pedit

Edits a polyline, 3D mesh, or vertex

VERSIONS

2.1 and later

SEQUENCE OF STEPS

Command: **Pedit**(↵)

To issue Pedit from the menu system: **Edit** | **Next** | **Pedit** *or* (Version 9 only) **Edit** pull-down | **Polyedit** *or* (Version 10 only) **Modify** pull-down | **Edit Polylines**

Select polyline: [*Select polyline or three-dimensional mesh.*]

The sequences beyond this point depend on the type of polyline object you are editing. See the following sections.

USAGE

You can use Pedit to edit two- or three-dimensional polylines or three-dimensional meshes, to change the location of individual vertices in a polyline or mesh, or to convert a non-polyline object into a polyline. The editing options available depend on the type of object you select. See the following sections for information about individual Pedit operations.

Pedit for Two-Dimensional or Three-Dimensional Polylines

Edits polylines

SEQUENCE OF STEPS

Command: **Pedit**(↵)

Select Polyline: [*Select two-dimensional or three-dimensional polyline.*]

If the object is a two-dimensional polyline, the following prompt appears:

Close/Join/Width/Edit vertex/Fit curve/Spline curve/Decurve/Undo/eXit <X>: <*option*>

If the object is a three-dimensional polyline, the following prompt appears:

Close/Edit vertex/Spline curve/Decurve/Undo/eXit <X>: <*option*>

If the object is a standard line or arc, the following prompt appears:

Entity selected is not a polyline

Do you want it to turn into one: <Y>: [*Enter **Y** or **N**.*]

OPTIONS

Close	Joins end points of an open polyline with a closing polyline segment. If the selected polyline is already closed, this option is replaced by Open in the prompt.
Open	Deletes last line segment in a closed polyline.
Join	Joins polylines, lines, and arcs. The objects to be joined must meet exactly end-to-end.
Width	Allows you to set the width of the entire polyline.
Edit vertex	Allows you to perform various edits on polyline vertices. See **Pedit/Edit** vertex in this chapter.
Fit curve	Changes a polyline made up of straight line segments into a smooth curve.
Spline curve	Changes a polyline made up of straight line segments into a smooth spline curve.
Decurve	Changes a smoothed polyline into one made up of straight line segments.
Undo	Undoes the last Pedit function issued.
eXit	Exits the Pedit command.

USAGE

Pedit allows you to modify the shape of two-dimensional and three-dimensional polylines, and three-dimensional meshes (see "Pedit for Three-Dimensional Meshes"). If the object you select is not a polyline, you are asked whether to turn it into one. This is a way of making a non-polyline object into a polyline. If the object you select is a three-dimensional polyline or a three-dimensional mesh, the first prompt is somewhat different than the one in the Sequence of Steps. For three-dimensional polylines, it is basically the same prompt without the Join, Width, and Fit curve options.

If you use the Spline curve option, you can adjust the amount of "pull" the vertex points exert on the curve by changing the Splinetype system variable. With Splinetype set to 5, the vertices exert a greater pull on the curve. With Splinetype set to 6 (the default), the vertices exert less pull. See **Setvar** for more details.

To help you edit a Spline curve, you can view both the curve and the defining vertex points by setting the Splframe system variable to 1.

You can adjust the smoothness of a spline curve with the Splinesegs system variable. Splinesegs determines the number of line segments used to draw the curve. A higher value generates more line segments, for a smoother curve but also a larger drawing file.

SEE ALSO

Setvar/Splinetype, Setvar/Splframe, Setvar/Splinesegs, Pline, Pedit/3D mesh, Pedit/Edit Vertex

Pedit/Edit Vertex

Edits vertices in polyline

VERSION

2.1 and later

SEQUENCE OF STEPS

Command: **Pedit**(↵)

Select polyline: [*Select polyline with cursor.*]

Close/Join/Width/Edit vertex/Fit curve/Decurve/Undo/eXit <X>: [*Enter* ***E****. An X appears on the selected polyline, indicating the vertex currently editable.*]

Next/Previous/Break/Insert/Move/Regen/Straighten/Tangent/Width/eXit <N>: [*Enter capitalized letter of function to use.*]

OPTIONS

Next Moves X marker to next vertex.

Previous Moves X marker to previous vertex.

Break Breaks polyline from marked vertex. Once you select **Break**, you can move the marker to another vertex to select the other end of the break. When this function is entered, the prompt changes to

Next/Previous/Go/eXit <N>:

allowing you to move in either direction along the polyline. Once the X marker is in position, enter **G** to initiate the break.

Insert Inserts new vertex. A rubber-banding line appears from the vertex being edited to the cursor. You can enter points using the cursor or by entering coordinates.

Move Allows relocation of vertex. A rubber-banding line appears from the xmarker to the cursor. Enter a new point using the cursor or by entering coordinates.

Regen Regenerates polyline. This may be required to see effects of some edits.

Straighten Straightens polyline between two vertices. When you enter this function, the prompt changes to

Next/Previous/Go/eXit <N>:

allowing you to move in either direction along the polyline. Once the X marker is in position, enter **G** to straighten the polyline.

Tangent Allows you to modify tangent direction of vertex. A rubber-banding line appears from the vertex to the cursor, indicating the new tangent direction. You can enter the new tangent angle by picking the direction using the cursor or by entering an angle value through the keyboard. This only affects curve-fitted or spline polylines.

Width — Allows you to vary the width of a polyline segment. When you enter this function, the prompt changes to

> Enter starting width <*current default width*>:

allowing you to enter a new width for the currently marked vertex. Once you enter a value, the prompt changes to:

> Enter ending width <*last value entered*>:

allowing you to enter a width for the next vertex.

eXit — Exits from vertex editing.

USAGE

You can relocate, remove, or move vertices in a polyline. You can also modify a polyline's width at a particular vertex and alter the tangent direction of a curved polyline through a vertex.

Once you invoke the Edit vertex function, an X appears on the polyline to indicate the vertex being edited. Entering ↵ moves the X to the next vertex. Entering **P** reverses the direction the X moves along the polyline. When inserting a new vertex into a polyline or using the width function, pay special attention to the direction in which the X moves when you select the Next function. This is the direction along the polyline in which the new vertex or the new ending width will be inserted.

If you select a three-dimensional polyline, all the edit options except Tangent and Width are available. Also, point input will accept three-dimensional points. You can issue Pedit from the Edit or Modify pull-down menu. In version 9, it is Polyedit on the Edit pull-down menu. In version 10, it is Edit Polylines on the Modify pull-down menu.

Pedit for Three-Dimensional Meshes

Edits three-dimensional meshes

VERSIONS

2.1 and later, three-dimensional options added in version 10

SEQUENCE OF STEPS

Command: **Pedit**(↵)

Select polyline: [*Pick three-dimensional mesh.*]

Edit vertex/Smooth surface/
Desmooth/Mclose/Nclose/Undo/eXit <X>: <*option*>

OPTIONS

Edit vertex — Allows you to relocate vertices of selected three-dimensional mesh. When you select this option, you get the prompt:

Vertex (m,n)

Next/Previous/Left/Right/Up/Down/
Move/REgen/eXit <N>: <*option*>

An X appears on the first vertex of the mesh, marking the vertex that will be moved with the Move option.

Next — Rapidly moves Edit vertex marker to next vertex.

Previous — Rapidly moves Edit vertex marker to previous vertex.

Left	Moves Edit vertex marker along the N direction of the mesh.
Right	Moves Edit vertex marker along the N direction of the mesh opposite to the Left option.
Up	Moves Edit vertex marker along the M direction of the mesh.
Down	Moves Edit vertex marker along the M direction of the mesh opposite to the Up direction.
Move	Moves location of currently marked vertex.
REgen	Redisplays mesh after a vertex has been moved.
Smooth surface	Generates B-spline or Bezier surface based on the mesh's vertex points. The type of surface generated depends on the Surftype system variable.
Desmooth	Returns smoothed surface back to regular mesh.
Mclose	Closes mesh in the M direction. If mesh is already closed, this option becomes Mopen.
Nclose	Closes mesh in the N direction. If mesh is already closed, this option becomes Nopen.
Undo	Undoes last Pedit option issued.

eXit Exits Edit vertex option or the Pedit command.

USAGE

When using Pedit on a three-dimensional mesh, you can either smooth the mesh or move the location of specific vertex points in the mesh.

You can use several system variables (see **Setvar**) to modify a three-dimensional mesh. You can use the Surftype variable in conjunction with the Smooth option to determine the type of smooth surface generated. A value of 5 gives you a quadratic B-spline surface, 6 gives you a cubic B-spline surface, and 8 gives you a Bezier surface. The default value for Surftype is 6.

The Surfu and Surfv system variables control the accuracy of the generated surface. Surfu controls the surface density in the M direction of the mesh; Surfv controls density in the N direction. The default value for these variables is 6.

The Splframe system variable determines whether the control mesh of a smoothed mesh is displayed. If it is set to 0, only the smoothed mesh is displayed. If it is set to 1, only the defining mesh is displayed.

SEE ALSO

Setvar/Surftype, /Surfu, /Surfv, and /Splframe

Redo

Reexecutes command reversed with Undo

VERSIONS

2.5 and later

SEQUENCE OF STEPS

Command: **Redo**(↵)

To issue Redo from the menu system: **Edit | Redo**

USAGE

If you change your mind about a command you have undone using Undo, Redo will restore the command.

SEE ALSO

U, Undo

Rotate

Rotates an object

VERSIONS

2.5 and later

SEQUENCE OF STEPS

Command: **Rotate**(↵)

To issue Rotate from the menu system: **Edit | Next | Rotate**

Select objects: [*Select objects to be rotated.*]

Base point: [*Pick point about which objects are to be rotated.*]

<Rotation angle>/Reference: [*Enter angle of rotation or* ***R*** *to specify a reference angle.*]

OPTIONS

Reference Allows you to specify the rotation angle in reference to the object's current angle. If you enter this option, you get the prompt

> Reference angle <0>: [*Enter current angle of object or pick a point representing the angle from the base point of the rotation.*]
>
> New angle: [*Enter new angle or pick angle with cursor.*]

USAGE

Rotate rotates an object or group of objects to a specified angle. You can also specify an angle relative to another angle.

SEE ALSO

Select

Scale

Changes the size of objects

VERSIONS

2.5 and later

SEQUENCE OF STEPS

Command: **Scale**(↵)

To issue Scale from the menu system: **Edit | Scale**

Select objects: [*Pick objects to be scaled.*]

Base point: [*Pick point of reference for scaling.*]

<Scale factor>/Reference: [*Enter scale factor, move the cursor to visually select new scale, or enter* ***R*** *to select the Reference option.*]

OPTIONS

Reference Allows you to specify a scale in relation to a known length.

USAGE

The Scale command allows you to change the size of objects in a drawing. You can scale a single object or an entire drawing. You can specify an exact scale or you can scale visually. You can also scale an object by reference. For example, suppose you have a box with sides 3 units long and you want to make the sides 4.3 units long. Using the Reference option, you can pick two end points of a side or enter a value for the reference length and then enter the new length, 4.3 units.

SEE ALSO

Block, Insert, Select

Select

Selects group of objects for later editing

VERSIONS

2.5 and later

SEQUENCE OF STEPS

Command: **Select**(↵)

To issue Select from the menu system: **Edit | Select**

Select objects: [*Select objects to be edited later using the usual selection options.*]

OPTIONS

Window	Selects objects completely enclosed by a rectangular window.
Crossing	Selects objects that are within or cross through a rectangular window.
Previous	Selects last set of objects selected for editing.
Last	Selects last object drawn or inserted.

Remove	Removes objects from the current selection of objects.
Add	Adds objects to the current selection of objects. You will usually use this option after you have issued the **R** option.
Multiple	Allows you to pick several objects at once before adding them to the current selection of objects.
Undo	Removes most recently added object from current selection of objects.
BOX	Allows you to use either a crossing or standard window, depending on the orientation of your window pick points. If points are picked from right to left, you will get a crossing window. If points are picked from left to right, you will get a standard window.
AUto	Allows you to select objects by picking them individually or by using a window, as in the BOX option. After you issue the AUto option, you can pick objects individually as usual. If a point void of object is picked, AutoCAD assumes you want to use the BOX option and a window appears allowing you to either use a crossing or standard window to select objects.
SIngle	Selects only the first picked object or the first group of windowed objects.

USAGE

The Select command operates exactly as does the *Select object* prompt in other commands. It allows you to select a group of objects using a variety of options. Once you select the objects, you are returned to the *Command* prompt. The objects selected become the most recent selection in AutoCAD's memory. You can then use the Previous option to pick this selection set when a later command prompts you to select objects. This is useful when you want several commands to process the same set of objects, as in a menu macro.

The Select command only maintains a selection set until you pick a different group of objects at another *Select object* prompt. To create a selection set that will be maintained for the duration of the current editing session, use a simple AutoLISP function. Do this by entering **(setq set1 (ssget))** at the *Command* prompt. You will be prompted to select objects. After you are done, you are returned to the *Command* prompt. Later, when you want to select this group of objects again, enter **!set1** at the *Select objects* prompt.

Stretch

Moves vertices of objects

VERSIONS

2.5 and later

SEQUENCE OF STEPS

Command: **Stretch**(↵)

To issue Stretch from the menu system: **Edit** | **Stretch** *or* **Edit** or **Modify** pull-down | **Stretch**

Select objects: [*Enter **C** to use a crossing window.*]

Select objects: [*Enter **R** to remove objects from the set of selected objects or press ↵ to confirm your selection.*]

Base point: [*Pick base reference point for the stretch.*]

New point: [*Pick second point in relation to the base point indicating the distance and direction you wish to move.*]

USAGE

Stretch allows you to move a group of objects, including any end points that may be connected to those objects. This way, you can maintain the continuity of connected lines while moving objects. If you issue Stretch from the keyboard, you must also enter **C** (for crossing window) at the *Select objects* prompt. You can then deselect objects with the *Remove object* selection option. See **Select** in this chapter.

Blocks and text will not be stretched. If a block's or text's insertion point is included in a crossing window, the entire block will be moved.

SEE ALSO

Move, Copy

Trim

Trims object to meet intersecting object

VERSIONS

2.5 and later

SEQUENCE OF STEPS

Command: **Trim**(↵)

To issue Trim from the menu system: **Edit** | **Trim** *or* **Edit** *or* **Modify** pull-down | **Trim**

Select cutting edge(s)... [*Pick objects to which you want to trim other objects.*]

Select objects: [*Pick objects you want to trim one at a time.*]

USAGE

Trim shortens an object to meet another object. At the *Select cutting edge* prompt, you can pick several objects that intersect the objects you want to trim. Once you've selected the cutting edges, press ↵ and the *Select object* prompt appears, allowing you to pick the objects to trim. You cannot trim objects within blocks or use blocks as cutting edges. In addition, cutting edges must intersect the objects to be trimmed. You can also use Trim to break a line, circle, or arc between two other objects.

You can only use Trim on objects that lie in a plane parallel to the current User Coordinate System. Also, if you are not viewing the current UCS in plan, you may get an erroneous result.

SEE ALSO

Change, Break

U

Undoes effects of last command

VERSIONS

2.5 and later

SEQUENCE OF STEPS

Command: **U**(↵)

USAGE

If you have executed a command that you wish to reverse, U will undo the most recent command. You can undo as many commands as you have issued during any given editing session. However, you cannot undo commands after a Plot or Prplot command has occurred.

The Auto, End, Control, and Group options under the Undo command affect the results of the U command.

SEE ALSO

Undo, Redo

Undo

Controls the Undo process

VERSIONS

2.5 and later

SEQUENCE OF STEPS

Command: **Undo**(↵)

To issue Undo from the menu system: **Edit** | **Undo**

Auto/Back/Control/End/Group/Mark/<*default number*>:
[*Enter option to use or number of commands to undo.*]

OPTIONS

Auto Makes AutoCAD view menu macros as a single command. If Auto is set to On, the effect of macros issued from a menu will be undone regardless of the number of commands the macro contains.

Back & Mark Allow you to experiment safely with a drawing by first marking a point in your editing session to which you can return. Once a mark has been issued, you can proceed with your experimental drawing addition. Then, you can use Back to undo all the commands back to the place that Mark was issued.

End & Group Allow you to mark a group of commands to be undone together. Issue the **Undo/Group** command and edit until you reach the point where you wish to end the group. Then, issue the **Undo/End** command. If you use the U command, the commands issued between the Undo/Group and the Undo/End commands will be treated as a single command and will all be undone at once.

Control Allows you to turn off the Undo feature to save disk space or to limit the Undo feature to single commands. You are prompted for All, None, or One. All fully enables the Undo feature, None disables Undo, and One restricts the Undo feature to a single command at a time.

USAGE

Undo allows you to control how much of a drawing is undone using the U command.

SEE ALSO

U, Redo

CHAPTER 6

Inquiry Commands

The commands in this chapter allow you to get information about your drawing. You can get general information about AutoCAD and the particular drawing file in which you are working, and specific information about commands and objects in your drawing. All of these commands can be found in the Inquiry side menu.

Area

Finds area within set of objects

VERSIONS

All versions

SEQUENCE OF STEPS

Command: **Area**(↵)

To issue Area from the menu system: **Inquiry** | **Area**

<First point>/Entity/Add/Subtract: [*Pick first point defining area or enter option.*]

If you select a point the following prompt appears:

Next Point: [*Pick next point*]

OPTIONS

Next point If you pick a point at the first prompt, you will be prompted for the next point. You can continue to select points to define the area from which you wish to obtain an area calculation. Once you are done defining an area, press ↵ at the *Next point* prompt.

Entity Allows you to select a circle or polyline for area calculation. If you pick an open polyline, AutoCAD calculates the area of the polyline as if its two end points were closed.

Add Allows you to keep running count of areas. Normally, Area returns you to the *Command* prompt as soon as an area has been calculated. If you enter the Add mode, once an area has been calculated, you are returned to the *Areas* command prompt and you can keep adding area values to the current area.

Subtract Allows you to subtract areas from a running count of areas.

USAGE

Area allows you to find an area by either defining it using line segments, by selecting lines and polylines defining the area, or by a combination of both. The Add option allows you to maintain a running count of several areas.

To find the area of a complex shape that includes arcs, convert the arc areas into polylines (see **Pedit**) before you issue the Area command. Area does not calculate areas for arcs, but it does for polylines. Then you can use the Entity option of the Area command and pick the polyline. Area will base its area calculation on the selected polyline. Add the polyline areas to the rectangular areas to get the total area of the shape.

Area will only calculate areas in a plane parallel to the current User Coordinate System. Also, you can only select objects that lie in a plane parallel to the current UCS.

SEE ALSO

List

Dblist

Lists properties of objects in drawing

VERSIONS

All versions

SEQUENCE OF STEPS

Command: **Dblist**(↵)

To issue Dblist from the menu system: **Inquiry | Dblist**

USAGE

Dblist lists the properties of all objects in a drawing. The screen will switch to Text mode and the list of objects will begin to scroll down the screen. You can stop the listing by pressing **Ctrl-C**. Dblist is similar to the List command.

SEE ALSO

List

Dist

Finds distance between two points

VERSIONS

All versions

SEQUENCE OF STEPS

Command: **Dist**(↵)

To issue Dist from the menu system: **Inquiry** | **Dist**

First point: [*Pick beginning point of distance.*]

Second point: [*Pick end point of distance.*]

USAGE

Dist gives you the distance between two points in either two-dimensional or three-dimensional space. It tells you the distance, angle in the current X-Y plane, angle *from* the current X-Y plane, and the distance in X, Y, and Z coordinate values.

Help

Displays information about AutoCAD commands

VERSIONS

All versions

SEQUENCE OF STEPS

Command: **Help**(↵)

To issue Help from the menu system: **Inquiry** *or* **Osnap** | **Help** *or* (Version 10 only) **Help** pull-down | **Help**

Command name (RETURN for list): [*Enter name of command in question or press ↵ for a list of commands and a brief description of point selection.*]

USAGE

Help gives you a brief description of how to use a particular command. By pressing ↵ at the *Command name* prompt, you can get a listing of available commands along with a description of the *Select object* options and coordinate input.

You can also use Help while in the middle of a command to get specific information about that command. To do this, enter **Help** preceded by an apostrophe at any prompt in the command.

You can use a question mark in place of Help.

Id

Gives coordinate of selected point

VERSIONS

All versions

SEQUENCE OF STEPS

Command: **Id**(↵)

To issue Id from the menu system: **Inquiry | Id**

Point: [*Pick point.*]

USAGE

Id displays the coordinates of a point by listing its X, Y, and Z coordinate values.

A point you select with the Id command becomes the last point in the current editing session. See Appendix A for more information about point selection.

List

Displays properties of objects

VERSIONS

All versions

SEQUENCE OF STEPS

Command: **List**(↵)

To issue List from the menu system: **Inquiry | List**

Select objects: [*Pick objects whose properties you wish to see.*]

USAGE

List displays most of the properties of an object, including coordinate location, color, layer, and line type. It will tell you if the object is a block or text. If the object is text, List will tell you its height, style, and width factor. If the object is a block, List will tell you its X, Y, and Z scale and insertion point. Attribute tags, defaults, and current values are also listed. If the object is a polyline, all of the coordinate values for all its vertices will be listed.

At times, the list may scroll off the screen. If this happens, you can press **Ctrl-S** to momentarily stop the scroll.

SEE ALSO

Dblist

Status

Displays general information about drawings

VERSIONS

All versions

SEQUENCE OF STEPS

Command: **Status**(↵)

To issue Status from the menu system: **Inquiry | Status**

0 entities in SAMPLE

Limits are	X: 0.0000	12.0000 (Off)
	Y: 0.0000	9.0000
Drawing uses	*Nothing*	
Display shows	X: 0.0000	14.7213
	Y: 0.0000	9.9692
Insertion base is	X: 0.0000	Y: 0.0000 Z: 0.0000
Snap resolution is	X: 1.0000	Y: 1.0000
Grid spacing is	X: 0.0000	Y: 0.0000

Current layer:	0	
Current color:	BYLAYER -- 7 (white)	
Current line type:	BYLAYER -- CONTINUOUS	
Current elevation:	0.0000	thickness: 0.0000

Axis off Fill on Grid off Ortho off Qtext off Snap off Tablet off

Object snap modes: None

Free RAM: 15800 bytes Free disk: 4696064 bytes

I/O page space: 40K bytes Extended I/O page space: 633K bytes

USAGE

Status displays the current settings of a drawing, including the drawing limits and the status of all drawing modes. It also displays the current memory usage. The preceding sequence of steps shows the status of a typical new file before you have drawn anything. You can adjust most of the settings shown by using the commands found in the Layer and Settings chapters. You can adjust the *Free RAM* and *Extended I/O page space* memory listings shown toward the bottom of the status display by using the DOS command SET before starting AutoCAD. See Appendix B for details on these memory options.

SEE ALSO

Time, Settings, Layers

Time

Displays information on file editing time

VERSIONS

2.5 and later

SEQUENCE OF STEPS

Command: **Time**(↵)

To issue Time from the menu system: **Inquiry** | **Time**

Current time: (*date and time*)

Drawing created: (*date and time*)

Drawing last updated: (*date and time*)

Time in drawing editor: (*days and time*)

Elapsed time: (*days and time*)

(*elapsed timer status*)

Display/On/Off/Reset: <*option*>

OPTIONS

Display	Redisplays time information
On	Sets elapsed timer on
Off	Sets elapsed timer off
Reset	Resets elapsed timer to 0

USAGE

Time allows you to keep track of the time you spend on a drawing. The time is displayed in "military" format, using the 24-hour count.

CHAPTER 7
Layering Commands

This chapter presents the two commands that enable you to work with layers in AutoCAD drawings: Layer and Ddlmodes. Layers organize your drawing by allowing you to separate different types of drawing components. You can give layers names of up to 31 characters, and you can assign them a color and line type (see **Color** and **Linetype** in Chapter 8). You can create an unlimited number of layers in a drawing, though in a new drawing, only one layer, numbered 0, exists.

Layers act like overlays on a drawing. For example, in a building plan you can keep the walls, plumbing, electrical, duct work, and furniture on different layers. When you need to show just the electrical and plumbing systems, you can turn off the furniture and duct work layers. Layers that are off will not be displayed or plotted.

Besides turning a layer off or on, you can also freeze or thaw it. Freezing not only makes a layer invisible, it also instructs AutoCAD to ignore the layer's contents when recalculating vectors during regeneration. By reducing the number of components AutoCAD has to recalculate, freezing layers can save a lot of time when you regenerate a complete drawing.

Freezing a layer and turning it off also affect blocks differently. As discussed in Chapter 1, a block is a set of objects grouped together to act like one object. A block can contain objects that are placed on different layers. For example, you can create a block of a room that has chairs and tables on one layer, walls on another layer, and doors and windows on a third layer. As a block, this room acts like a single object, and you can assign it a color, line type, and layer even though it is made up of component objects that reside on different layers and have their own color and line type assignments. If you insert this room block into a frozen layer, the entire block will be frozen. If you insert it into a layer that has been turned off, it will still be displayed. If the block contains component objects that are on a frozen or turned off layer, the block will be displayed minus those components.

You can issue the Layer command directly from the root menu for quick access to this organizational tool. You can also access layers from the Settings pull-down menu by selecting **Modify Layer**. Picking **Layer** from the pull-down menu is the same as entering the **Ddlmodes** command from the keyboard or from the Layer menu. To use the pull-down menu or the Ddlmodes command, your system must support the AutoDesk Advanced User Interface (AUI).

Layer

Controls layers

VERSIONS

All versions

SEQUENCE OF STEPS

Command: **Layer**(↵)

To issue Layer from the menu system: **Root** | **Layer**

?/Make/Set/New/ON/OFF/Color/Ltype/Freeze/Thaw: *<option>*

OPTIONS

?	Displays list of existing layers
Make	Creates new layer and makes it current
Set	Makes an existing layer the current layer
New	Creates new layer
ON	Turns on layers that are off
OFF	Turns layers off
Color	Sets color of a layer
Ltype	Sets line type of a layer
Freeze	Freezes one or more layers
Thaw	Thaws or "unfreezes" one or more layers

USAGE

The Layer command allows you to create new layers, assign colors and line types to layers, and set the current layer. Layer also allows you to control which layers are displayed.

All of the Layer options except Make, Set, and New allow you to enter wildcard characters (question marks and asterisks). For example, if you want to turn off all layers whose name begins with G, you can enter **G*** at the *Layers to turn off* prompt.

Freeze/Thaw and ON/OFF both control whether a layer is displayed or not. Freeze differs from OFF, however, in that it makes AutoCAD ignore objects on frozen layers. This allows AutoCAD to produce faster regenerations. Freeze also affects blocks differently from OFF.

Layer 0, the default layer when you open a new file, is given the color White (number 7) and the continuous line type assignment. Layer 0 also has some unique properties. If you include objects on that layer in a block, those objects will take on the color and line type of the layer on which the block is inserted. For example, if you draw a chair in layer 0, turn that chair into a block, and insert it into a layer whose color is red, the chair will become red. The objects must be created with the Byblock color (see **Color**).

SEE ALSO

Color, Ddlmodes, Linetype, Regen, Regenauto

Ddlmodes

Displays Modify Layer dialog box

VERSIONS

9 and later

SEQUENCE OF STEPS

Command: **Ddlmodes**(↵)

To issue Ddlmodes from the menu system:
(version 10) **Settings** pull-down | **Modify Layer** *or*
(version 9) **Modes** pull-down | **Modify Layer**

OPTIONS

Current	Selects current layer
Layer name	Changes existing layer name
ON	Turns layer on or off
Frozen	Freezes or thaws a layer
Color	Changes color of a layer
Linetype	Changes line type of a layer
Up	Scrolls list of layers up one position
Page up	Scrolls list of layers up one page
Down	Scrolls list of layers down one position
Page down	Scrolls list of layers down one page
New layer	Adds new layer
OK	Makes current the settings in the dialog box and closes the dialog box
Cancel	Ignores any changes made to the dialog box and closes the dialog box

USAGE

If you have a display that supports the Advanced User Interface, Ddlmodes displays a dialog box from which you can control layers. You can also access the Modify Layer dialog box by picking **Modify Layer** from the Settings pull-down menu or, for version 9, from the Modes pull-down menu.

If you select the **Color** or **Linetype** pick box, you get another dialog box showing a list of available colors or line types from which to choose.

Ddlmode differs from the Layer command in that line types are not automatically loaded when you select a line type for a layer. If you want to use the Modify Layer dialog box to select line types, you must first load the desired line types using the Linetype command.

SEE ALSO

Layer, Rename, Linetype

CHAPTER 8

Settings Commands

This chapter covers the commands on the Settings menu. These commands control the various modes available in AutoCAD, such as the display of grids and the cursor. Many of these commands are also available on the Settings pull-down menu. You can toggle on and off a few settings commands by using the functions keys.

Aperture

Sets Osnap target box

VERSIONS

2.0 and later

SEQUENCE OF STEPS

Command: **Aperture**(↵)

To issue Aperture from the menu system: **Settings | Aperture**

Object snap target height (1-50 pixels) <5>: [*Enter desired size of Osnap target in pixels.*]

USAGE

With Aperture you can set the size of the Osnap target box to your personal preference. A smaller value will produce a smaller target box. Once set, the target size becomes part of AutoCAD's configuration. Also, if you have a high resolution display, the target box may be too small. Aperture allows you to enlarge it.

SEE ALSO

Osnap, Osnap overrides

Axis

Controls axis displayed markings

VERSIONS

All versions

SEQUENCE OF STEPS

Command: **Axis**(↵)

To issue Axis from the menu system: **Settings | Axis**

Tick spacing(X) or ON/OFF/Snap/Aspect <default setting>: [*Enter spacing of tick marks or an option.*]

OPTIONS

Tick spacing(X)	Allows you to set spacing of axis tick marks.
ON/OFF	Toggles Axis command on or off.
Snap	Sets axis tick mark to match Snap setting.
Aspect	Allows you to set X and Y tick mark spacing to different values.

USAGE

Axis displays tick marks along the bottom and right-hand edge of the drawing area. You can use these marks to determine distances and relative locations. The marks can reflect the Snap setting or a multiple thereof.

If you follow the spacing value with an X at the *Tick spacing* prompt, the value entered will represent a multiple of the current Snap setting. If set to 0, the tick marks will reflect the Snap settings.

If you set Axis to be a multiple of the Snap mode and change the Snap distance, the Axis mode will remain at the previous Snap setting.

SEE ALSO

Setvar/Axismode, Setvar/Axisunit, Ddrmodes

Blipmode or Blips

Controls display's marking blips

VERSIONS

2.1 and later

SEQUENCE OF STEPS

Command: **Blipmode**(↵)

To issue Blipmode from the menu system: **Settings | Blips**

ON/OFF *<current setting>*: *<option>*

OPTIONS

ON Displays blips when you enter points.

OFF Suppresses blips when you enter points.

USAGE

When you draw with AutoCAD, tiny crosses, or "blips," appear where you select points. These blips are not part of your drawing but are to help you easily locate points that you have previously selected. You can suppress these blips either out of personal preference or because you have written a macro that does not require blips.

SEE ALSO

Setvar/Blipmode

Color

Sets default color

VERSIONS

2.5 and later

SEQUENCE OF STEPS

Command: **Color**(↵)

To issue Color from the menu system: **Settings | Color**

New entity color <*current default*>: [Entire desired color.]

OPTIONS

The following is a list of acceptable AutoCAD color names. In addition, you can enter a number that corresponds to a color. You can enter any number from 1 to 255. The color that is displayed will depend on your particular display adapter and monitor, but the first seven colors are the same for most display systems. Some display adapters can display the full range of 256 colors while others simply repeat the first 16 colors.

red 1

yellow 2

green	3
cyan	4
blue	5
magenta	6
white	7
Bylayer	No corresponding number
Byblock	No corresponding number

USAGE

The Color command allows you to set the color of objects being drawn. Once you select a color with the Color command, all objects will be given the selected color regardless of their layers, unless you specify Bylayer as the color. Objects you drew before using the Color command are not affected.

Bylayer is a color option that gives objects the color of the layer on which they are placed and is the default color setting. Byblock is a color option that works on objects used in blocks. If an object that is part of a block is assigned the Byblock color, it will take on the color of the layer in which the block is placed.

Assign colors to objects carefully, especially if you use colors to distinguish different layers. Objects that are assigned a color different from their layer color can create confusion.

SEE ALSO

Layer, Change/Properties

Ddemodes

Opens the entity creation dialog box

VERSIONS

9 plus a display that supports the Advanced User Interface

SEQUENCE OF STEPS

Command: **Ddemodes**(↵)

To issue Ddemodes from the menu system: **Settings** pull-down | **Entity Creation** *or* **Modes** pull-down | **Entity Creation**

OPTIONS

When you issue Ddemodes, a dialog box with the following options appears. These options are in the form of input boxes that allow you to either check an option or enter a distance or coordinate value.

Color Allows you to set the current default color for objects being drawn. The default is Bylayer, which creates an object with the current layer's color.

Layer name Allows you to set the current layer.

Linetype Allows you to set the current default line type for objects being drawn. The default is Bylayer, which creates an object with the current layer's line type.

Elevation Allows you to set the current default elevation of objects being drawn. This elevation value is the distance in the Z axis from the X-Y plane of the current User Coordinate System.

Thickness Allows you to set the default thickness of objects being drawn. This value is a distance in the Z axis of the object.

OK Implements the settings displayed in the dialog box and exits the dialog box.

Cancel Exits the dialog box without implementing any changes.

USAGE

Ddemodes allows you to set several entity creation modes at once. You can set the default color, line type, elevation, and thickness of objects being drawn as well as the current default layer. Normally, you set these settings using the Color, Linetype, Elev, and Layer commands individually.

SEE ALSO

Color, Linetype, Elev, Layer, Change

Ddrmodes

Opens drawing mode's dialog box

VERSIONS

9 plus a display that supports the Advanced User Interface

SEQUENCE OF STEPS

Command: **Ddrmodes**(↵)

To issue Ddrmodes from the menu system: **Settings** pull-down | **Drawing Aids** *or* **Modes** pull-down | **Drawing Aids**

OPTIONS

When you issue Ddrmodes, the following options appear as input boxes that allow you to either check an option or enter a distance or coordinate value.

X Spacing	Sets spacing in the X axis for the mode under which the input box is found.
Y Spacing	Sets spacing in the Y axis for the mode under which the input box is found.
Snap angle	Sets snap angle.
Snap X Base	Sets Snap base point's X coordinate.
Snap Y Base	Sets Snap base point's Y coordinate.
Snap	Toggles Snap mode on or off. The F9 function key or the Ctrl-B keys perform the same function.
Grid	Toggles Grid mode on or off. The F7 function key or the Ctrl-G keys perform the same function.
Axis	Toggles Axis mode on or off.

Ortho	Toggles Ortho mode on or off. The F9 function key or the Ctrl-O keys perform the same function.
Blips	Toggles Blip mode on or off.
Isoplane Left	Moves an isometric cursor to the left plane. The Ctrl-E keys shift the cursor to the next Isoplane.
Isoplane Top	Moves an isometric cursor to the top plane. The Ctrl-E keys shift the cursor to the next Isoplane.
Isoplane Right	Moves an isometric cursor to the right plane. The Ctrl-E keys shift the cursor to the next Isoplane.
Isometric	Toggles the Isometric snap mode on or off.
OK	Implements the settings displayed in the dialog box and exits the dialog box.
Cancel	Exits the dialog box without implementing any changes.

USAGE

Ddrmodes allows you to change several mode settings at once. This saves you from having to enter a lengthy set of commands and responses.

SEE ALSO

Snap, Snap/Style, Grid, Axis, Ortho, Isoplane, Blipmode

Dragmode

Controls drags function

VERSIONS

2.0 and later

SEQUENCE OF STEPS

Command: **Dragmode**(↵)

To issue Dragmode from the menu system: **Settings | Dragmode**

ON/OFF/Auto <*current setting*>: [Enter desired setting.]

OPTIONS

ON Enables the Drag mode so that objects will be dragged whenever you issue the Drag command modifier.

OFF Disables the Drag mode so that no dragging will occur.

Auto Causes all commands that allow dragging to automatically drag objects, whether or not you issue the Drag command modifier.

USAGE

When you move, copy, stretch, or insert objects, it is often helpful to see them as they are being moved. The Drag command modifier shows you a temporary image of the selected objects in their position relative to your cursor. As your cursor moves, so does the temporary image. Dragmode enables you to control when the Drag facility is used. The default setting is Auto. You can also use Drag with several of the drawing commands to help you visualize the object before you actually complete it.

When you edit large sets of objects, the Drag function can slow down the editing process. It takes time for AutoCAD to refresh the temporary image, especially if the image is complex. For this reason, you may want to set Dragmode on. This way, you can use the Drag function when appropriate and not use it when you are editing large groups of objects.

SEE ALSO

Drag

Elev

Sets elevation and thickness

VERSIONS

2.0 and later

SEQUENCE OF STEPS

Command: **Elev**(↵)

To issue Elev from the menu system: **Settings | Elev**

New current elevation <*current default*>: [Enter desired elevation.]

New current thickness <*current default*>: [Enter desired thickness.]

OPTIONS

New current elevation Allows you to set the current default elevation in the Z axis.

New current thickness Allows you to set the current default thickness in the Z axis.

USAGE

The Elev command allows you to set the default Z axis elevation and thickness of objects being drawn. Normally, objects will be placed at a 0 elevation. Once you enter an elevation or thickness with the Elev command, all objects will be given the selected option value. Objects you drew before using the Elev command are not affected. You can also change the elevation of an existing object with the Change or Move command.

SEE ALSO

Ddemodes, Change, Move

Grid

Controls display of a grid

VERSIONS

All versions

SEQUENCE OF STEPS

Command: **Grid**(↵)

To issue Grid from the menu system: **Settings | Grid**

Grid spacing(X) or ON/OFF/Snap/Aspect *<default value>*: [*Enter desired grid spacing or other option.*]

OPTIONS

Grid spacing(X)	Allows you to enter the desired grid spacing in drawing units or 0 if you want the grid spacing to reflect the Snap setting.
ON	Turns the grid display on. The F7 key performs the same function.
OFF	Turns the grid display off. The F7 key performs the same function.
Snap	Sets the grid spacing to reflect the Snap spacing.
Aspect	Allows you to specify a grid spacing in the Y axis that is different from the spacing in the X axis.

USAGE

The Grid command can aid your drafting by displaying an array of points at a specified distance in the current User Coordinate System. You can use these points as a reference when drawing objects to specific distances. You can set the grid to match the Snap spacing or to an entirely different setting. Since the grid is only displayed within the limits of the drawing, you can use it to visually determine the limits of your drawing.

If you follow the grid spacing value with an X at the *Grid spacing* prompt, AutoCAD will interpret the value as a multiple of the Snap setting. For example, if you enter a **2** at the *Grid spacing* prompt, the grid points will be two units apart. If you enter **2X**, the grid points will be twice as far apart as the Snap settings.

At times, a grid setting may obscure the view of your drawing. If this happens, AutoCAD will automatically turn the grid mode off and display the message *Grid too dense to display.*

SEE ALSO

Ddrmodes

Handles

Tags objects alphanumerically

VERSIONS

10

SEQUENCE OF STEPS

Command: **Handles**(↵)

To issue Handles from the menu system: **Settings | Handles**

Handles are disabled

ON/DESTROY: [Enter desired option]

OPTIONS

ON Enables the Handles function, giving every object drawn an alphanumeric name.

DESTROY Disables the Handles function, destroying any currently existing handles in the drawing.

USAGE

If you enable the Handles function, you can access each object in a drawing by its name. When you use the List command, you see the selected object's handle in addition to the other information List provides. If you are programming in AutoLISP, you can identify entities using the Handent AutoLISP function.

Handle information is written to DXF files and therefore can help you extract database information from a drawing.

SEE ALSO

List, DXFout, Setvar/Handles

Limits

Sets drawing area

VERSIONS

All versions

SEQUENCE OF STEPS

Command: **Limits**(↵)

To issue Limits from the menu system: **Settings | Limits**

ON/OFF/<lower left corner> <0.0000,0.0000>: [*Enter coordinate for lower-left corner or ON/OFF option.*]

OPTIONS

ON Turns on the limit-checking function. This function keeps your drawing activity within the drawing limits.

OFF Turns off the limit-checking function, allowing you to draw objects regardless of their location in relation to the drawing limits.

<lower left corner> Allows you to set the limits of the drawing by entering the lower-left and upper-right corner of the desired drawing limits.

USAGE

You use Limits to determine the boundaries of the drawing. The limits can be thought of as the drawing "sheet." If you use a grid, it will appear only within the limits. With Limit-checking on, you are forced to keep your drawing activities within the limits.

You can also use Limits to control the virtual screen area. Turning on the limit-checking feature and then performing a Zoom/All makes the virtual screen conform to the limits of the drawing.

The Setup option on the root menu will set the limits of your drawing automatically according to the sheet size and drawing scale you select.

SEE ALSO

Viewres, Regen, Zoom, Setvar/Limcheck, Setvar/Limmin, Setvar/Limmax

Linetype

Controls default line types

VERSIONS

2.0 and later

SEQUENCE OF STEPS

Command: **Linetype**(↵)

To issue Linetype from the menu system: **Settings | Linetype**

?/Create/Load/Set: <*option*>

OPTIONS

? Lists available line types in a specified external line type file.

Create Allows you to create a new line type.

Load Loads a line type from a specified line type file.

Set Allows you to set the current default line type.

USAGE

Linetype enables you to control the type of line you can draw. The default line type is continuous, but you can choose from several other types, such as a dotted or dashed line or a combination of the two (see Figure 8.1). Several predefined line types are stored in a file called Acad.LIN. You can list these line types by entering a question mark at the *Linetype* prompt.

You can also use the Create option to create your own line types and store them in Acad.LIN or in another file you create. When using this option, you are first prompted for a line type name. This name can be any alphanumeric string of 31 characters or less. You are then prompted for the name of the file in which you wish to store your line type. Next, you are asked to enter descriptive text. This can be any verbal description of the line type. Finally, you are prompted to enter the pattern on the next line. You will see the letter "A" followed by a comma and the cursor. To define a line type pattern, enter a string of numeric values separated by commas. These values should alternate between positive and negative—the positive values representing the "drawn" portion of the line and the negative values representing the "pen-up" or blank portion of the line. These values should represent the actual lengths of lines as they are to appear when plotted.

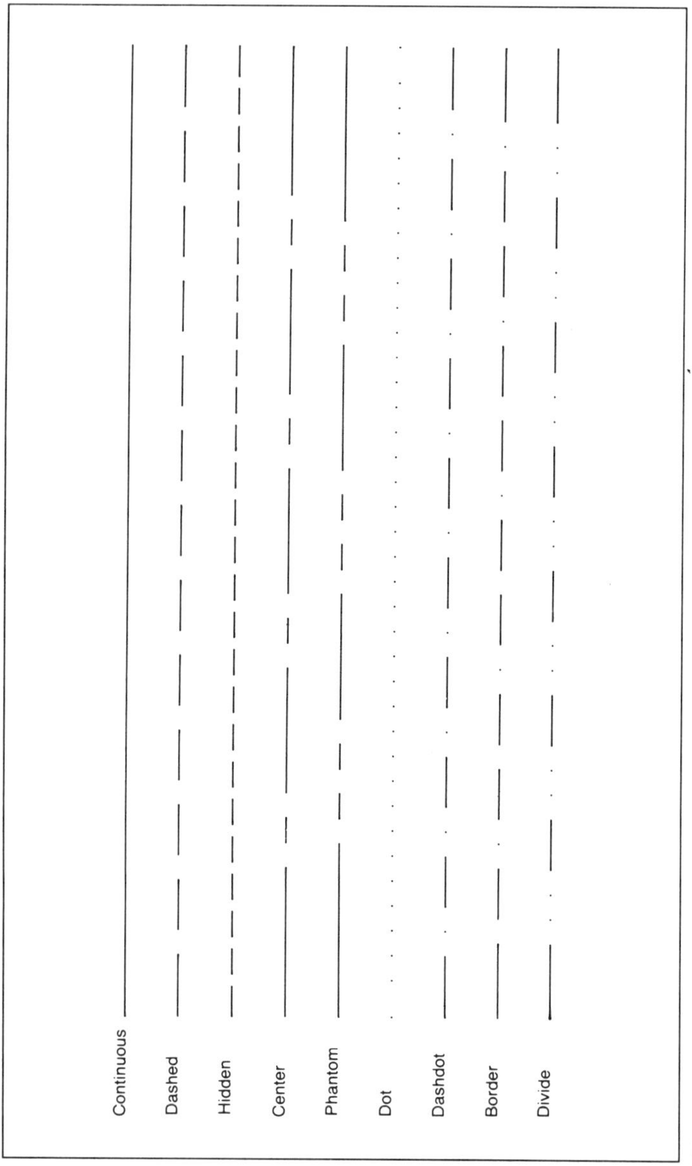

Continuous

Dashed

Hidden

Center

Phantom

Dot

Dashdot

Border

Divide

Figure 8.1: The standard AutoCAD line types

You can adjust the overall scale of these lines with the Ltscale command. If you want a dot in a line type, use 0 for the appropriate value.

You can assign line types to layers or to individual objects. You can make the scale of the line types correspond with the scale of your drawing by using the Ltscale command.

At times, a line type may appear continuous even though it is a noncontinuous type. Several things can affect the appearance of line types. The first is an incorrect Ltscale setting. If the drawing is of a scale other than 1:1, the Ltscale must be set to correspond with your drawing scale. A drawing at a scale of 1/4" equals 1′ would require that the Ltscale be set to 48, for example. A low Viewres value can also affect the on-screen appearance of line types by making them appear continuous even though they plot as a noncontinuous line type.

SEE ALSO

Viewres, Ltscale, Layer, Ddemodes

Ltscale

Sets line type scale

VERSIONS

2.0 and later

SEQUENCE OF STEPS

Command: **Ltscale**(↵)

To issue Ltscale from the menu system: **Settings | Next | Ltscale**

New scale factor <*current default*>: [Enter desired scale factor.]

If Regenauto is on, the drawing will regenerate once you enter a new scale factor.

USAGE

Ltscale allows you to control the scale of line types. Normally, noncontinuous line types are defined at a 1:1 scale. This means that if the drawing is at a 1:1 scale, the line types will appear as they are originally defined. When a drawing's scale is something other than 1:1, the line types will appear to be smaller or larger than they were originally defined. Dashes and spaces will appear larger or smaller. Ltscale brings the line type into conformity with the scale of your drawing by globally adjusting all line type definitions to the value given to Ltscale.

Ltscale forces a drawing regeneration. If Regenauto is off, you won't see the effects of Ltscale until you issue **Regen**.

SEE ALSO

Linetype

Osnap

Controls Object snap function

VERSIONS

2.0 and later

SEQUENCE OF STEPS

Command: **Osnap**(↵)

To issue Osnap from the menu system: **Settings | Next | Osnap**

Object snap modes: [*Enter desired default Object snap mode(s).*]

OPTIONS

CENter	Picks center of circles and arcs.
ENDpoint	Picks end point of objects.
INSert	Picks insertion point of blocks and text.
INTersect	Picks intersection of objects.
MIDpoint	Picks midpoint of lines.
NEArest	Picks point on an object nearest to the cursor.
NODe	Picks a point object.

PERpend	Picks point on an object perpendicular to the last point.
QUAdrant	Picks a cardinal point on an arc or circle.
QuickOsnap	Modifier that shortens the time it takes AutoCAD to find an object snap point. Quick does not work in conjunction with INTersect.
Tangent	Picks a tangent point on a circle or arc.
NONE	Disables the current default Object snap mode.

USAGE

Osnap sets the current default Object snap mode, allowing you to pick specific geometric points on an object. You can have several Object snap modes active at once if you enter their names separated by commas. For example, if you want to be able to select end points and midpoints automatically, enter **END,MID** at the *Osnap* prompt.

You can also use the Osnap overrides whenever you are prompted to select a point or object. Enter the first three letters of the name of the desired override or pick the override from the Tools pull-down menu or the Asterisks side menu. Unlike the Osnap mode settings, the overrides are active only at the time they are issued.

SEE ALSO

Aperture

Qtext

Disables text display

VERSIONS

2.0 and later

SEQUENCE OF STEPS

Command: **Qtext**(↵)

To issue Qtext from the menu system: **Settings** | **Next** | **Qtext**

ON/OFF <Off>: [enter desired option.]

OPTIONS

ON Turns Qtext mode on

OFF Turns Qtext mode off

USAGE

Qtext helps reduce drawing regeneration and redraw times by making text appear as a rectangular box instead of readable text. The rectangle approximates the height and length of text. This can be useful if you want to edit only the graphics in a drawing that contains much text. You can still enter and change text with Qtext on. Figures 8.2 and 8.3 illustrate the effect of Qtext.

Qtext forces a regeneration. If Regenauto is off, you do not see the effects of Qtext until you issue a Regen command.

SEE ALSO

Regen, Dtext

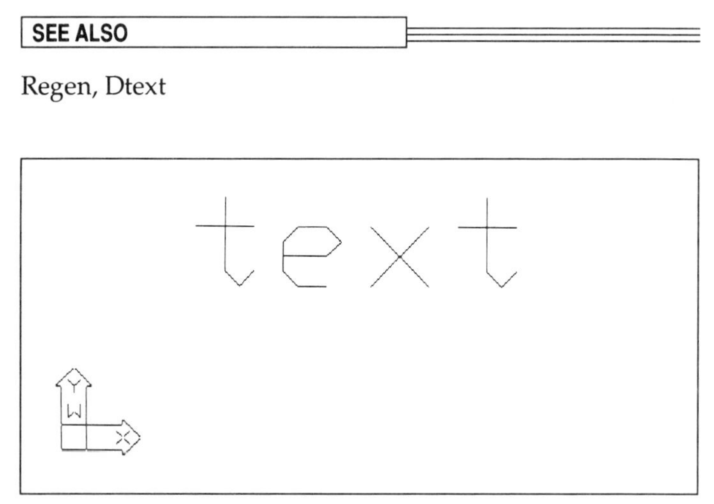

Figure 8.2: Text with Qtext off

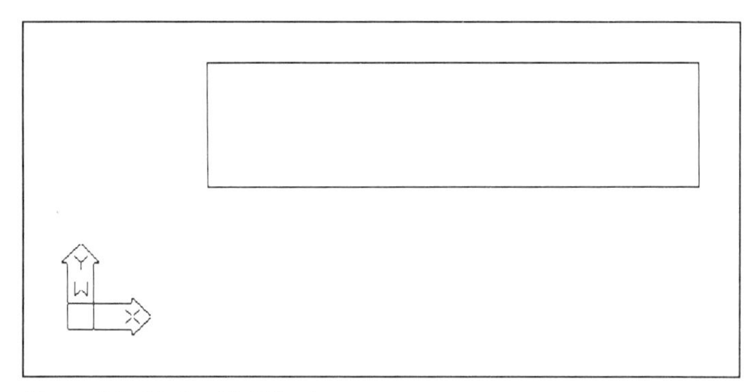

Figure 8.3: Text with Qtext on

Setvar

Accesses system variables

VERSIONS

2.5 and later

SEQUENCE OF STEPS

Command: **Setvar**(↵)

To issue Setvar from the menu system: **Settings | Next | Setvar**

Variable name or ?: [*Enter desired system variable name or a question mark for a list of variables.*]

OPTIONS

Table 8.1 lists all of the system variables that you can access through Setvar. They fall into three categories: adjustable variables, read-only variables, and variables accessible only through Setvar. You can set an adjustable variable by issuing the **Setvar** command and the name of the desired variable. A prompt asks for an integer value. The meaning of that value depends on the nature of the variable.

USAGE

Setvar offers a means of accessing the AutoCAD system variables. Most of these variables are accessible through the commands they are associated with. At times, however, you will want to use Setvar to read or change them while you are in another command. You can do this because Setvar is a

ADJUSTABLE VARIABLES

You can adjust these variables either through the Setvar command or through the commands associated with the variable. For example, you can adjust the first three variables with the Units command, or with Setvar.

Variable	Description
Aflags	Controls the attribute mode settings: 1 = invisible, 2 = constant, 4 = verify, 8 = preset. For more than one setting, use the sum of the desired settings. See **Attdef**.
Angbase	Controls the direction of the 0 angle. Can also be set with the Units command.
Angdir	Controls the positive direction of angles: 0 = counterclockwise, 1 = clockwise. Can also be set with the Units command.
Aperture	Controls the Osnap cursor target height in pixels. Can also be set with the Aperture command.
Attmode	Controls the attribute display mode: 0 = off, 1 = normal, 2 = on. Can also be set with the Attdisp command.
Aunits	Controls angular units: 0 = decimal degrees, 1 = degrees-minutes-seconds, 2 = grads, 3 = radians, 4 = surveyors' units. Can also be set with the Units command.
Auprec	Controls the precision of angular units determined by decimal place. Can also be set with the Units command.
Axismode	Controls the axis mode: 0 = off, 1 = on. Can also be set with the Axis command.
Axisunit	Controls the X and Y axis spacing. Can also be set with the Axis command.

Table 8.1: Setvar System Variables

Variable	Description
Blipmode	Controls the appearance of blips: 0 = off, 1 = on. See **Blipmode**.
Chamfera	Controls first chamfer distance. See **Chamfer**.
Chamferb	Controls second chamfer distance. See **Chamfer**.
Coords	Controls coordinate readout: 0 = coordinates are displayed only when points are picked. 1 = absolute coordinates are dynamically displayed as cursor moves. 2 = distance and angle are displayed during commands that accept relative distance input. Also controlled by the F6 function key.
Dragmode	Controls dragging: 0 = no dragging, 1 = on if requested, 2 = automatic drag. See **Dragmode**.
Elevation	Controls current three-dimensional elevation. See **Elev**.
Filletrad	Controls fillet radius. See **Fillet**.
Fillmode	Controls fill status: 0 = off, 1 = on. See **Fill**.
Gridmode	Controls grid: 0 = off, 1 = on. See **Grid**.
Gridunit	Controls grid spacing. See **Grid**.
Insbase	Controls insertion base point of current drawing. See **Base**.
Limcheck	Controls limit checking: 0 = no checking, 1 = checking. See **Limits**.
Limmax	Controls the coordinate of drawing's upper-right limit. See **Limits**.
Limmin	Controls the coordinate of drawing's lower-left limit. See **Limits**.

Table 8.1: Setvar System Variables (continued)

Ltscale	Controls the line type scale factor. See **Ltscale**.
Lunits	Controls unit styles: 1 = scientific, 2 = decimal, 3 = engineering, 4 = architectural, 5 = fractional. See **Units**.
Luprec	Controls unit accuracy by decimal place or size of denominator. See **Units**.
Orthomode	Controls the Ortho mode: 0 = off, 1 = on. See **Ortho**.
Osmode	Sets the current default Osnap mode: 0 = none, 1 = end point, 2 = midpoint, 4 = center, 8 = node, 16 = quadrant, 32 = intersection, 64 = insert, 128 = perpendicular, 256 = tangent, 512 = nearest, 1024 = quick. If more than one mode is required, enter the sum of those modes. See **Osnap**.
Qtextmode	Controls the Quick text mode: 0 = off, 1 = on. See **Qtext** command.
Regenmode	Controls the Regenauto mode: 0 = off, 1 = on. See **Regenauto**.
Sketchinc	Controls the sketch record increment. See **Sketch**.
Snapang	Controls snap and grid angle. See **Snap**.
Snapbase	Controls snap, grid, and hatch pattern origin. See **Snap**.
Snapisopair	Controls isometric plane: 0 = left, 1 = top, 2 = right. See **Snap** command.
Snapmode	Controls Snap toggle: 0 = off, 1 = on. See **Snap** command.

Table 8.1: Setvar System Variables (continued)

Snapstyl	Controls Snap style: 0 = standard, 1 = isometric. See **Snap**.
Snapunit	Controls Snap spacing given in *x* and *y* values. See **Snap**.
Textsize	Controls default text height. See **Dtext**, **Text**, and **Style**.
Thickness	Controls three-dimensional thickness of objects being drawn. See **Elev**.
Tracewid	Controls trace width. See **Trace**.

READ-ONLY VARIABLES

You can read these variables either through their associated commands or through Setvar. Rather than setting or adjusting some parameter of a drawing or of your AutoCAD system, they simply display the specified information.

Acadver	Displays the AutoCAD version number.
Area	Displays the current area being computed. See **Area**.
Backz	Displays the distance from the Dview target to the back clipping plane. See **Dview**.
Cdate	Displays calendar date/time read from DOS. See **Time**.
Cecolor	Displays current object color. See **Color**.
Celtype	Displays current object line type. See **Linetype**.
Clayer	Displays current layer. See **Layer** and **Ddlmode**.
Date	Displays Julian date/time. See **Time**.

Table 8.1: Setvar System Variables (continued)

Distance	Displays last distance read using Dist. See **Dist**.
Dwgname	Displays drawing name. See **Status**.
Frontz	Displays the distance from the Dview target to the front clipping plane. See **Dview**.
Handles	Displays the status of the Handles command. 0 = off, 1 = on. See **Handles**.
Lastangle	Displays the end angle of last arc or line. See **Pline/Length**.
Lastpoint	Displays coordinates of last point entered. Same point referenced by at sign (@). See Appendix A.
Lenslength	Displays the current lens focal length used during the Dview command Zoom option.
Menuname	Displays the current menu file name. See **Menu**.
Perimeter	Displays the perimeter value currently being read by Area, List, or Dblist. See **Area**, **List**, or **Dblist**.
Popups	Displays the availability of the Advanced User Interface. 0 = not available, 1 = available.
Target	Displays the coordinate of the target point used in the Dview command.
Tdcreate	Displays time and date of drawing creation. See **Time**.
Tdindwg	Displays total editing time. See **Time**.
Tdupdate	Displays time and date of last save. See **Time**.

Table 8.1: Setvar System Variables (continued)

Tdusrtimer	Displays user-elapsed time. See **Time**.
Textstyle	Displays the current text style. See **Style**.
Ucsname	Displays the name of the current UCS. See **UCS**.
Ucsorg	Displays the current UCS origin point. See **UCS**.
Ucsxdir	Displays the X direction of the current UCS. See **UCS**.
Ucsydir	Displays the Y direction of the current UCS. See **UCS**.
Viewdir	Displays the view direction of the current view port. See **Dview**.
Viewtwist	Displays the view twist angle for the current view port. See **Dview**.
Vpointx	Displays the *x* value of the current three-dimensional viewpoint. See **Vpoint**.
Vpointy	Displays the *y* value of the current three-dimensional viewpoint. See **Vpoint**.
Vpointz	Displays the *z* value of the current three-dimensional viewpoint. See **Vpoint**.
Worlducs	Displays the status of the World Coordinate System. 0 = WCS is not current, 1 = WCS is current. See **UCS**.

Table 8.1: Setvar System Variables (continued)

VARIABLES ACCESSIBLE ONLY THROUGH SETVAR

You can access the following variables only through the Setvar command.

Adjustable Variables
You can alter these variables, but only through the Setvar command.

Attdia	Controls the attribute dialog box for the Insert command: 0 = no dialog box, 1 = dialog box.
Attreq	Controls the prompt for attributes. 0 = no prompt or dialog box for attributes. Attributes use default values. 1 = normal prompt or dialog box upon attribute insertion.
Cmdecho	Used with AutoLISP to control what is displayed on the prompt line. See the AutoLISP manual for details.
Dragp1	Controls regen-drag input sampling rate.
Dragp2	Controls fast-drag input sampling rate. Higher values force the display of more of the dragged image during cursor movement while lower values display less.
Expert	Controls prompts, depending on level of user's expertise. 0 issues normal prompts. 1 suppresses *About to Regen* and *Really want to turn the current light off?* prompts. 2 suppresses previous prompts plus *Block already defined* and *A drawing with this name already exists*. 3 suppresses previous prompts plus line type warnings. 4 suppresses previous prompts plus UCS and Vports *Save* warnings.

Table 8.1: Setvar System Variables (continued)

Flatland	Controls AutoCAD's handling of three-dimensional functions and objects as they relate to Object snaps, DXF formats, and AutoLISP. 0 = functions take advantage of version 10's advanced features, 1 = functions operate as they did prior to version 10.
Highlight	Controls object-selection ghosting: 0 = no ghosting, 1 = ghosting.
Menuecho	Controls the display of commands and prompts issued from the menu. A value of 1 suppresses display of commands entered from menu (can be toggled on or off with Ctrl-P); 2 suppresses display of commands and command prompts when command is issued from AutoLISP macro; 3 is a combination of options 1 and 2; 4 disables Ctrl-P menu echo toggle.
Mirrtext	Controls text mirroring: 0 = no text mirroring, 1 = text mirroring.
Pdmode	Controls the type of symbol used as a point during the Point command. Several point styles are available. See **Point**.
Pdsize	Controls the size of the symbol set by Pdmode.
Pickbox	Controls the size of the object-selection box. You can enter integer values to control the box height in pixels.
Skpoly	Controls whether the Sketch command uses regular lines or polylines. 0 = line, 1 = polyline.

Table 8.1: Setvar System Variables (continued)

Splframe	Controls the display of spline vertices, surface fit three-dimensional meshes, and invisible edges of 3dfaces. 0 = no display of Spline vertices of invisible 3dface edges. Displays only defining mesh or surface fit mesh. 1 = display of Spline vertices or invisible 3dface edges. Displays only surface fit mesh.
Splinesegs	Controls the number of line segments used for each spline patch.
Spline type	Controls the type of curved line generated by the Pedit Spline command. 5 = quadratic B-spline, 6 = Cubic B-spline.
Surftab1	Controls the number of mesh control points for the Rulesurf and Tabsurf commands and the number of mesh points in the M direction for the Revsurf and Edgesurf commands.
Surftab2	Controls the number of mesh control points in the N direction for the Revsurf and Edgesurf commands.
Surftype	Controls the type of surface fitting generated by the Pedit Smooth command. 5 = quadratic B-spline, 6 = cubic B-spline, and 8 = Bezier surface.
Surfu	Controls the accuracy of the smoothed surface models in the M direction.
Surfv	Controls the accuracy of the smoothed surface models in the N direction.

Table 8.1: Setvar System Variables (continued)

Texteval	Controls whether prompts for text and attribute input to commands are taken literally or as AutoLISP expressions. 0 = literal, 1 = text you input with parentheses and exclamation points will be interpreted as AutoLISP expression. Dtext takes all input literally, regardless of this setting.
Ucsfollow	Controls whether changing the current UCS automatically displays the plan view of the new current UCS. 0 = displayed view does not change, 1 = automatic display of new current UCS in plan.
Useri*1-5*	Five variables for storing integers for custom applications.
Userr*1-5*	Five variables for storing real numbers for custom applications.
Worldview	Controls whether point input to the Dview and Vpoint commands is relative to the WCS or the current UCS. 0 = commands use the current UCS to interpret point value input, 1 = commands use UCS to interpret point value input.

Read-Only Variables
These variables can be read only through the Setvar command, unlike the variables in the first two sections of this table.

Acadprefix	Displays the name of the directory saved in the DOS environment using the DOS command SET.
Dwgprefix	Displays drive and directory prefix for drawing file.

Table 8.1: Setvar System Variables (continued)

Extmax	Displays upper-right corner coordinate of drawing extent.
Extmin	Displays lower-left corner coordinate of drawing extent.
Screensize	Reads the size of the graphics screen in pixels.
Tempprefix	Displays the name of the directory where temporary AutoCAD files are saved.
Viewctr	Displays the center coordinate of the current view.
Viewsize	Displays the height of the current view in drawing units.
Vsmax	Displays the three-dimensional coordinate of the upper-right corner of the current view port's virtual screen relative to the current UCS.
Vsmin	Displays the three-dimensional coordinate of the lower-left corner of the current view port's virtual screen relative to the current UCS.

Table 8.1: Setvar System Variables (continued)

transparent command that you can issue at any time by entering **'Setvar**. You can also access these system variables through the AutoLISP interpreter with the Setvar and Getvar AutoLISP functions.

Snap

Controls snap settings

VERSIONS

All versions

SEQUENCE OF STEPS

Command: **Snap**(↵)

To issue Snap from the menu system: **Settings | Next | Snap**

Snap spacing or ON/OFF/Aspect/Rotate/Style <*default spacing*>: [*Enter desired Snap spacing or option.*]

OPTIONS

Snap spacing Allows you to enter the desired Snap spacing. The Snap mode will be turned on and the new Snap settings will take effect.

ON Turns on the Snap mode. Has the same effect as pressing the F9 function key or the Ctrl-B keys.

OFF Turns off the Snap mode. Has the same effect as pressing the F9 function key or the Ctrl-B keys.

Aspect Allows you to enter a Y axis Snap spacing different from the X axis Snap spacing.

Rotate Allows you to rotate the Snap points and the AutoCAD cursor to an angle other than 0 and 90 degrees.

Style Allows you to choose between the standard orthagonal snap style and an isometric snap style.

USAGE

The Snap command controls the settings for the Snap mode, which allows you to accurately place the cursor by forcing the cursor to move in specified increments. For example, if Snap is set to 0.25 and the Snap mode is turned on, the cursor will only move in 0.25 unit increments. Normally, these snap increments or points are aligned with the X Y axis and are evenly spaced. However, you can rotate the Snap points to a different angle. In doing so, you also rotate the cursor. Use the Aspect option if you want to set the Snap points to be different in the X and Y axis. Finally, you can use the Snap command to set up Snap points for isometric drawings.

If you use the Rotate option to rotate the cursor, the Ortho mode will conform to the new cursor angle. This option also allows you to specify a Snap origin, allowing you to accurately place hatch patterns.

If you use the Isometric style option, you can use the Isoplane command to control the cursor orientation. Also, the Ellipse command allows you to draw isometric ellipses.

SEE ALSO

Hatch, Isoplane, Ellipse, Setvar, Ddrmodes

Style

Sets current text style

VERSIONS

2.0 and later

SEQUENCE OF STEPS

Command: **Style**(↵)

To issue Style from the menu system: **Options** pull-down | **Fonts** *or* **Settings** | **Next** | **Style**

Text style name (or ?) <*current style*>: [*Enter style name or a question mark for list of available styles.*]

Font file <*default font file*>: [*Enter font file name or ↵ to accept default.*]

Height <*default height*>: [*Enter desired height or ↵ to accept default.*]

Width factor <*default width factor*>: [*Enter desired width factor or ↵ to accept default.*]

Obliquing angle <*default angle*>: [*Enter desired width obliquing angle or ↵ to accept default.*]

Backwards? <N>: [*Enter **Y** if you want the text to read backward or ↵ to accept N, the default.*]

Upside-down? <N>: [*Enter **Y** if you want the text to read upside down or ↵ to accept N, the default.*]

Vertical? <N>: [*Enter **Y** if you want the text to read vertically or ↵ to accept N, the default.*]

OPTIONS

Text style name	Allows you to either enter a new name to define a new style or the name of an existing style to redefine the style.
Font file	Allows you to choose from several "fonts," or type styles. You can select from a set of predefined fonts from the Styles/Fonts menu or from the Fonts icon menu found on the Options pull-down menu.
Height	Allows you to determine a fixed height for the style being defined. A 0 value allows you to determine text height as it is entered.
Width factor	Allows you to make the style appear expanded or compressed.
Obliquing angle	Allows you to "italicize" the style.
Backwards	Allows you to make the style appear backwards.
Upside down	Allows you to make the style appear upside down.
Vertical	Allows you to make the style appear vertical.

USAGE

Style allows you to create a text style by determining the AutoCAD font on which it is based, its height, width factor, and obliquing angle. You can also make a font appear backwards, upside down, or vertical. See Figure 8.4 for a list of the standard AutoCAD fonts and Figure 8.5 for tables of the symbol, Greek, and Cyrillic fonts. Style also allows you to modify an existing text style. If you modify a style's font, text previously entered in that style will be updated to reflect the modification. If any other style option is modified, previously entered text will not be affected. Once you use the Style command, the style created or modified will become the new current style.

A 0 value at the *Height* prompt will cause AutoCAD to prompt you for a text height whenever you use this style with the Dtext and Text commands.

At the *Width factor* prompt, a value of 1 will generate normal text. A greater value will expand the style while a smaller value will compress it.

At the *Obliquing angle* prompt, a value of 0 will generate normal text while a greater value will slant the style to the right, as in an italic typeface. A negative value will slant the style to the left.

If you pick **Fonts** from the Options pull-down menu, you get a set of icon menus that display the various standard fonts available (see Figure 8.6). Once you pick a font from an icon menu, AutoCAD automatically enters a style name and font at the first two prompts, leaving you to enter the style height, width factor, obliquing angle, and so on.

SEE ALSO

Dtext, Text, Qtext, Change

AutoCAD Font	Font Description
This is Txt	
This is Monotxt	
This is Simplex	(Old version of Roman Simplex)
This is Complex	(Old version of Roman Complex)
This is Italic	(Old version of Italic Complex)
This is Romans	(Roman Simplex)
This is Romand	(Roman double stroke)
This is Romanc	(Roman Complex)
This is Romant	(Roman triple stroke)
This is Scripts	(Script Simplex)
This is Scriptc	(Script Complex)
This is Italicc	(Italic Complex)
This is Italict	(Italic triple stroke)
Τηισ ισ Γρεεκσ	(This is Greeks – Greek Simplex)
Τηισ ισ Γρεεκχ	(This is Greekc – Greek Complex)
Узит ит Вшсиллив	(This is Cyrillic – Alphabetical)
Тхис ис Чйрилтлч	(This is Cyriltlc – Transliteration)
This is Gothice	(Gothic English)
Thiſ iſ Gothicg	(Gothic German)
This is Gothici	(Gothic Italian)

Figure 8.4: The AutoCAD script fonts

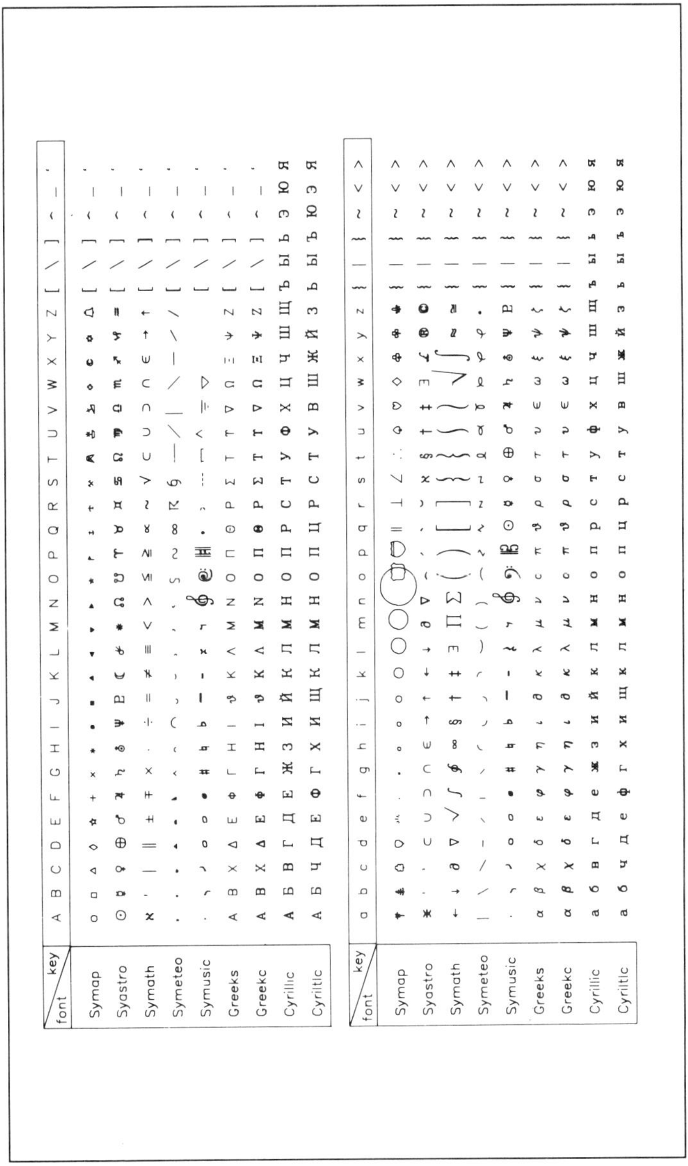

font \ key	A	B	C	D	E	F	G	H	I	J	K	L	M	N	O	P	Q	R	S	T	U	V	W	X	Y	Z	[	\	]	^	_	`
Symap	○	□	△	◇	☆	+	×	*	•	■	▲	◀	▼	▶	✱	⚑	‡	†	✕	[illegible]	[illegible]	[illegible]	◈	©	✿	🔔	[	\	]	^	_	`
Syastro	⊙	☿	♀	⊕	♂	♃	♄	♅	♆	♇	☾	☄	✸	☊	☋	♈	♉	♊	♋	♌	♍	♎	♏	♐	♑	♒	[	\	]	^	_	`
Symath	ℵ	′	|	‖	±	∓	×	·	÷	=	≠	≡	<	>	≤	≥	∝	∼	√	⊂	∪	⊃	∩	∈	→	↑	[	\	]	^	_	`
Symeteo	·	·	•	▲	▬	◢	^	⌃	⌒	◡	‿	›	′	‵	ʃ	∼	∞	☈	ϭ	—	/	|	\	—	⁄	/	[	\	]	^	_	`
Symusic	·	╮	╯	○	○	●	♯	♮	♭	▬	-	𝄪	𝄾	𝄞	𝄢	𝄡	·	›	---	⎴	^	≡	▽				[	\	]	^	_	`
Greeks	A	B	X	Δ	E	Φ	Γ	H	I	ϑ	K	Λ	M	N	O	Π	Θ	P	Σ	T	Υ	∇	Ω	Ξ	Ψ	Z	[	\	]	^	_	`
Greekc	A	B	X	Δ	E	Φ	Γ	H	I	ϑ	K	Λ	M	N	O	Π	Θ	P	Σ	T	Υ	∇	Ω	Ξ	Ψ	Z	[	\	]	^	_	`
Cyrillic	А	Б	В	Г	Д	Е	Ж	З	И	Й	К	Л	М	Н	О	П	Р	С	Т	У	Ф	Х	Ц	Ч	Ш	Щ	Ъ	Ы	Ь	Э	Ю	Я
Cyriltlc	А	Б	Ч	Д	Е	Ф	Г	Х	И	Щ	К	Л	М	Н	О	П	Ц	Р	С	Т	У	В	Ш	Ж	Й	З	Ь	Ы	Ъ	Ю	Э	Я

font \ key	a	b	c	d	e	f	g	h	i	j	k	l	m	n	o	p	q	r	s	t	u	v	w	x	y	z	{	|	}	~	<	>
Symap	↟	🌲	⌂	♢	[illegible]	·	•	∘	∘	○	○	◯	◯	◯	🛡	🛡	‖	⊥	∠	∴	♤	♡	◇	♧	♣	♠	{	|	}	~	<	>
Syastro	✳	′	′	⊂	∪	⊃	∩	∈	→	↑	←	↓	∂	∇	⌢	´	`	˘	ℵ	§	†	‡	∃	£	®	©	{	|	}	~	<	>
Symath	←	↓	∂	∇	√	∫	∮	∞	§	†	‡	∃	∏	∑	(	)	[	]	{	}	(	)	√	∫	≈	≅	{	|	}	~	<	>
Symeteo	|	\	╲	–	⁄	ı	╲	⌜	◟	◞	◝	‿	(	)	⌢	≀	∿	∼	~	ℓ	∝	ɣ	℘	φ	φ	•	{	|	}	~	<	>
Symusic	·	╮	╯	○	○	●	♯	♮	♭	▬	-	𝄽	𝄾	𝄞	𝄢	𝄡	⊙	☿	♀	⊕	♂	♃	♄	♅	♆	♇	{	|	}	~	<	>
Greeks	α	β	χ	δ	ε	φ	γ	η	ι	∂	κ	λ	μ	ν	ο	π	ϑ	ρ	σ	τ	υ	∈	ω	ξ	ψ	ζ	{	|	}	~	<	>
Greekc	α	β	χ	δ	ε	φ	γ	η	ι	∂	κ	λ	μ	ν	ο	π	ϑ	ρ	σ	τ	υ	∈	ω	ξ	ψ	ζ	{	|	}	~	<	>
Cyrillic	а	б	в	г	д	е	ж	з	и	й	к	л	м	н	о	п	р	с	т	у	ф	х	ц	ч	ш	щ	ъ	ы	ь	э	ю	я
Cyriltlc	а	б	ч	д	е	ф	г	х	и	щ	к	л	м	н	о	п	ц	р	с	т	у	в	ш	ж	й	з	ь	ы	ъ	э	ю	я

Figure 8.5: The AutoCAD symbol fonts

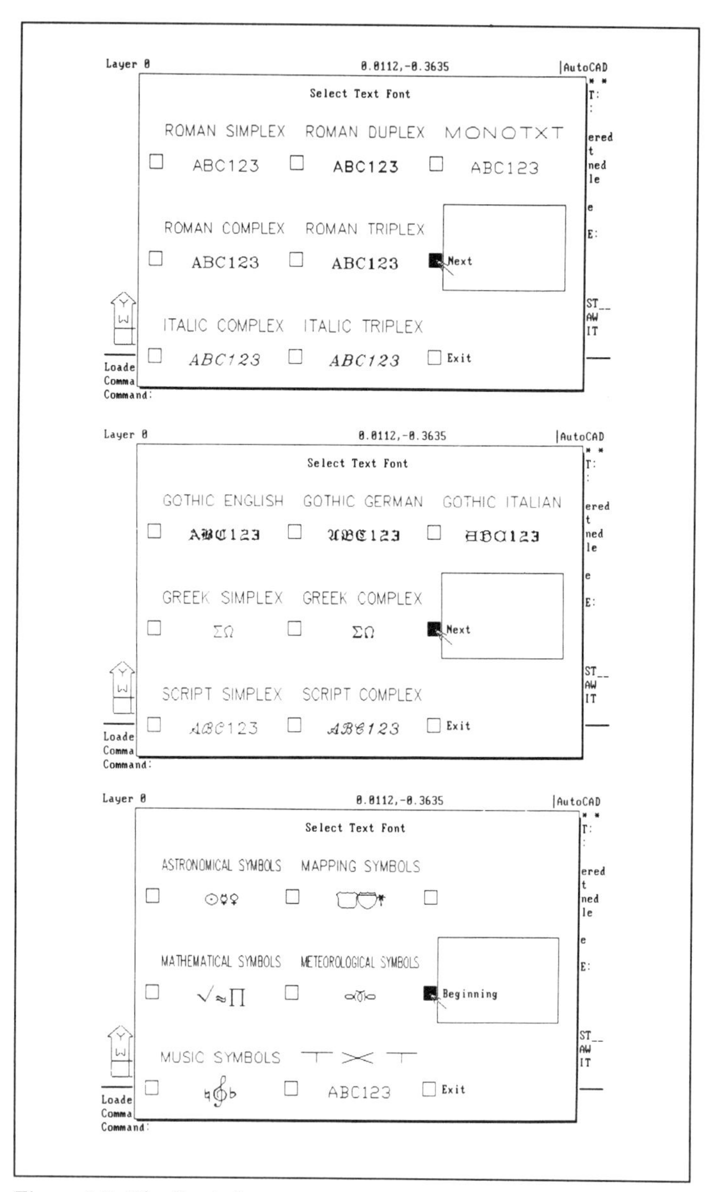

Figure 8.6: The Fonts icon menus

Tablet

Controls digitizing tablet

VERSIONS

All versions

SEQUENCE OF STEPS

Command: **Tablet**(↵)

To issue Tablet from the menu system: **Settings | Next | Tablet**

Option (ON/OFF/CAL/CFG): [Enter desired option.]

If you do not have a digitizing tablet, you will get the message:

Your pointing device cannot be used as a tablet.

OPTIONS

ON If a tablet has been calibrated, ON will toggle the Calibrated mode on. In this mode, you cannot access the screen menus. The F10 function key performs the same function.

OFF If a tablet has been calibrated, OFF will toggle the Calibrated mode off. You will then be able to access the screen menus. The F10 function key performs the same function.

CAL Allows you to calibrate a tablet.

CFG Allows you to configure your digitizing tablet for a tablet menu like the one provided by AutoCAD.

USAGE

Tablet is only useful if you have a digitizing tablet. Use it to set up your tablet for accurate tracing by marking two known locations on your drawing to be traced. Then you can place the drawing on your tablet and use the CAL option under the Tablet command to tell AutoCAD the coordinate location of those two points. From then on, any movement on the drawing will correspond to the movement of the cursor in AutoCAD.

The CAL or Calibrate option allows you to make a specific distance on the tablet correspond to a distance in your AutoCAD drawing. You will be asked to pick a first known point on the tablet and enter its corresponding coordinate in your AutoCAD drawing. This point should be at one end of a line of a known length; one end of a building plan wall known to be ten feet long, for example. Then you are asked to pick a second known point on your tablet and enter its corresponding coordinate in your drawing. This second point should be the other end of the line of known length; the other end of the wall in the preceding example. For best results, the line of known length should be as long as possible and should be horizontal or vertical, not diagonal. You may want to include a graphic scale in your drawing to be digitized just for the purpose of calibrating your tablet. Also, if you have configured your tablet to have menus and a small screen pointing area, to calibrate the tablet you will have to reconfigure it so that its entire surface is designated for the screen pointing area.

The CFG or Configure option allows you to control the location and format of tablet menus as well as the pointing area on your tablet. You are first prompted for the number of tablet menus you want. The AutoCAD tablet menu contains four. Then you are prompted to pick the upper-left, lower-left, and lower-right corners of the tablet menus. The

AutoCAD template shows a black dot at these corners. Next, you are prompted for the number of columns and rows that each menu contains. Finally, you are asked if you want to specify the screen pointing area. This is the area on the tablet used for actual drawing. If you answer yes to this prompt, you are prompted to pick the lower-left and upper-right corners of the pointing area.

SEE ALSO

Sketch

Ucsicon

Controls UCS icon

VERSIONS

10

SEQUENCE OF STEPS

Command: **Ucsicon**(↵)

To issue Ucsion from the menu system: **Settings | Next | Ucsion**

ON/OFF/All/Noorign/ORigin <ON>: [Enter desired option]

OPTIONS

ON — Turns the UCS icon on.

OFF — Turns the UCS icon off.

All — If you use multiple view ports, All forces the Ucsicon settings to take effect in all view ports. Otherwise, the settings will only affect the active view port.

Noorigin — When Ucsicon is set to on, Noorigin places the UCS icon in the lower-left corner of the drawing area, regardless of the current UCS's origin location.

ORigin — When Ucsicon is set to on, ORigin places the UCS icon at the origin of the current UCS. If the origin is off the screen, the UCS icon will appear in the lower-left corner of the drawing area.

USAGE

Ucsicon controls the display and location of the UCS icon. The UCS icon tells you the orientation of the current UCS. It displays an X and Y showing the positive X and Y directions. It also displays a W when the WCS is the current default coordinate system. If the current UCS plane is perpendicular to your current view, the UCS icon displays a broken pencil telling you that you will have difficulty drawing in the current view. The UCS icon changes to a cube when you are displaying a perspective view.

SEE ALSO

UCS, Viewports, Setvar/Ucsicon

Units

Controls measurement system

VERSIONS

All versions, some options added later

SEQUENCE OF STEPS

Command: **Units**(↵)

To issue Units from the menu system: **Settings** | **Next** | **Units**

Systems of units: (Examples)

1. Scientific	1.55E+01
2. Decimal	15.50
3. Engineering	1'-3.50"
4. Architectural	1'-3 1/2"
5. Fractional	15 1/2

With the exception of Engineering and Architectural modes, you can use these modes with any basic unit of measurement. For example, Decimal mode is perfect for metric units as well as decimal English units.

Enter choice, 1 to 5 <2>: [*Enter the number corresponding to the desired unit system.*]

Number of digits to right of decimal point (0 to 8): <4>: [Enter desired number.]

Systems of angle measure: (Examples)

1. Decimal degrees	45.0000
2. Degrees/minutes/seconds	45d0'0"
3. Grads	50.0000g
4. Radians	0.7854r
5. Surveyor's units	N 45d0'0" E

Enter choice, 1 to 5 <1>: [*Enter the number corresponding to the desired angle measure system.*]

Number of fractional places for display of angle (0 to 8) <0>: [Enter desired number.]

Direction for angle 0:

East	3 o'clock	=	0
North	12 o'clock	=	90
West	9 o'clock	=	180
South	6 o'clock	=	270

Enter direction for angle 0 <0>: [*Enter desired angle for the 0 degree direction.*]

Do you want angle measured clockwise <N>: [*Enter* ***Y*** *if you want angles measured clockwise, otherwise press ↵.*]

OPTIONS

System of units Sets format of units that AutoCAD will accept as input.

System of angle measure Sets format of angle measurement AutoCAD will accept as input.

Direction for angle 0 Sets direction for the 0 angle.

USAGE

With Units, you can set AutoCAD to the unit format appropriate to the drawing. For example, if you are drawing an architectural floor plan, you can set up AutoCAD to accept and display distances using feet, inches, and fractional inches. You can also set up AutoCAD to accept and display angles as degrees, minutes, and seconds of arc rather than the default decimal degrees.

The Setup option on the root menu automatically adjusts the Units settings based on the options you select. If you do not like the default settings created by Setup, you can use Units to fine-tune your settings.

SEE ALSO

Setvar

Vports

Controls view ports

VERSIONS

10

SEQUENCE OF STEPS

Command: **Vports**(↵)

To issue Vports from the menu system: **Settings | Next | Vports** *or* **Diplay** pull-down | **Set Viewports**

Save/Restore/Delete/Join/Single/?/2/<3>/4: <*option*>

OPTIONS

Save	Saves the current view port arrangement.
Restore	Restores a saved view port arrangement.
Delete	Deletes a saved view port arrangement.
Join	Joins two adjacent view ports of the same size to make one larger view port.
Single	Changes the display to a single view port.
?	Displays a list of saved view port arrangements along with each view port's coordinate location.
2	Splits the display to show two view ports. You are prompted for a horizontal or vertical split.
3	Changes the display to show three view ports.
4	Changes the display to show four equal view ports.

USAGE

Vports allows you to display multiple views, or *view ports*, of your drawing at once. Each view port can contain any type of view you like. For example, you can display a perspective view in one view port and a plan view of the same drawing in another view port. Or you can have an overall view of the drawing in one port and a close-up of a particular area in another.

Only one view port is active once. That is, you can only work in one view port at a time. To change active view ports, pick any point inside the desired view port. The border around the selected view port will thicken to show you which one is currently active. Also, the standard cursor appears only in the active view port. When you move the cursor into an inactive view port, it changes into an arrow. Although only one view port is active at any given time, any edits made in one view port are immediately reflected in the other view ports. Also, most edit and draw commands started in one view port can be completed in another view port.

Each view port has its own virtual display within which you can pan and zoom at redraw speeds. For this reason, the Regen and Redraw commands affect only the active view port. To regenerate or redraw all the view ports at once, use the Regenall and Redrawall commands.

If you use the 3 option, the display will be split into three view ports, two of equal size and the third taking half of the screen. You are prompted for a horizontal or vertical split or Above, Below, Left, or Right. These options allow you to place the larger of the three view ports at the top, bottom, left, or right half of the drawing area.

You can pick from several predefined view port arrangements by selecting one from an icon menu. You can access the Viewports icon menu by picking the **Set Viewports** option on the Display pull-down menu.

SEE ALSO

Regen, Regenall, Redraw, Redrawall, Viewres

CHAPTER 9

Plotting Commands

This chapter covers the Plot and Prplot commands, found in the Plot menu. These commands allow you to get hard copy of your drawings. The Plot command is intended for plotters and laser printers while the Prplot command works with dot matrix printers. If you are using a laser printer, the pen assignment options described in this chapter do not apply. You may get the listing of entity colors to pens, but you will not get the pen assignment prompts. However, you can use the *Pen width* prompt to set the width of standard lines.

Plot

Plots drawings

VERSIONS

All versions

SEQUENCE OF STEPS

Command: **Plot**(↵)

To issue Plot from the menu system: **Plot** | **Plot** *or* **Files** pull-down | **Plot** *or* **Main** | **3**

What to plot -- Display, Extents, Limits, View or Window <default>: [Enter desired option.]

Pen width is 0.010

Plot will be written to a selected file

Sizes are in inches

Plot origin is at (0.00, 0.00)

Plotting area is 11.00 wide by 8.50 high (MAX size)

Plot is NOT rotated 90 degrees

Area fill will NOT be adjusted for pen width

Hidden lines will NOT be removed

Plot will be scaled to fit available area

Do you want to change anything? <N> [*Enter **Y** if you want to change the default plotter settings shown above.*]

You will get the following series of prompts. Enter **N** to skip the following prompts until you get the *Write plot to a file* prompt.

Entity Color	Pen No.	Line Type	Pen Speed	Entity Color	Pen No.	Line Type	Pen Speed
1 (red)	1	0	60	9	1	0	60
2 (yellow)	1	0	60	10	1	0	60
3 (green)	1	0	60	11	1	0	60
4 (cyan)	1	0	60	12	1	0	60
5 (blue)	1	0	60	13	1	0	60
6 (magenta)	1	0	60	14	1	0	60
7 (white)	1	0	60	15	1	0	60
8	1	0					

Line types 0 = continuous line

1 = ...

2 = —— —— —— ——

3 = ——— ——— ——— ———

4 = ——— . ——— . ——— .

5 = —— - —— - —— - —— -

6 = —— - - —— - - —— - - —— - -

Do you want to change any of the above parameters? <N> [*Enter **Y** to change plotter pen assignments.*]

Enter values, Blank=Next value, Cn=Color n, S=Show current values, X=Exit

Entity Color	Pen No.	Line Type	Pen Speed	
1 (red)	1	0	60	Pen number <1>:

[*Enter ↵ to go to the next options, line type and pen speed, or enter a pen number corresponding to the entity color shown at the far left, or enter **C** followed by an entity color number to select another entity color or **S** to display the current pen settings or **X** to exit the pen setup and continue with the rest of the plotter setup.*]

Write the plot to a file? <N> [*Enter **Y** to create a plot file or press ↵ to plot the drawing.*]

Size units (Inches or Millimeters) <I>: [*Enter desired unit equivalent.*]

Plot origin in Inches <0.00,0.00>: [*Enter location of plot origin on plotter sheet.*]

Standard values for plotting size

Size	Width	Height
A	10.50	8.00
MAX	11.00	8.50

Enter the Size or Width,Height (in Inches) <MAX>: [*Enter desired sheet size.*]

Rotate 2D plots 90 degrees clockwise? <N> [*Enter **Y** if you want a two-dimensional plot rotated 90 degrees on the plotted sheet.*]

Pen width <0.010>: [*Enter width of pen used for solid fills.*]

Adjust area fill boundaries for pen width? <N> [*Enter **Y** if you want the plotter to compensate for pen width on solid filled areas.*]

Remove hidden lines? <N> [*Enter **Y** if you want a three-dimensional view to be plotted with hidden lines removed.*]

Specify scale by entering:

Plotted Inches=Drawing Units or Fit or ? <F>: [*Enter scale factor for plot or **F** to force drawing to fit entirely on sheet.*]

Effective plotting area: [*A value will appear showing you the width and height of the final plotted image. The size of the image will depend on the sheet size entered at the* Standard values for plotting size *prompt plus the scale factor.*]

Enter file name for plot <JUNK>: [*If this prompt appears, enter desired plot file name.*]

Processing vector [*Numbers will appear as AutoCAD sends information to the plotter.*]

Plot complete.

Press RETURN to continue: [*Press ↵ to return to the drawing editor.*]

OPTIONS

What to plot Lets you use the standard display selection options to select part of drawing to plot.

Do you want to change anything? Lets you change current default plotter settings.

Do you want to change ... parameters? If you answer **Y** to the previous prompt, this prompt allows you to coordinate the drawing colors with plotter pens. An **X** at any time during the following three prompts will save the current settings, exit the pen parameters options, and continue the plotter setup prompts.

Pen number If you answer **Y** to the previous prompt, this prompt allows you to set a plotter pen to correspond with a drawing color.

Line type After you answer the previous prompt, this prompt allows you to select a line type that is available on your plotter. Not all plotter configuration will offer this option.

Pen speed After you answer the previous prompt, this prompt allows you to control the plotter pen speed.

Write the plot to a file... After you exit the pen parameters options, this prompt allows you to send the plot information to a file rather than a plotter.

Size units... Allows you to choose between inches and metric units.

Plot origin... Allows you to specify the location of the drawing on the plotter media by specifying an origin location other than the default plotter origin.

Enter the size... Allows you to determine the final drawing sheet size.

Rotate 2D plots... Allows you to select the orientation of the plot on the plotter media. This affects only two-dimensional drawings.

Pen width... Allows you to specify pen widths so AutoCAD can adjust for area fills.

Adjust fill... Tells AutoCAD to adjust area fills for pen widths. If you respond **Y** to this prompt, AutoCAD will offset the border of a filled area by half the pen width so that the area will plot accurately.

Remove hidden lines... Lets you plot a three-dimensional drawing with hidden lines removed.

Specify scale... Allows you to specify the scale of your drawing.

Enter name of file for plot This prompt only appears if you answer **Y** to the plot to file prompt. It allows you to enter a plot file name.

USAGE

Plot allows you to send your drawing to your plotter in order to get hard copy. You can control the plotter pen selection and speed as well as where and how the drawing appears on the plotter media. You also use Plot to tell AutoCAD how much to reduce a scale drawing in order to make it fit onto the media. Once you change any of the plotter settings, AutoCAD automatically saves the new settings, which become the default settings.

Since some plotters do not have built-in line types, the **Select linetype** option may not appear on your plotter.

If you respond **Y** to the *Write the plot to a file* prompt, AutoCAD creates a file on your disk to which it sends the plot information. Plotting to a file will take less time. You can plot the drawing later by downloading the file to your plotter. This capability can be useful if your plotter is in a remote location.

At the *Enter the size* prompt, the available sizes for your plotter will be displayed and you can either enter the corresponding size at the prompt or enter a custom size.

The *Pen width* prompt works in conjunction with the *Adjust fill* prompt, allowing your plotter to compensate for the pen width during area fills. If you respond with a **Y** at the *Adjust fill* prompt, AutoCAD will use the *Pen width* value to offset the outline of any filled areas to half the pen width. This will cause the edge of filled areas to be drawn to the center line of the fill outline.

Also, if you are using a laser printer, the *Pen width* value determines the thickness of a typical line.

If your drawing is to a scale other than 1:1, you must enter the scale at the *Specify scale* prompt to get an accurate scale drawing. The Fit option at this prompt will make a drawing fit within the area specified in the *Enter size* prompt.

You can also issue the Plot command from the AutoCAD main menu as option 3, Plot a drawing.

At times, even though all of your plotter settings are correct, your plot may not appear in the proper location on your sheet or the drawing may not be plotted at all. This often occurs when you are plotting from the main menu and

AutoCAD does not recognize changes to the extents of the drawing. If you have this problem with a plot, open the file to be plotted and issue a **Zoom/Extents**. Let the drawing complete the regeneration process (it will probably regenerate twice), and try plotting again. If the problem persists, double-check your size units, plot origin, plot size, and plot scale settings.

SEE ALSO

Prplot

Prplot

Sends drawing to printer

VERSIONS

2.0 and later

SEQUENCE OF STEPS

Command: **Prplot**(↵)

To issue Prplot from the menu system: **Plot** | **Printer** *or* **File** pull-down | **Print** *or* **Main** | **4**

USAGE

Prplot sends your drawing to a dot matrix printer for hard copy output. The options are the same as for the Plot command, except options related to pens. You can also issue this command from the AutoCAD main menu under option 4, Printer plot a drawing.

SEE ALSO

Plot

CHAPTER 10

The UCS Command

This chapter covers the UCS command, which controls the User Coordinate System function. You can issue the UCS command from the root menu or the Settings pull-down menu. The User Coordinate System enables you to draw three-dimensional objects using all the standard two-dimensional drawing commands. It does this by allowing you to define two-dimensional planes in three-dimensional space. If you master this command, you will master AutoCAD's three-dimensional drawing capabilities.

You can also use the UCS command in two-dimensional drawings to set up *local coordinate systems.* A local coordinate system is one whose origin is a point of reference other than the overall drawing origin. For example, a surveyor may want to measure distances and angles using a monument's location on an AutoCAD map. With the UCS command, you can easily set up a coordinate system with its origin on the monument and in the desired orientation. Another example is the builder who wants to locate exact points in relation to a corner of a room. You could set up a UCS using the corner of a room as the UCS's origin so that you could pick points in relation to that corner using AutoCAD's Coordinate readout. Each room of the building could have its own coordinate system.

The Follow option on the UCS menu is not an actual AutoCAD command, nor is it a UCS option. It is a system variable that you can access with the Setvar command.

Follow is included in the UCS menu for your convenience. (See **Setvar**.)

The Rename command on the UCS menu is actually a macro that starts the Rename command and then automatically selects the Rename UCS option. (See **Rename**.)

Dducs

Displays UCS dialog

VERSIONS

10

SEQUENCE OF STEPS

Command: **Dducs**(↵)

To issue Dducs from the menu system: **Settings** pull-down | **UCS Dialog**

OPTIONS

Current	Allows you to select UCS to make current.
UCS Name	Displays names of defined UCS's and allows you to change UCS names.
List	Displays information about UCS.
Delete	Deletes UCS.

Define new current UCS	Displays dialog box that allows you to define a new UCS. Options on the Define new current UCS dialog box are the same as those for the UCS command.
Up	Scrolls the UCS list up one position.
Page up	Scrolls the UCS list up one page.
Down	Scrolls the UCS list down one position.
Page down	Scrolls the UCS list down one page.
OK	Changes the current UCS settings to those shown in the dialog box and closes the dialog box.
Cancel	Ignores any changes entered into the dialog box and closes the dialog box.

USAGE

If your computer supports the Advanced User Interface, you can use the Dducs command in place of the UCS to control and create User Coordinate Systems.

SEE ALSO

UCS, Elev, Thickness, Vpoint, Dview, Plan, Setvar/ Ucsfollow, Rename

UCS

Controls User Coordinate System

VERSIONS

10

SEQUENCE OF STEPS

Command: **UCS**(↵)

To issue UCS from the menu system: **Root | UCS**

Origin/ZAxis/3point/Entity/View/X/Y/Z/Prev/Restore/Save/Del/?/<World>: *<option>*

OPTIONS

Origin Allows you to determine the origin of a UCS.

ZAxis Allows you to define the direction of the Z coordinate axis. You are prompted for an origin for the UCS and for a point along the Z axis of the UCS.

3point Allows you to define a UCS by selecting three points: the origin, a point along the positive direction of the X axis, and a point along the positive direction of the Y axis.

Entity	Allows you to define a UCS based on the orientation of an object. The way the object was originally created affects the orientation of the UCS.
View	Allows you to define a UCS parallel to your current view. The origin of the current UCS will be used as the origin of the new UCS.
X/Y/Z	Allows you to define a UCS by rotating the current UCS about its X, Y, or Z axis.
Prev	Places you in the previously defined UCS. The UCS Previous option under the Settings pull-down menu has the same effect.
Restore	Restores a saved UCS.
Save	Saves a UCS for later recall.
Del	Deletes a previously saved UCS.
?	Displays a list of currently saved UCS's.
World	Returns you to the World Coordinate System.

USAGE

The User Coordinate System, or UCS, is a tool for creating and editing three-dimensional drawings. A UCS can be described as a plane in three-dimensional space on which you can draw. Using the UCS command, you can create and shift between as many UCS's as you like. This enables you to draw three-dimensional images while still using all the standard AutoCAD two-dimensional drawing and editing commands. There are also specialized three-dimensional drawing commands for creating three-dimensional surfaces. You can issue these three-dimensional commands independently of the UCS. In general, however, objects are drawn on or parallel to the plane of a UCS.

The World Coordinate System, or WCS, is the base from which all other UCS's are defined; WCS is itself considered a UCS. The WCS is the "drawing surface" on which you do most of your two-dimensional drawing. It is the default coordinate system when you open a new file.

If you want to draw an orthagonal three-dimensional object, you can select from several predefined UCS's by picking **UCS options** from the Settings pull-down menu. An icon menu will appear, showing you several predefined UCS's. Once you pick an option, you are prompted for an origin. This allows you either to accurately place the plane on a three-dimensional object you may have already started or to specify coordinates for the UCS origin.

When you use the Entities option, the way the selected entity was created will affect the orientation of the UCS. Table 10.1 describes how a UCS will be generated depending on the object selected.

SEE ALSO

Plan, Elev, Thickness, Vpoint, Dview, Ucsicon, Setvar/Ucsfollow, Dducs, Rename

OBJECT TYPE	UCS ORIENTATION
Arc	The center of the arc establishes the UCS origin. The X axis of the UCS passes through the pick point on the arc.
Circle	The center of the circle establishes the UCS origin. The X axis of the UCS passes through the pick point on the circle.

Table 10.1: UCS Generation Based on Entities

OBJECT TYPE	UCS ORIENTATION
Dimension	The midpoint of the dimension text establishes the UCS origin. The X axis of the UCS is parallel to the X axis that was active when the dimension was drawn.
Line	The end point nearest the pick point establishes the origin of the UCS, and the XZ plane of the UCS contains the line.
Point	The point location establishes the UCS origin. The UCS orientation is arbitrary.
2D Polyline	The starting point of the polyline establishes the UCS origin. The X axis is determined by the direction from the first point to the next vertex.
Solid	The first point of the solid establishes the origin of the UCS. The second point of the solid establishes the X axis.
Trace	The direction of the trace establishes the X axis of the UCS with the beginning point setting the origin.
3Dface	The first point of the 3Dface establishes the origin. The first and second points establish the X axis. The plane defined by the face determines the orientation of the UCS.
Shapes, Text, Blocks, Attributes, and Attribute Definitions	The insertion point establishes the origin of the UCS. The object's rotation angle establishes the X axis.

Table 10.1: UCS Generation Based on Entities (continued)

CHAPTER 11

Utility Commands

This chapter presents commands found in the Utility menu. You use these commands for general file maintenance and file import and export. This chapter also covers the Script and Slide commands. Script runs a sequence of commands and responses in AutoCAD—much like the batch file in DOS. Slides are like snapshots of drawing views that you can display at any time in AutoCAD. Finally, the chapter covers the external commands, which access DOS operations such as Dir and Type.

Attext

Extracts attribute information

VERSIONS

All versions

SEQUENCE OF STEPS

Command: **Attext**(↵)

To issue Attext from the menu system: **Attext | Utility**

CDF, SDF or DXF Attribute extract (or Entities)? <C>: [*Enter format of extracted file or* **E** *to select specific attributes for extraction.*]

Template file: [*Enter name of external template file.*]

Extract file name <drawing name>: [*Enter name of file to hold extracted information.*]

OPTIONS

CDF Creates an ASCII file using commas to delimit fields.

SDF Creates an ASCII file using spaces to delimit fields.

DXF Creates an abbreviated AutoCAD DXF file containing only the block reference, attribute, and end of sequence entities.

Entities Prompts you to select objects. You can then select specific attributes to extract. Once you are done with the selection, the *Attribute extract* prompt reappears.

USAGE

Attext converts attribute information into external ASCII text files. You can then bring these files into database or spreadsheet programs for analysis. For this reason, Attext allows you to choose from three standard database and spreadsheet file formats. If you select CDF (comma-delimited format), each attribute is treated as a field of a record, and all of the attributes in a block are treated as one record. The field values are separated by commas, and character fields are enclosed in quotes. Some database programs, such as dBASE III, III PLUS, and IV, can read this format without any alteration.

If you select SDF (space-delimited format), each attribute is treated as a field of a record, and all attributes in a block are treated as one record. The field values are given a fixed width, and character fields are not given special treatment. Many microcomputer database programs, dBASE included, can read this format without alteration. If you open this file using a word processor, the attribute values will appear in a row and column fashion—the rows are the records and the columns are the fields.

If you select DXF, the attribute information is written in the Autodesk DXF format. This format is designed to exchange data between different CADD programs and generally cannot be read by database or spreadsheet programs.

Before you can extract attribute values with Attext, you need to create a *template* file, an external ASCII file containing a list of attribute tags you wish to extract. Template files, which have the extension .TXT, also contain a code describing the characteristics of the attribute associated with the tag. The code denotes character and numeric values as well as the number of characters for string values or the number of placeholders for numeric values. For example, if you expect the value entered for a numeric attribute whose tag is *cost* to be five characters long with two decimal places, include the following line in the template file:

```
cost   N005002
```

The attribute tag *cost* is followed by the code N005002. The N denotes a numeric value. The next three characters indicate the number of digits the value will hold, in this case five. The last three characters indicate the number of decimal places the number will require, in this case two. If you want to extract a character attribute, you might include the following line in the template file:

```
name   C030000
```

The attribute tag *name* is followed by the code C030000. The C denotes a character value. The next three characters indicate the number of characters you expect for the attribute value, in this case 30. The last three characters are always zeroes in character attributes, since character values have no decimal places.

Follow the last line in the template file by a ↵ or you will get an error message when you try to use the template file.

You can also extract information about the block that contains the attributes. Table 11.1 shows the format that you use in the template file to extract block information. A template file that contains these codes must also contain at least one attribute tag because AutoCAD must know which attribute it is extracting before it can tell what block the attribute is associated with.

SEE ALSO

Attdef, Attedit

DXF/DXB

Working with the DXF and DXB file formats

The following commands deal with the DXF and DXB data exchange file formats for AutoCAD and other programs such as AutoSketch and AutoShade. The DXF format was developed by Autodesk and has become the standard for data exchange between microcomputer CADD programs.

TAG	CODE	DESCRIPTION
BL:LEVEL	N*000000*	Level of nesting for block
BL:NAME	C*000000*	Block name
BL:X	N*000000*	X value for block insertion point
BL:Y	N*000000*	Y value for block insertion point
BL:Z	N*000000*	Z value for block insertion point
BL:NUMBER	N*000000*	Block counter
BL:HANDLE	C*000000*	Block handle
BL:LAYER	C*000000*	Name of layer block is on
BL:ORIENT	N*000000*	Block rotation angle
BL:XSCALE	N*000000*	Block X scale
BL:YSCALE	N*000000*	Block Y scale
BL:ZSCALE	N*000000*	Block Z scale
BL:XEXTRUDE	N*000000*	X value for block extrusion direction
BL:YEXTRUDE	N*000000*	Y value for block extrusion direction
BL:ZEXTRUDE	N*000000*	Z value for block extrusion direction

Note: Italicized zeros indicate adjustable variables.

***Table 11.1:** Template tags and codes for extracting information about blocks*

Dxfin

Imports DXF files

VERSIONS

All versions

SEQUENCE OF STEPS

Command: **Dxfin**(↵)

To issue Dxfin from the menu system: **Utility|Dxf/Dxb | Dxfin**

File name <current file name>: [*Enter name of DXF file to import.*]

USAGE

Dxfin imports drawing files in the AutoCAD DXF format. These are ASCII files with the extension .DXF. They contain a code that allows AutoCAD to import complete drawing information. Many microcomputer-based CADD programs as well as some minicomputer CADD programs offer a DXF converter so that you can export files to AutoCAD. DXF is the format that you use to import AutoSketch files.

To import an entire DXF file, open a new file that does not contain any nameable variable definitions such as layers, line types, text styles, views, and so on. Issue the Dxfin command before you do anything else. If the current file already contains nameable variables, only the drawn objects in the imported file will be imported. Line types, layers, and so on will not be imported. When you enter the name of the DXF file you wish to import, do not include the .DXF extension.

SEE ALSO

Dxfout, Dxbin

Dxfout

Creates a DXF file

VERSIONS

All versions

SEQUENCE OF STEPS

Command: **Dxfout**(↵)

To issue Dxfout from the menu system: **Utility|Dxf/Dxb | Dxfout**

File name <default current file name>: [*Enter file name or press ↵ for default.*]

Enter decimal places of accuracy (0 to 16)/Entities/Binary <6>: [*Enter a value representing the decimal place accuracy of your DXF file or press ↵ to accept the default, 6*]

OPTIONS

(0 to 16) Controls the decimal accuracy of the DXF file to be created. The default value is 6.

Entities Allows you to select specific objects or a portion of the current drawing to be exported. You are then prompted to select objects.

Binary Creates a binary version of the DXF file. Do not confuse this with the DXB file format.

USAGE

Dxfout creates a copy of your current file in the DXF file format for export to other programs (see **Dxfin**, the Usage section). You can also create a binary version of the DXF format, which is highly compressed compared with the ASCII version. The binary version will also have the .DXF extension. Do not confuse this binary DXF file format with the DXB file format generated by AutoShade and the AutoCAD ADI plotter option.

There are many programs that make use of DXF files. Some are converters that translate DXF files into formats readable by desktop publishing programs, paint programs, or other CADD programs. These can allow you to render or manipulate an AutoCAD drawing in ways not offered by AutoCAD. Other programs are available that use DXF files for analysis or for generating database information.

SEE ALSO

Dxfin, Dxbin

Dxbin

Imports DXB files

VERSIONS

2.1 and later

SEQUENCE OF STEPS

Command: **Dxbin**(↵)

To issue Dxbin from the menu system: **Utility|Dxf/Dxb | Dxbin**

DXB file: [*Enter DXB file name.*]

USAGE

Dxbin imports files in the DXB file format. Unlike the DXF file format, DXB is a binary file format that contains a limited amount of drawing information. It is the main format used by AutoShade to export files to AutoCAD.

You can also use Dxbin to convert AutoCAD three-dimensional views, both perspective and orthogonal, into two-dimensional drawings by configuring AutoCAD's plotter option to an ADI plotter that produces DXB files. You will then be able to generate DXB plot files of any three-dimensional view and import these files into AutoCAD as two-dimensional images. Since PageMaker accepts DXB files, this is also one way of exporting AutoCAD drawings to PageMaker.

SEE ALSO

Dxfout, Dxfin

End

Exits and saves files

VERSIONS

All versions

SEQUENCE OF STEPS

Command: **End**(↵)

To issue End from the menu system: **Utility** | **End** *or* **File** pull-down | **End**

USAGE

End simultaneously exits and saves a file. All edits up to the point when you issue the End command will be saved. If you pick **End** from the Utility menu, you must also pick **Yes** from the End menu that then appears.

SEE ALSO

Quit, Save

Files

Offers DOS file maintenance

VERSIONS

All versions

SEQUENCE OF STEPS

Command: **Files**(↵)

To issue Files from the menu system: **Utility | Files**

File Utility Menu

0. Exit File Utility Menu
1. List Drawing files
2. List user specified files
3. Delete files
4. Rename files
5. Copy file

Enter selection (0 to 5) <0>: [*Enter number corresponding to desired option.*]

OPTIONS

Exit File Utility Menu Exits the Files command.

List Drawing files Lists all drawing files in a directory you specify.

List user specified files Lists files you specify in the directory you specify. Accepts wildcard specifications.

Delete files Deletes files you specify. Accepts wildcard specifications.

Rename files Renames files. Prompts you for current file name and then for new name.

Copy file Copies files.

USAGE

Files allows you to manipulate files on your disk without having to exit AutoCAD. You can list all or specified files, delete them, rename them, or copy them.

SEE ALSO

External Commands

Igesin/out

Working with the IGES file format

Igesin and Igesout allow you to import and export files in the IGES file format. IGES, or Initial Graphics Exchange Standard, is a file format standard for CADD drawings.

Igesin

Imports IGES files

VERSIONS

2.5 and later

SEQUENCE OF STEPS

Command: **Igesin**(↵)

To issue Igesin from the menu system: **Utility|Iges | Igesin**

File name: [*Enter IGES file names.*]

USAGE

Use Igesin to import files in the IGES format.

SEE ALSO

Igesout

Igesout

Creates an IGES file

VERSIONS

2.5 and later

SEQUENCE OF STEPS

Command: **Igesout**(↵)

To issue Igesout from the menu system: **Utility|Iges | Igesout**

File name: [*Enter IGES file name.*]

USAGE

Igesout makes a copy of your current file in the IGES format.

SEE ALSO

Igesin

Menu

Loads a menu file

VERSIONS

All versions

SEQUENCE OF STEPS

Command: **Menu**(↵)

To issue Menu from the menu system: **Utility | Menu**

Menu file name or . for none <acad>: [*Enter menu file name.*]

USAGE

You can create your own menu using a text editor that can read and write ASCII files. You use the Menu command to load your custom menu file. Once you have loaded a menu into a drawing, that drawing file will include the menu file name. The next time you open the drawing file, AutoCAD will also attempt to load the last menu used with the file.

If you use one of Autodesk's Template overlays, you can use the Arch... or Mech... options on the Change Template menu that appears when you pick **Menu** from the Utility menu to switch to those templates.

Purge

Deletes unused variables

VERSIONS

2.0 and later

SEQUENCE OF STEPS

Command: **Purge**(↵)

To issue Purge from the menu system: **Utility | Purge**

Purge unused Blocks/LAyers/LTypes/SHapes/ STyles/All: [*Enter option to purge from the file.*]

When you enter the variable type name at the *Purge* prompt, you can purge or keep each unused variable. The All option will display all variables, regardless of type.

USAGE

A drawing may accumulate blocks, layers, and other elements that are no longer used or needed. These unused objects and settings can increase the size of the drawing file, making the drawing slow to load and difficult to transport. Purge allows you to eliminate these unused drawing elements, reducing the size of the file. You can only use this command as the first command after you open the file.

Version 10 allows you to use Purge later in an editing session as long as you haven't made any changes to the drawing's database. This means that you can use commands that affect the display of the drawing and still use Purge afterward, but if you use a drawing or editing command, you must close the file and then reopen it before you can use the Purge command.

SEE ALSO

Wblock

Quit

Exits file without saving edits

VERSIONS

All versions

SEQUENCE OF STEPS

Command: **Quit**(↵)

To issue Quit from the menu system: **Utility** | **Quit** *or* **Files** pull-down | **Quit**

Really want to discard all changes to drawing? [*Enter* ***Y*** *to exit or* ↵ *to abort Quit command.*]

USAGE

Quit will exit a drawing without saving the most recent edits. The file will revert to its condition when you last saved it with the Save or End command. If you pick **Quit** from the Utility menu, Quit will not be issued until you pick **Yes** from the Quit menu that then appears. Once you pick **Yes**, a Yes response is automatically entered at the *Really want to discard file* prompt and you exit the drawing.

SEE ALSO

Save, End

Rename

Renames nameable drawing elements

VERSIONS

2.0 and later

SEQUENCE OF STEPS

Command: **Rename**(↵)

To issue Rename from the menu system: **Utility** | **Rename**

Block/LAyer/LType/Style/Ucs/VIew/VPort: [*Enter type of drawing element to rename.*]

USAGE

Rename will rename any of the drawing elements you give at the *Rename* prompt.

Script

Executes Script files

VERSIONS

All versions

SEQUENCE OF STEPS

Command: **Script**(↵)

To issue Script from the menu system: **Utility** | **Script**

Script file <current file name>: [*Enter script file name.*]

OPTIONS

Delay *<time in milliseconds>* When included in a script file, Delay makes AutoCAD pause for the number of milliseconds indicated.

Rscript When included at the end of a Script file, Rscript will repeat the script continuously.

Resume Restarts a Script file that has been interrupted with the Backspace or Ctrl-C key.

Backspace *or Ctrl-C* Interrupts Script file processing.

USAGE

Script allows you to "play back" a set of AutoCAD commands and responses recorded in a Script file. Script files, like DOS batch files, are lists of commands and responses that you enter exactly as you would while in the AutoCAD drawing editor. You can use Script files to set up frequently used macros to save lengthy keyboard entries, or to automate a presentation.

SEE ALSO

Slides

Slides

Working with Slide files

The commands on the Slides submenu allow you to store and retrieve "snapshot" images or slides of drawing views. These slides are stored on your disk as individual files with the .SLD extension. (Versions 9 and 10 allow you to combine several slides into a file known as a *slide library*.) You cannot edit slides, nor can you use the Zoom or Pan commands over them. However, you can view slides regardless of which file you are in. This enables you to view a slide of one drawing while working on another.

You can also use slides to create presentations. By combining slides with scripts, you can set up your computer to display a series of slides as a form of animated presentation.

You use slides in conjunction with the AutoCAD Slidelib.EXE external program to create icon menus.

Mslide

Makes a Slide file

VERSIONS

All versions

SEQUENCE OF STEPS

Command: **Mslide**(↵)

To issue Mslide from the menu system: **Utility|Slides | Mslide**

File name <current file name>: [*Enter desired file name, excluding extension.*]

USAGE

Mslides saves the current view in a Slide file. (Slide files have .SLD extensions.)

SEE ALSO

Vslide

Vslide

Displays Slide files

VERSIONS

All versions

SEQUENCE OF STEPS

Command: **Vslide**(↵)

To issue Vslide from the menu system: **Utility|Slides | Vslide**

File name <current file name>: [*Enter name of slide file to be displayed, excluding extension.*]

USAGE

Vslide will display a Slide file. For versions up to 2.6, slides are always individual files with the extension .SLD. Versions 9 and 10 offer a slide library facility that combines a set of slides into one file. Slide library files have .SLB extensions. To view a slide from a slide library, enter the slide library name followed by the slide's name in parentheses, as in **library(slide)**.

SEE ALSO

Mslide, Slidelib.EXE

Slidelib.EXE

Combines slides into one file

VERSIONS

9 and later

SEQUENCE OF STEPS

C:/acad> **Slidelib** *slide-library-name* **<** *list* (↵)

USAGE

Slidelib.EXE is an external AutoCAD program that runs independently from AutoCAD. It can be found on one of your AutoCAD support disks. Use it to combine several slide files into a slide library file. You use slide libraries to create icon menus and to help organize slide files. Before you can create a slide library, you must create an ASCII file containing a list of slide file names to include in the library. Do not include the .SLD extension in the list of names. You can give the list any name and extension. Then you can issue the Slidelib program from the DOS prompt in the manner just shown.

SEE ALSO

Vslide, Mslide

External Commands

Access to DOS

You use the following set of commands to access DOS while in AutoCAD. You can perform several standard DOS functions and temporarily exit AutoCAD to run small programs.

The external command function operates via an external DOS text file called Acad.PGP, which is included in your AutoCAD package. Each external command is given a line written in a special code. You can include your own custom external commands by adding to this file with a word processor that reads and writes ASCII files. Here is a listing of the standard Acad.PGP file.

```
CATALOG,DIR /W,30000,*Files: ,0
DEL,DEL,30000,File to delete: ,0
DIR,DIR,30000,File specification: ,0
EDIT,EDLIN,42000,File to edit: ,0
SH,,30000,*DOS Command: ,0
SHELL,,127000,*DOS Command: ,0
TYPE,TYPE,30000,File to list: ,0
```

Each entry is a line of items separated by commas. The first item is the name of the command as it is to be entered at the AutoCAD *Command* prompt. The next item is the actual command as entered at the DOS prompt. Next is the amount of memory in bytes to allocate to the command. (The amount of memory will depend on the requirements of the command. Usually 30K is enough for most DOS functions. The maximum allowable is 127K.) Following that is the prompt, if any, to appear after the command is issued. An asterisk preceding the prompt tells AutoCAD to accept spaces in the response to the prompt. The prompt response will be appended to the preceding command. If no prompt is needed, this item can be blank. Finally, the 0 is a return code, which is usually 0. Other return codes are reserved for special programming.

Catalog

Lists files

VERSIONS

2.1 and later

SEQUENCE OF STEPS

Command: **Catalog**(↵)

To issue Catalog from the menu system: **Utility|External Command | Catalog**

Files: [*Enter standard DOS file names; wildcard characters accepted.*]

USAGE

Catalog displays a list of files in any specified drive or directory. You get the same list in DOS when you enter **dir /w**. At the *Files* prompt, you can enter any drive letter, directory name, or wildcard character, as you would in DOS. If you give no specifications, you will get a list of the current drive.

SEE ALSO

Dir, Files

Del

Deletes files

VERSIONS

2.1 and later

SEQUENCE OF STEPS

Command: **Del**(↵)

To issue Del from the menu system: **Utility|External Command | Del**

File to delete: [*Enter file name.*]

USAGE

Del deletes files from a specified disk. At the *Files to delete* prompt, you can enter any drive letter or directory name, as you would in DOS.

SEE ALSO

Files

Dir

Lists files

VERSIONS

2.1 and later

SEQUENCE OF STEPS

Command: **Dir**(↵)

To issue Dir from the menu system: **Utility|External Command | Dir**

File specification: [*Enter standard DOS file names; wildcard characters accepted.*]

USAGE

Dir displays a list of files in any specified drive or directory. You get the same list in DOS when you enter **dir**. At the *File specification* prompt, you can enter any drive letter or directory name, as you would in DOS. You can also add the standard DOS Dir command switches, such as /P or /W. If you give no specifications, you will get a list of the current drive.

SEE ALSO

Catalog, Files

Edit

Opens DOS line editor Edlin

VERSIONS

2.5 and later

SEQUENCE OF STEPS

Command: **Edit**(↵)

To issue Edit from the menu system: **Utility|External Command | Edit**

File to edit: [*Enter DOS or ASCII file name.*]

USAGE

Edit opens a specified file using the DOS Edlin line editor. You can then edit the file using all of the Edlin commands. The Edlin.COM file must be in the default drive and directory before this command will work. See your DOS manual for details on Edlin.

You can use this command when you need to create an ASCII file for the Attext or Script commands.

SEE ALSO

Attext, Script, and Edlin in your DOS manual

SH

Small shell to DOS

VERSIONS

2.1 and later

SEQUENCE OF STEPS

Command: **Sh**(↵)

To issue Sh from the menu system: **Utility|External Command | Sh**

DOS Command: [*Enter standard DOS command or press ↵ to enter DOS.*]

USAGE

Sh allows you to use any DOS command without exiting AutoCAD. It sets aside a small amount of memory with which to run DOS commands or other commands external to AutoCAD. There are internal and external DOS commands. Internal DOS commands reside in RAM and can be accessed regardless of your current drive and directory location. External DOS commands are actually files on your hard disk. To use them, you must either specify the drive and directory where the external command can be found or set a path to that drive and directory before you start AutoCAD.

If you press ↵ at the *DOS Command* prompt, the DOS prompt appears and you can enter any number of external commands. You must enter **Exit** to return to the AutoCAD *Command* prompt.

SEE ALSO

Shell

Shell

Large shell to DOS

VERSIONS

2.1 and later

SEQUENCE OF STEPS

Command: **Shell**(↵)

To issue Shell from the menu system: **Utility|External Command | Shell**

DOS Command: [*Enter standard DOS command or press ↵ to enter DOS.*]

USAGE

Shell allows you to use any DOS command and to run other programs with low memory requirements without exiting AutoCAD. If you want to use external DOS commands or programs, be sure you either specify the drive and directory where the commands or programs are located or set a path to the appropriate drive and directory before you start AutoCAD. Shell differs from Sh in that it allows the external commands to use larger amounts of memory. You can run programs that use 120K of RAM or less.

If you press ↵ at the *DOS command* prompt, the DOS prompt appears and you can enter any number of external commands. You must enter **Exit** to return to the AutoCAD *Command* prompt.

SEE ALSO

Sh

Type

Displays DOS file contents

VERSIONS

2.1 and later

SEQUENCE OF STEPS

Command: **Type**(↵)

To issue Type from the menu system: **Utility|External Command | Type**

File to list: [*Enter DOS or ASCII file name.*]

USAGE

Type performs the same function as the DOS command TYPE. It will display the contents of a DOS text file or ASCII file. If the DOS More.COM file is available, you can use the DOS command modifier | **more** to display large files.

CHAPTER 12

Commands for Three-Dimensional Operations

This chapter presents the commands that generate three-dimensional surfaces and objects. These commands are on the 3D menu and on the 3D construction icon menu, which you access from the Draw pull-down menu.

A three-dimensional surface in AutoCAD takes the form of a mesh. This mesh has an M and N direction, which are roughly equivalent to the X and Y axes of a coordinate system. However, the M and N directions are not necessarily perpendicular to each other nor do they lie in a single plan (see Figure 12.1). These direction designations do not act as actual axes of a coordinate system; they are meant to help you edit the surface.

All of the three-dimensional surfaces use 3dfaces as their basic component. *3dfaces* are solid objects defined by four points in space. Although they are solid, they will appear as transparent or wire frame objects until you remove hidden lines from the drawing. AutoCAD creates surfaces by joining several 3dfaces to form a larger and more complex surface. This means that a bowl-shaped mesh, for example, will be made up of facets, each facet being a 3dface. A three-dimensional surface acts like a single object but can be broken into its component 3dfaces with the Explode command.

You can control the number of 3dfaces used to create a three-dimensional surface by adjusting the Surftab1 and Surftab2 system variables. You can set these variables using the Setvar command or by picking **Surftab1** or **Surftab2** from the 3D construction icon menu found on the Draw pull-down menu. A detailed description of how these variables affect the surfaces is given under each command. See **Setvar** for more information on these system variables.

Finally, you can use the point filters described in Appendix A to enter points in three-dimensional space while drawing three-dimensional objects.

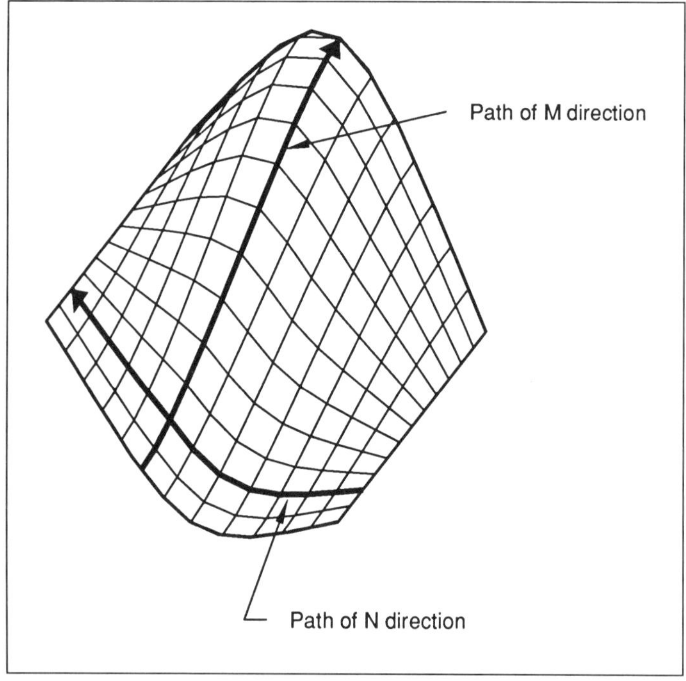

Figure 12.1: The M and N directions of a three-dimensional mesh

Edgesurf

Draws surface based on four edges

VERSIONS

10

SEQUENCE OF STEPS

Command: **Edgesurf**(↵)

To issue Edgesurf from the menu system:

3D|Edgesurf
or
Draw pull-down|**3D construction**| **Edge Defined surface patch** icon

Select edge 1:

Select edge 2:

Select edge 3:

Select edge 4:

USAGE

Edgesurf draws a three-dimensional surface based on four contiguous objects. These objects can be lines, arcs, polylines, or three-dimensional polylines, but they must join exactly end-to-end. The type of surface generated is called a *Coons surface patch* (see Figure 12.2).

The first edge selected becomes the M direction of the mesh while the direction indicated by the edges adjoining the first become the N direction. The end point on the object closest to the first point picked becomes the origin of the M and N directions.

You can control the number of facets used to generate the mesh by setting the Surftab1 and Surftab2 system variables. Surftab1 controls the number of facets in the M direction; Surftab2 controls the facets in the N direction. Increasing the number of facets gives a smoother-looking mesh but also increases the size of the drawing considerably, which in turn increases file-opening and redrawing and regeneration times. See *Setvar* for details.

SEE ALSO

Setvar/Surftab1, Surftab2, Pedit

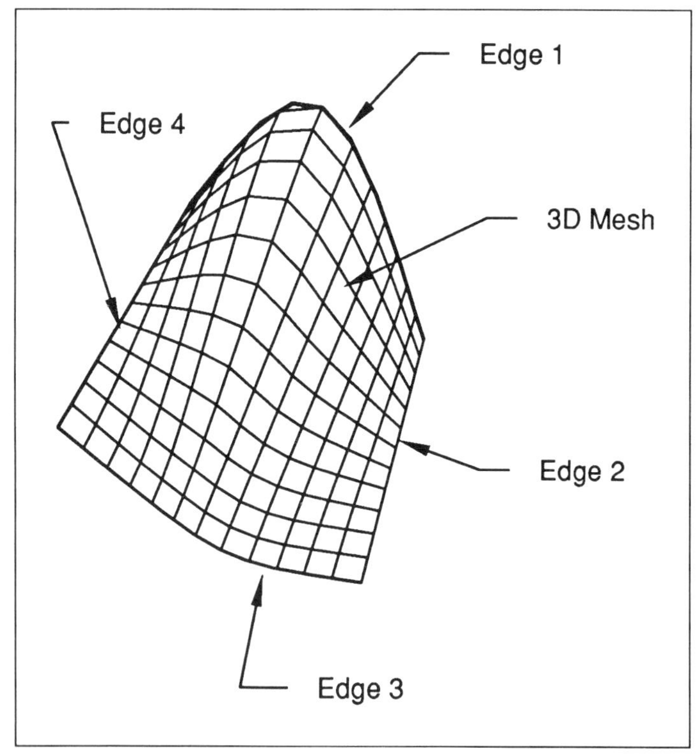

Figure 12.2: A Coons surface patch

Revsurf

Draws circular extrusion

VERSIONS

10

SEQUENCE OF STEPS

Command: **Revsurf**(↵)

To issue Revsurf from the menu system:

3D|Revsurf
or
Draw pull-down|**3D construction|Surface of Revolution** icon

Select path curve: [*Pick arc line, arc, circle, two-dimensional or three-dimensional polyline defining shape to be extruded.*]

Select Axis of revolution: [*Pick line representing axis of rotation.*]

Starting Angle <0>: [*Enter angle from object selected as path curve where extrusion starts.*]

Included angle (+=ccw, −=cw) <Full circle>: [*Enter angle of extrusion.*]

USAGE

Revsurf draws an extruded curved surface rotated about an axis like a bell, globe, or drinking glass (see Figure 12.3). Before you can use Revsurf, you must define the shape of the extrusion and an axis of rotation. You can define this shape using arcs, lines, circles, or two-dimensional or three-dimensional polylines. The axis of rotation can be a line.

At the first prompt, select the object defining the extrusion. At the next prompt, pick the line indicating the axis of rotation. The point you pick on this line will determine the positive and negative directions of the rotation. You can use the "right-hand rule" illustrated in Figure 12.4 to determine the positive direction of the rotation. Imagine placing your right hand on the axis line so that your thumb points away from the end closest to the pick point. The rest of your fingers will point in the positive rotation direction. The rotation direction determines the N direction of the surface while the axis of rotation defines the M direction.

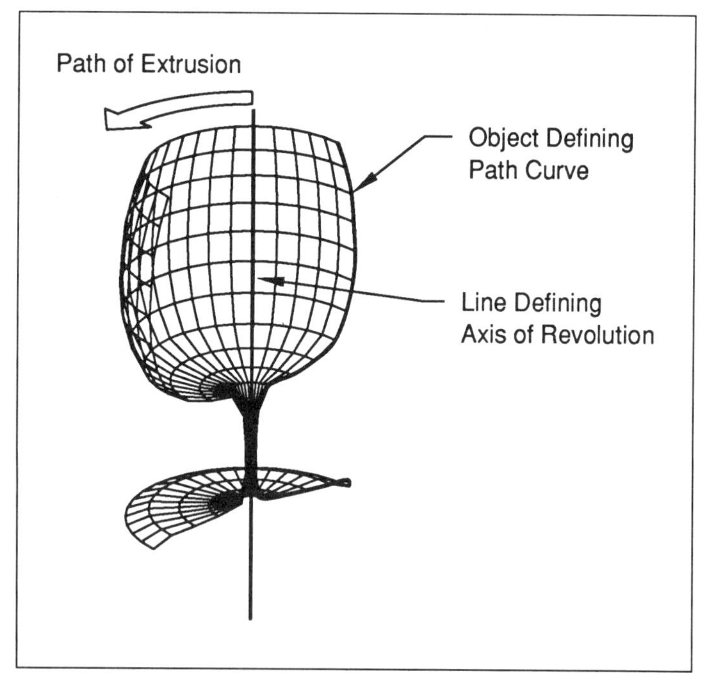

Figure 12.3: Extruded curved surface drawn by Revsurf

You can control the number of facets used to create the revsurf by setting the Surftab1 and Surftab2 system variables. Surftab1 controls the number of facets in the M direction while Surftab2 controls the facets in the N direction. See **Setvar** for details.

SEE ALSO

Pedit

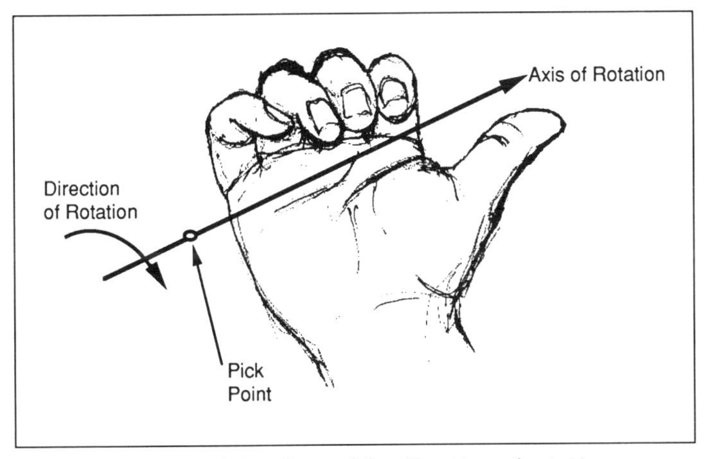

Figure 12.4: Determining the positive direction of rotation

Rulesurf

Draws surface based on two edges

VERSIONS

10

SEQUENCE OF STEPS

Command: **Rulesurf**(↵)

To issue Rulesurf from the menu system:

3D|Rulesurf
or
Draw pull-down|**3D construction|Ruled Surface** icon

Select first defining curve: [*Pick first curve.*]

Select second defining curve: [*Pick second curve.*]

USAGE

Rulesurf generates a surface based on two curves. Before you can use Rulesurf, you must draw two curves defining opposite ends of the desired surface (see Figure 12.5). The

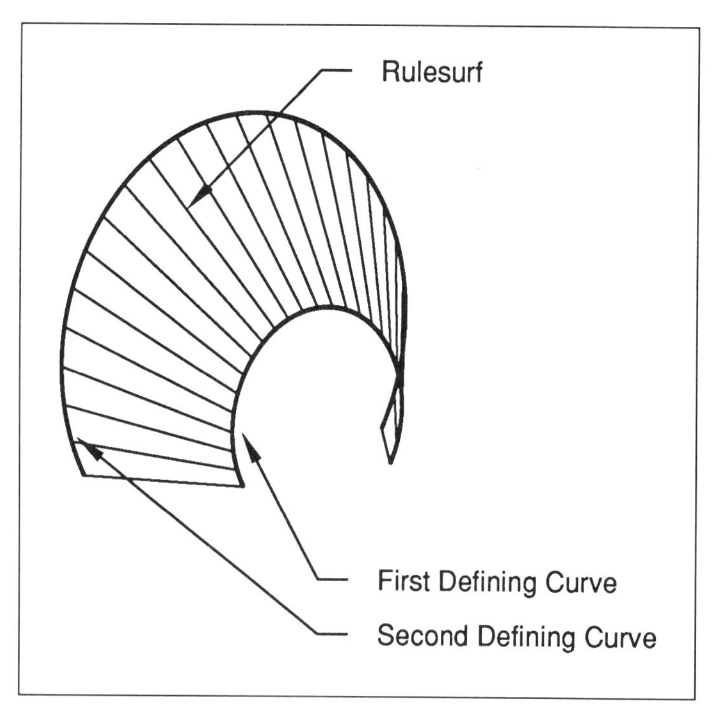

Figure 12.5: Defining the opposite ends of a surface for Rulesurf

defining curves can be points, lines, arcs, circles, or two-dimensional or three-dimensional polylines.

The location of your pick points on the defining curves will affect the way the surface is generated. If you want the surface to be drawn straight between the two defining curves, pick points near the same position on each curve. If you want the surface to cross between the two defining curves, in a corkscrew fashion, pick points at opposite positions on the curves (see Figure 12.6).

The Surftab1 system variable controls the number of faces used to generate the surface.

SEE ALSO

Setvar/Surftab1, Pedit

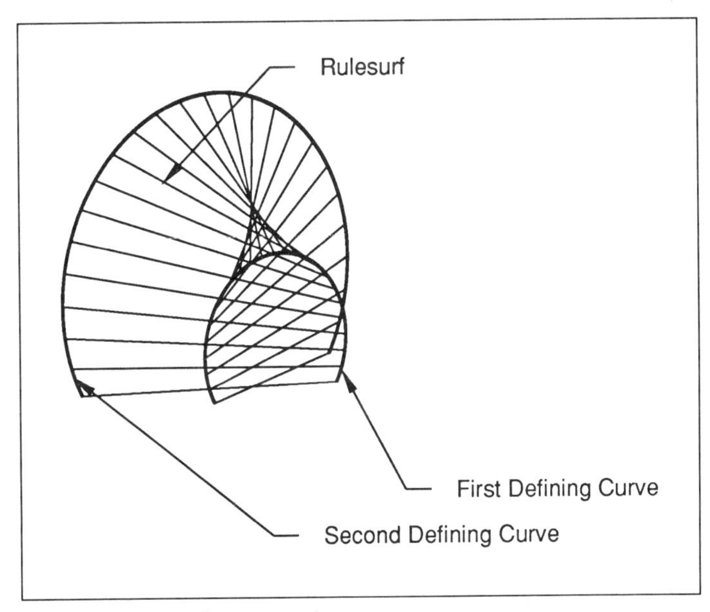

Figure 12.6: A corkscrew surface

Tabsurf

Draws straight line extrusion

VERSIONS

10

SEQUENCE OF STEPS

Command: **Tabsurf**(↵)

To issue Tabsurf from the menu system:

3D|Tabsurf
or
Draw pull-down|**3D construction|Tabulated Surface** icon

Select path curve: [*Pick curve defining surface shape.*]

Selecting direction vector: [*Pick line defining direction of extrusion.*]

USAGE

Tabsurf draws a surface by extruding a curve in a straight line (see Figure 12.7). Before you can use Tabsurf, you must draw a curve defining the extruded shape and a line defining the direction of the extrusion (the direction vector). The point at which you pick the direction vector at the *Select direction vector* prompt determines the direction of the extrusion. The end point nearest the pick point is the base of the direction vector, and the other end indicates the direction of the extrusion. You can draw the curve with a line, arc, circle, or two-dimensional or three-dimensional polyline. The direction vector can be a three-dimensional line. Tabsurf has an effect similar to changing the thickness of an object, but extrusions using Tabsurf are not limited to the Z axis.

The Surftab1 system variable will affect the number of facets used to form the surface.

SEE ALSO

Setvar/Surftab1, Pedit

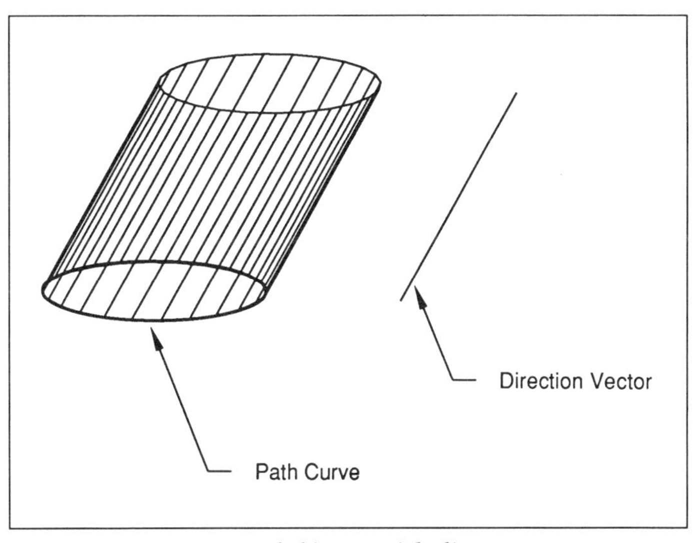

Figure 12.7: A curve extruded in a straight line

3dface

Draws a single 3dface

VERSIONS

10

SEQUENCE OF STEPS

Command: **3dface**(↵)

To issue 3dface from the menu system: **3D|3dface**

First point: [*Pick first corner.*]

Second point: [*Pick second corner.*]

Third point: [*Pick third corner.*]

Fourth point: [*Pick fourth corner.*]

Third point: [*Continue to pick pairs of points defining more faces or press ↵ to end command.*]

OPTIONS

Invisible Makes an edge of the 3dface invisible

USAGE

3dface allows you to draw a single 3dface in three-dimensional space. As mentioned, 3dfaces are surfaces defined by four points in space picked in a circular fashion. Though they appear transparent, they are treated as opaque when you remove hidden lines from a drawing. You can create adjoining 3dfaces by entering more points after the first face is defined. You are prompted for additional third and fourth points to allow the addition of more 3dfaces.

At times, you may want to hide the joint line between joined 3dfaces. You can use the Invisible option to do so. As you pick the defining points, enter **I** just before you pick the first point of the side to be made invisible (see Figure 12.8).

You can make invisible edges visible for editing by setting the Splframe system variable to any nonzero value. See **Setvar** for more on Splframe. Also see **Edge** in Appendix C.

SEE ALSO

Setvar/Splframe

3dmesh

Draws three-dimensional surface from point input

VERSIONS

10

SEQUENCE OF STEPS

Command: **3dmesh**(↵)

To issue 3dmesh from the menu system: **3D|Mesh**

Mesh M size: [*Enter number of vertices in M direction.*]

Mesh N size: [*Enter number of vertices in N direction.*]

Vertex (0,0): [*Enter X,Y,Z coordinate value for first vertex in mesh.*]

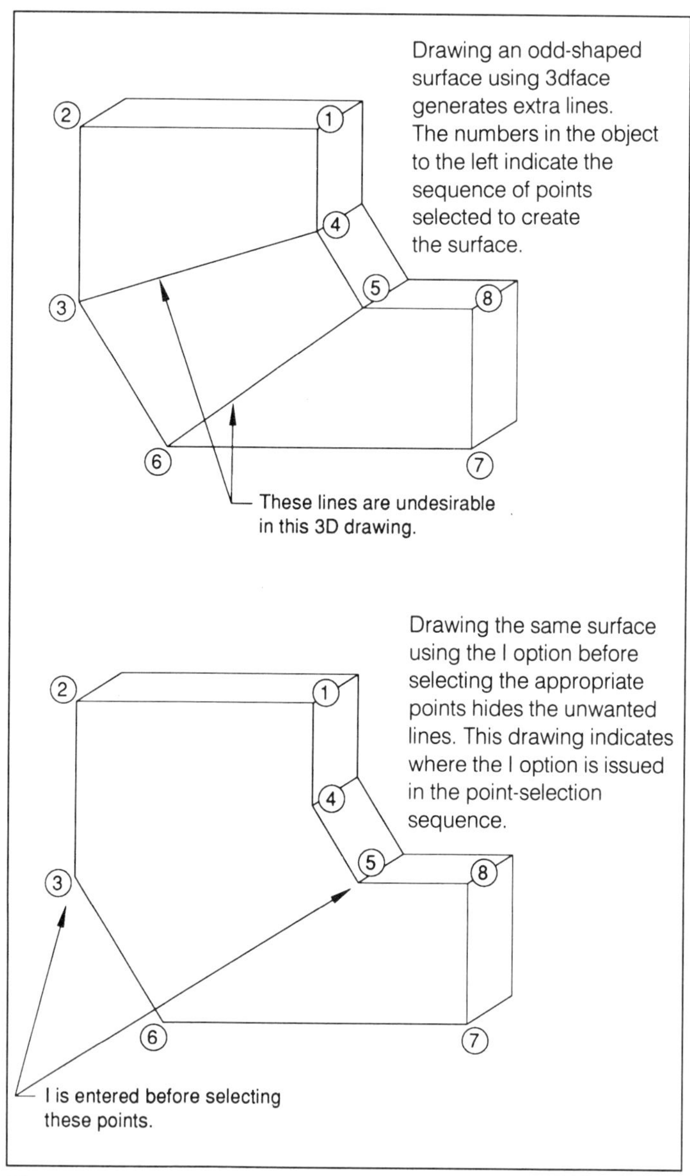

Drawing an odd-shaped surface using 3dface generates extra lines. The numbers in the object to the left indicate the sequence of points selected to create the surface.
1
2
3
4
5
6
7
8
These lines are undesirable in this 3D drawing.
Drawing the same surface using the I option before selecting the appropriate points hides the unwanted lines. This drawing indicates where the I option is issued in the point-selection sequence.
1
2
3
4
5
6
7
8
I is entered before selecting these points.

Figure 12.8: Hiding the joined edge of multiple 3dfaces

Vertex (0,1): [*Enter X,Y,Z coordinate value for next vertex in the N direction of the mesh.*]

Vertex (0,2): [*Continue to enter X,Y,Z coordinates values for vertices.*]

.

.

.

USAGE

3dmesh draws a three-dimensional surface using coordinate values you specify. This is useful when you are drawing three-dimensional models of a topography or for finite element analysis. You can also use 3dmesh with AutoLISP.

To use 3dmesh to generate a topographic model, make a list of your X,Y,Z coordinate values in a rectangular array. Arrange the coordinates roughly as they would appear in plan. Be sure you fill any blanks in the array with dummy or neutral coordinate values. Start the 3dmesh command and use the number of columns for the mesh M size and the number of rows for the N size. At the *Vertex* prompts, enter the coordinate values row by row, starting at the lower-left corner of your array and reading from left to right. Be sure to include any dummy values. When you finish the first row, start entering the next row. Continue in this way until you are done. Figure 12.9 illustrates a finished topographic model generated with 3dmesh.

SEE ALSO

Pedit

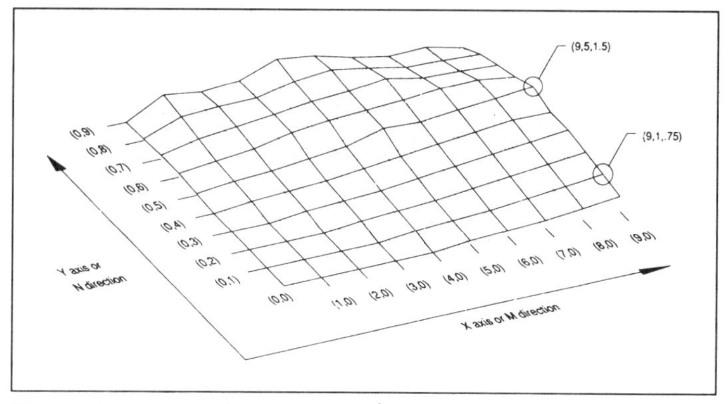

Figure 12.9: A sample drawing of a three-dimensional mesh

3dpoly

Draws three-dimensional polyline

VERSIONS

10

SEQUENCE OF STEPS

Command: **3dpoly**(↵)

To issue 3dpoly from the menu system: **3D|3dpoly**

From point: [*Pick beginning point.*]

Close/Undo/<Endpoint of line>: [*Pick next point of line.*]

Close/Undo/<Endpoint of line>: [*Continue to pick points for additional line segments or press ↵ to end command.*]

OPTIONS

Close Connects the first point with the last point in a series of line segments.

Undo Moves back one line segment in a series of line segments.

USAGE

Unlike the standard polyline, 3dpoly allows you to draw a polyline in three-dimensional space using X, Y, and Z coordinates or by picking object snap points. Three-dimensional polylines behave like standard polylines, except that you cannot give three-dimensional polylines a width or use arc segments. Nor can you use the Pedit command's Fit curve option. To create a smooth curve using three-dimensional polylines, use the Spline Pedit option.

SEE ALSO

Pedit, Pline

3dobjects

The following three-dimensional object commands are on the 3dobjects menu, which you access from the 3D menu. You can access the same commands from an icon menu that appears when you pick **3D construction** from the Draw menu. These commands are actually AutoLISP functions that are loaded when you first pick **3dobjects** or **3D construction** from the menu system. Until these functions are loaded, you cannot enter them through the keyboard.

Box

Draws a box

VERSIONS

10

SEQUENCE OF STEPS

Command: **Box**(↵)

To issue Box from the menu system:
3D|3dobjects|Box
or
Draw pull-down|**3D construction**|**box** icon

Corner of box: [*Pick first corner of box.*]

Length: [*Enter length of the box or visually select a length using the rubber-banding line.*]

Cube/<Width>: [*Enter* ***C*** *to draw a cube or enter a width of the box or visually select a width using the rubber-banding line.*]

Height: [*If you enter a width in the previous prompt, enter a box height or visually select a height using the rubber-banding line.*]

Rotation angle about Z axis: [*Enter an angle for the box location or visually select a width using the rubber-banding line.*]

USAGE

Box draws a three-dimensional box with its base on the plane of the current UCS, as illustrated in Figure 12.10. You can specify width, length, and height using your cursor or by entering X, Y, and Z coordinate values.

SEE ALSO

Explode, Pedit

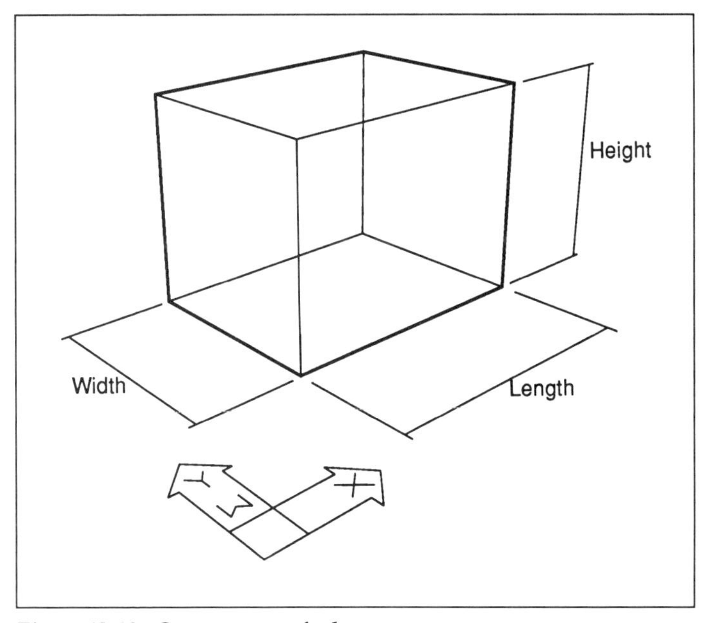

Figure 12.10: Components of a box

Cone

Draws a cone

VERSIONS

10

SEQUENCE OF STEPS

Command: **Cone**(↵)

To issue Cone from the menu system:
3D|3dobjects|Cone
or
Draw pull-down| **3D construction|cone** icon

Base center point: [*Enter center of cone base.*]

Diameter/<radius> of base: [*Enter **D** to enter diameter of base or enter radius or visually select radius using rubber-banding line.*]

Diameter/<radius> of top <0>: [*Enter **D** to enter diameter of top of cone or enter radius dimension or visually select radius of top using rubber-banding line.*]

Height: [*Enter height of cone.*]

Number of segments <16>: [*Enter number of 3dface segments used to generate cone or press ↵ to accept the default.*]

USAGE

Cone draws a three-dimensional cone with its base on the plane of the current UCS, as illustrated in Figure 12.11. You can specify the diameter or radius of its base and top as well as its height and the number of facets used to construct the cone.

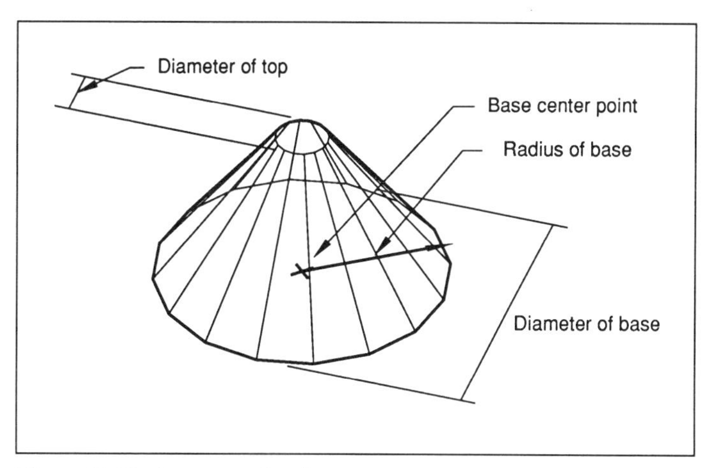

Figure 12.11: Components of a cone

Version 9 has a similar Cone AutoLISP function but you can only access it via the 3D Objects option from the Options pull-down menu.

SEE ALSO

Explode, Pedit

Dish

Draws a dish shape

VERSIONS

10

SEQUENCE OF STEPS

Command: **Dish**(↵)

To issue Dish from the menu system:
3D|3dobjects|Dish
or
Draw pull-down|**3D construction|bottom hemisphere** icon

Center of dish: [*Pick center point of dish.*]

Diameter/<radius>: [*Enter* ***D*** *to enter diameter or enter radius value or visually select radius using the rubber-banding line.*]

Number of longitudinal segments <16>: [*Enter number of segments defining dish in plane of current UCS.*]

Number of latitudinal segments <8>: [*Enter number of segments defining dish in Z axis of current UCS.*]

USAGE

Dish draws a three-dimensional hemisphere as a dish, with its equator on the plane of the current UCS, as illustrated in Figure 12.12. The dish is generated in the current UCS. You can specify the center of the dish as well as its diameter or radius and the number of segments used for its longitudinal and latitudinal directions.

Version 9 has a similar Dish AutoLISP function, but you can only access it via the 3D Objects option on the Options pull-down menu.

SEE ALSO

Explode, Pedit

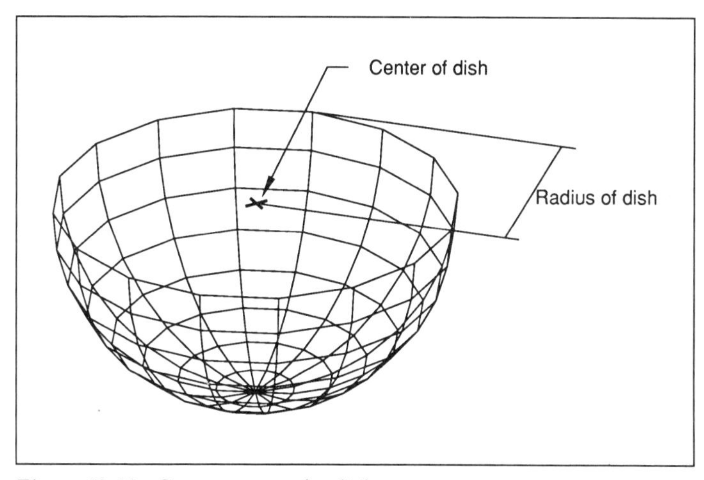

Figure 12.12: Components of a dish

Dome

Draws a dome shape

VERSIONS

10

SEQUENCE OF STEPS

Command: **Dome**(↵)

To issue Dome from the menu system:
3D|3dobjects|Dome
or
Draw pull-down|**3D construction|dome** icon

Center of dome: [*Pick center of dome.*]

Diameter/<radius>: [*Enter **D** to enter dome diameter or enter radius value or visually select radius using the rubber-banding line.*]

Number of longitudinal segments <16>: [*Enter number of segments defining dome in the plane of the current UCS.*]

Number of latitudinal segments <8>: [*Enter number of segments defining dome in the Z axis.*]

USAGE

Dome draws a three-dimensional hemisphere as a dome, with its base on the plane of the current UCS, as illustrated in Figure 12.13. The dome is generated in the current UCS. You can specify the center of the dome as well as its diameter or radius and the number of segments used for its longitudinal and latitudinal directions.

Version 9 has a similar Dome AutoLISP function, but you can only access it via the 3D Objects option from the Options pull-down menu.

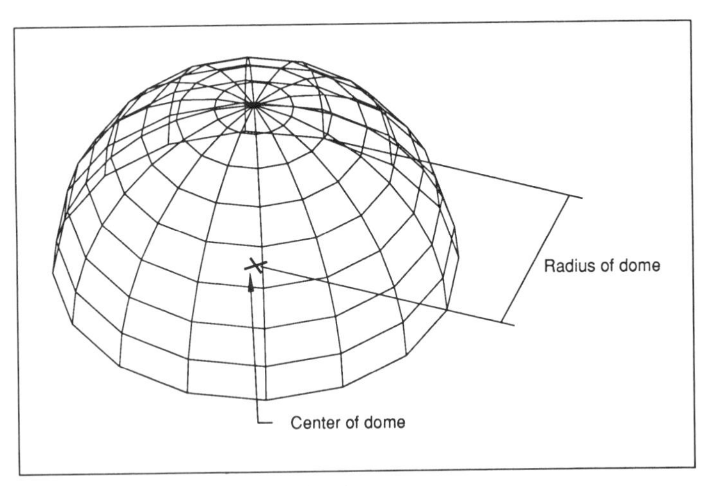

Figure 12.13: Components of a dome

SEE ALSO

Explode, Pedit

Mesh

Draws 3dmesh with straight edges

VERSIONS

10

SEQUENCE OF STEPS

Command: **Mesh**(↵)

To issue Mesh from the menu system:
3D|3dobjects|Mesh
or
Draw pull-down|**3D construction|mesh** icon

First corner: [*Pick or enter first corner of mesh.*]

Second corner: [*Pick or enter second corner.*]

Third corner: [*Pick or enter third corner.*]

Fourth corner: [*Pick or enter fourth corner.*]

Mesh M size: [*Enter number of vertices in M direction.*]

Mesh N size: [*Enter number of vertices in N direction.*]

USAGE

Mesh draws a 3dmesh defined by four corner points. These points define the four straight edges of the mesh and can be specified by either picking points using the X,Y,Z point filters (see Appendix A) or by entering X,Y,Z point values. You can also determine the number of vertices in the mesh in both the M and N direction. The direction indicated by the first two corners is the N direction (see Figure 12.14).

SEE ALSO

Explode, Pedit

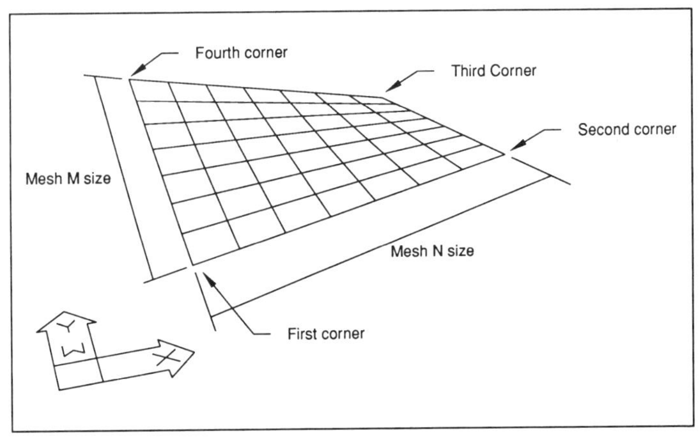

Figure 12.14: Components of a mesh

Pyramid

Draws pyramid shape

VERSION

10

SEQUENCE OF STEPS

Command: **Pyramid**(↵)

To issue Pyramid from the menu system:
3D|3dobjects|Pyramid
or
Draw pull-down|**3D construction|pyramid** icon

First base point: [*Pick or enter first corner of base.*]

Second base point: [*Pick or enter second corner of base.*]

Third base point: [*Pick or enter third corner of base.*]

Tetrahedron/<Fourth base point>: [*Enter **Tetrahedron** or **T** if the base is to be a tetrahedron in plan or pick a fourth corner.*]

Ridge/Top/<Apex point>: [*Enter X, Y, and Z coordinates for the Apex of the pyramid or enter **R** to define a ridge or **T** to define a four-sided top.*]

USAGE

Pyramid draws a pyramid shape based on points you enter for the base and apex. The base of the pyramid is placed on the current UCS. You can also draw a truncated pyramid by using the Top option. This option will prompt you for four points defining the top of the pyramid. These four points need not be on a plane parallel to the base of the pyramid. The Ridge option allows you to define the top of the pyramid as a ridge rather than a point. This option prompts you to select two points defining the ridge (see Figure 12.15).

Sphere

Draws sphere

VERSION

10

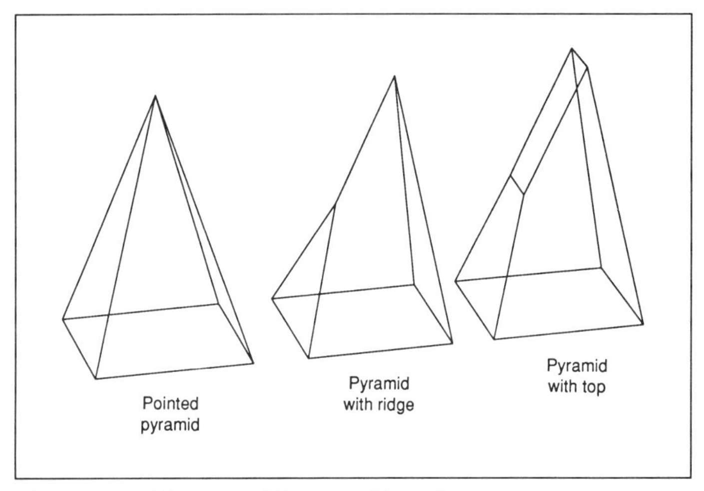

Figure 12.15: Three possible pyramid configurations

SEQUENCE OF STEPS

Command: **Sphere**(↵)

To issue Sphere from the menu system:
3D|3dobjects|Sphere
or
Draw pull-down|**3D construction|sphere** icon

Center of sphere: *<center of sphere>*

Diameter/<radius>: [*Enter radius or* ***D*** *to define diameter.*]

Number of longitudinal segments <16>: [*Enter number of segments defining sphere in the plane of the current UCS.*]

Number of latitudinal segments <16>: [*Enter number of segments defining sphere in the Z axis.*]

USAGE

Sphere draws a faceted sphere with its equator on the plane of the current UCS. You can specify the center point and its radius or diameter. You can also determine the number of facets used to draw the sphere (see Figure 12.16).

Version 9 has a similar AutoLISP function found on the 3D Objects icon menu. This menu is displayed when you pick 3D Objects from the Options pull-down menu.

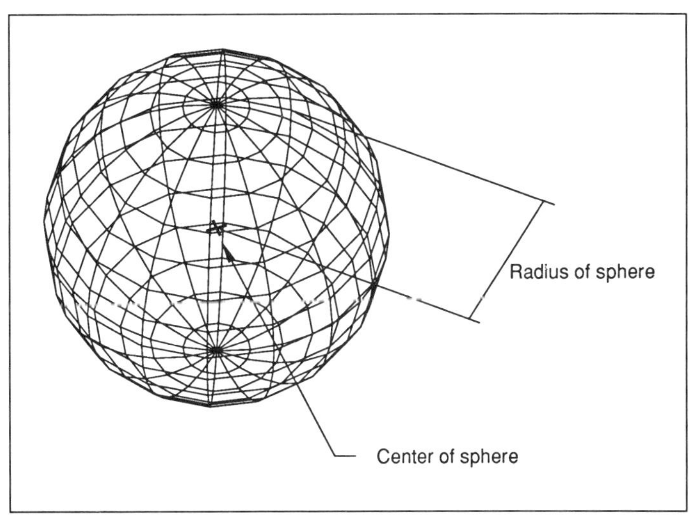

Figure 12.16: Components of a sphere

Torus

Draws torus shape

VERSION

10

SEQUENCE OF STEPS

Command: **Torus**(↵)

To issue Torus from the menu system:
3D|3dobjects|Torus
or
Draw pull-down|**3D construction|torus** icon

Center of torus: [*Pick center of torus.*]

Diameter/<radius> of torus: [*Enter radius of torus.*]

Diameter/<radius> of tube: [*Enter radius of tube comprising torus.*]

Segments around tube circumference <16>: [*Enter number of facets used to define tube.*]

Segments around torus circumference <16>: [*Enter number of tube segments used to define torus.*]

USAGE

Torus draws a three-dimensional doughnut shape or circular tube in the plane of the current UCS. You can specify an overall diameter or radius of the torus as well as the diameter or radius of the tube itself. You can also specify the number of facets used to define the tube's shape and the number of tube segments used to define the torus. Figure 12.17 illustrates the components of a torus.

Wedge

Draws wedge shape

VERSIONS

10

SEQUENCE OF STEPS

Command: **Wedge**(↵)

To issue Wedge from the menu system:
3D|3dobjects|Wedge
or
Draw pull-down|**3D construction|wedge** icon

Corner of wedge: [*Pick a corner for the wider edge of the wedge.*]

Length: [*Enter length of wedge.*]

Width: [*Enter width of wedge.*]

Height: [*Enter height of wedge.*]

Rotation angle about Z axis: [*Enter rotation angle of wedge in plan.*]

USAGE

Wedge draws a three-dimensional wedge shape with its base on the current UCS. The wedge's base is drawn in the plane

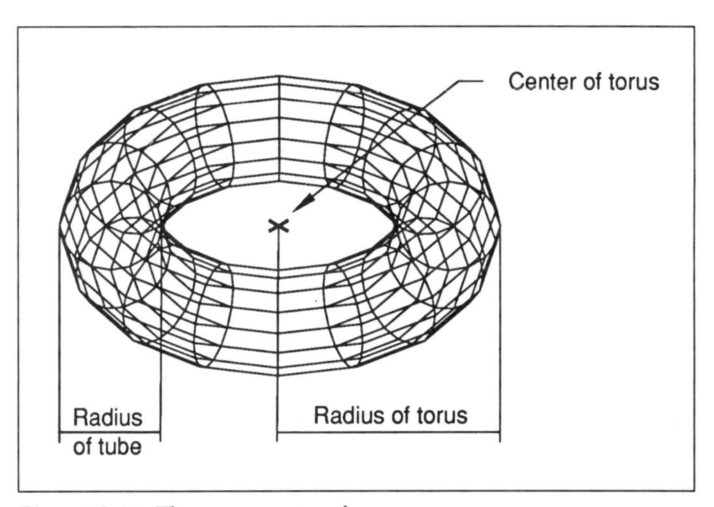

Figure 12.17: The components of a torus

of the current UCS. You can specify the length, width, and height of the wide portion of the wedge (see Figure 12.18).

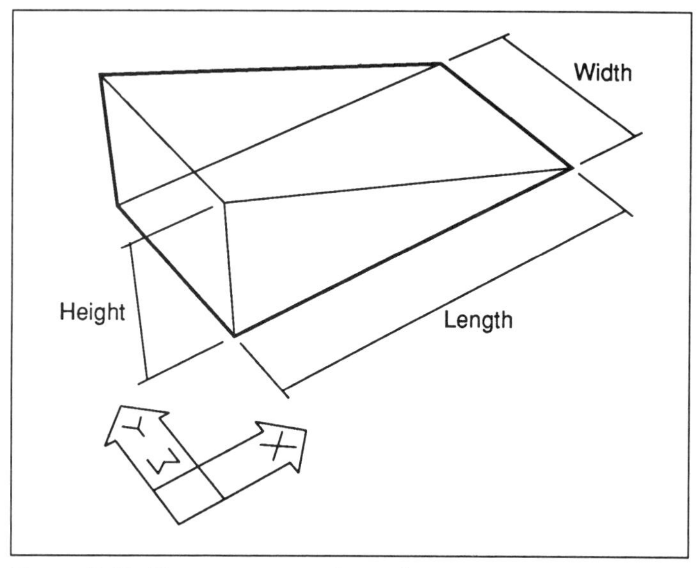

Figure 12.18: The components of a wedge

Hide

Removes hidden lines

VERSIONS

2.1 and later

SEQUENCE OF STEPS

Command: **Hide**(↵)

To issue Hide from the menu system: **Display|Vpoint|Hide|Yes** or **Display** pull-down|**Vpoint3D|Hide icon**. For version 9, **3D|Hide** or **Display** pull-down|**3D View|Hide icon**.

Removing hidden lines: <*number of vectors hidden*>

USAGE

Hide will remove hidden lines on an orthogonal three-dimensional view. Once you issue Hide, the *Removing hidden lines* prompt appears followed by a series of numbers. Those numbers count off the lines as they are hidden. In a complex three-dimensional drawing, Hide can take from several minutes to several hours. For this reason, you may want to use the Mslide command to save a three-dimensional view with hidden lines removed. To remove hidden lines in a perspective view, use the Hide option under the Dview command.

CHAPTER 13

Ashade Commands

This chapter presents commands you use to set up three-dimensional views for export to AutoShade, the surface shading program by Autodesk. These commands are actually AutoLISP functions, and they are loaded from disk when you first pick **Ashade** from the root menu or the Options pull-down menu. You cannot enter the commands through the keyboard until the functions have been loaded. Also, if certain AutoShade files are not present on the default directory, these functions will not work properly. These files are Camera.DWG, Clapper.DWG, Direct.DWG, Overhead.DWG, and Shot.DWG. You must have a copy of AutoShade on a directory in your disk drive and have a DOS path set to that directory.

If you pick **Ashade** from the Options pull-down menu, you get an icon menu containing the options found on the Ashade menu. Version 10 users will have an extra function called Camview, described later in this chapter. Otherwise, there is no difference in the AutoShade functions in versions 9 and 10.

Several Ashade functions insert blocks into your drawing to help identify camera and light locations. These blocks are placed on a special layer called Ashade. You can freeze, or turn off, the Ashade layer to hide these blocks when you do not need them.

Meeting AutoShade's Hardware Requirements

AutoShade does not work on as many different types of hardware as AutoCAD. To use AutoShade, you will need an IBM PC/XT, AT, or PS/2 compatible with at least 640K of memory and with a math coprocessor installed. Most AutoCAD users will already have this equipment.

You will also need an IBM EGA or PGC (Professional Graphics Controller) display adapter or compatible, or a Hercules display or compatible. The PGC gives the best results but is the most costly of the display options. An Orchid Turbo PGA is also an excellent display option. Both the PGC and the Orchid Turbo PGA offer 256 colors, which produce smooth, natural shading of your model. Some display systems using the AutoCAD Device Interface will also work, but since AutoShade is relatively new, only recently written ADI display devices will work with it. Check with your dealer for more information on your ADI display.

A mouse is highly recommended but you can use the cursor keys if you don't have one. A Microsoft mouse or compatible is supported, or any input device that uses the ADI. Other options are the Koala pad, which is like a small digitizing tablet, and the joystick.

Output devices are limited to some ADI-supported devices and PostScript printers, such as the Apple LaserWriter or QMS PS 800 series laser printers. You can also use a color PostScript printer when they become available. If you want high-resolution shaded images, Linotronic 300 typesetters can output very high-resolution AutoShade prints. Because of its flexibility, the PostScript printer will be the device of choice for most AutoShade users. If you have an ADI input or output device, check with the manufacturer to determine whether it will work with AutoShade.

You cannot get AutoShade hard copy from plotters. Plotters are designed to output line drawings but produce poor shaded images, so AutoShade does not support them. You can, however, produce perspective wire frame images with

AutoShade that can be sent back to AutoCAD and then plotted through AutoCAD's output options.

Using the AutoShade Camera

AutoShade uses the analogy of a camera to set up and view your three-dimensional model. First, you set up the "shots" of your model while in AutoCAD by establishing your lighting, camera position, and view angle. Then you take your "pictures." Once you have taken as many pictures as you need, you send your film to AutoShade for "processing." In this case, the pictures are called *scenes* and the film is a file on your disk that contains information about your model, plus information about the scenes you have created.

An exception to the camera analogy is that scenes can be manipulated *after* they have been taken. AutoShade can change camera locations. It can also adjust light intensities and the amount of light reflected by your model. You can even adjust the type of lens your camera uses. This means that if you want a wide-angle view of a scene, you can change a setting in AutoShade to allow a wider view.

Light

Places a light source

VERSIONS

9 and 10

SEQUENCE OF STEPS

Command: **Light**(↵)

To issue Light from the menu system: **Ashade | Light** *or* **Options** pull-down|**Ashade**| **Point** or **Directed** icon

Enter light name: *<name for light>*

Point source or Directed <P>: [*Enter desired option. If you pick* ***Point*** *or* ***Directed*** *from the icon menu, this prompt is not presented.*]

Enter light location: [*If you entered* ***P*** *at the previous prompt, or if you picked* ***Point*** *from the Ashade icon menu, pick location for light source.*]

If you entered **D** for directed at the *Point source or Directed* prompt, or if you picked **Directed** from the icon menu, the *Enter light location* prompt is preceded by the following prompt:

Light aim point: [*Pick point to which directed light is aimed.*]

USAGE

Light places a light source in your three-dimensional drawing which AutoShade uses to determine how to shade the drawing. If you pick **Lights** from the Ashade menu or enter **Lights** at the *Command* prompt, you are first prompted for a light name. You can place as many light sources as you like, regardless of the number of scenes you want to create. You must, however, use the Light command for each light source you place in the drawing. You should be able to identify each light source individually by name. Next, if you picked **Lights** from the Ashade menu, you are prompted for the type of light source you want. You can choose between a *point source,* which is like a light bulb, and a *directed source,* which is like a spot light. If you choose a directed source, you are prompted for its aim point. Finally, you are prompted for the light location.

If you pick **Point** or **Directed** from the Ashade icon menu, you will not get the *Point or Directed* prompt, since you make that choice by picking one or the other directly from the icon menu.

Once you complete the sequence of steps, a block representing the light source is inserted into your drawing, showing the location and direction of your light source. This block will display the name you entered at the *Enter light name* prompt. You get a different block depending on whether you use a point or directed light source (see Figure 13.1). When picking the location and aim of the light source, you can use the point filters to select a point in three-dimensional space (see Appendix A). Later, while in AutoShade, you can adjust lighting intensity as well as the surface reflectance of your three-dimensional drawing.

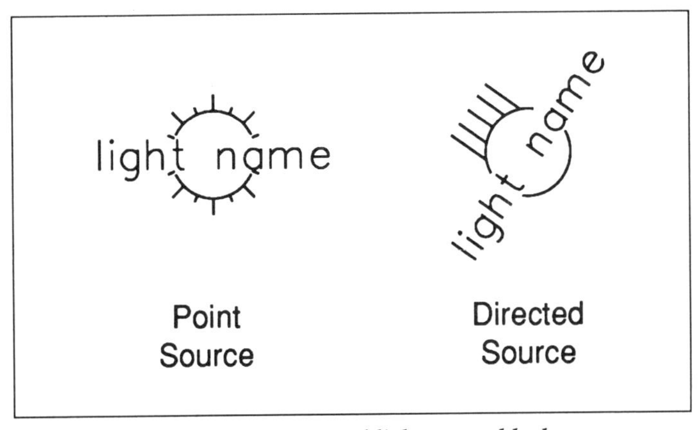

Figure 13.1: The point and directed light source blocks

Camera

Places a camera

VERSIONS

9 and 10

SEQUENCE OF STEPS

Command:**Camera**(↵)

To issue Camera from the menu system:
Ashade|**Camera** *or* **Options** pull-down|**Ashade**|
Camera icon

Enter camera name: *<desired name>*

Enter target point: *<center of camera view>*

Enter camera location: *<camera location>*

USAGE

Camera sets up your view. You are first prompted for the camera name. Since you can place several cameras in one drawing, name the cameras to help you keep track of them. You are then prompted for the *target point*. This is the point to which the camera is aimed. Finally, you are prompted for the camera location or your point of view. A block representing the camera is inserted at the camera location. This block will display the name you entered at the *Enter camera name* prompt. When picking the camera location, you can use the point filters to select a point in three-dimensional space (see Appendix A). Later, in AutoShade, you can adjust the camera's focal length, image frame, and position.

Scene

Creates a scene

VERSIONS

9 and 10

SEQUENCE OF STEPS

Command:**Scene**(↵)

To issue Scene from the menu system: **Ashade** | **Action** | **Scene** *or* **Options** pull-down|**Ashade**|**Scene** icon

Enter scene name: [*Enter name of scene for later identification in AutoShade.*]

Select the camera: [*Pick camera or enter its name.*]

Select a light: [*Pick light source or enter its name.*]

Select a light: [*Continue to pick light sources if desired.*]

Enter scene location: [*Pick location of scene clapper.*]

USAGE

Scene allows you to combine a camera with light sources to create a scene for AutoShade. You can create several scenes using different lighting schemes and camera positions and then save them to disk using the Filmroll function described later in this chapter. You can then view and edit your scenes in AutoShade.

Each time you create a scene, a block is inserted in the form of a clapper (see Figure 13.2). This block displays a list of the camera and lights used for the scene. This clapper block helps you keep track of scenes and their associated camera and lights; its location is not of significance. When selecting a scene name, you may want to use the same name as the camera, since you can only use one camera per scene.

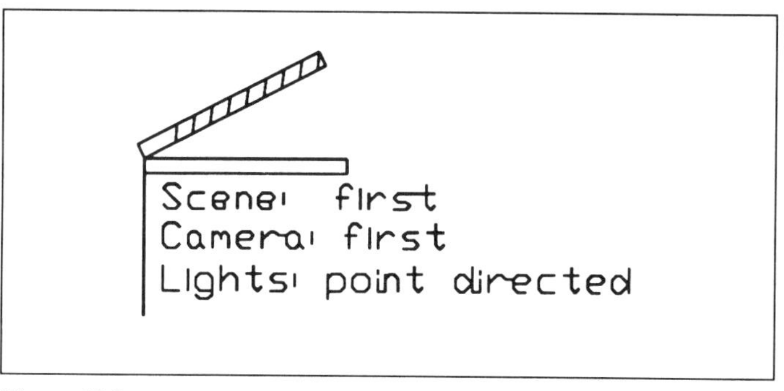

Figure 13.2:

Camview

Previews a camera's view

VERSIONS

10

SEQUENCE OF STEPS

Command: **Camview**(↵)

To issue Camview from the menu system: **Ashade** | **Camview** *or* **Options** pull-down|**Ashade**|**Camview** icon

Select the camera: <*camera*>

USAGE

Camview gives you an unshaded preview of what you will see in AutoShade. If you select the camera you wish to preview, AutoCAD automatically adjusts your display to show the perspective view from that camera.

Filmroll

Saves scenes to a file

VERSIONS

9 and 10

SEQUENCE OF STEPS

Command: **Filmroll**(↵)

To issue Filmroll from the menu system: **Ashade** | **Action** | **Filmroll** *or* **Options** pull-down|**Ashade**| **Filmroll** icon

Enter filmroll file name <*current file name*>: [*Enter desired file name for filmroll.*]

Creating the filmroll file

Filmroll file created

USAGE

Filmroll saves to a file on disk all scenes created by the Scene Ashade AutoLISP function. The scenes are saved in a format that the AutoShade program can read. Once they are imported to AutoShade, you can shade your three-dimensional drawing by adjusting lighting intensities, the surface reflectance of your object, the camera settings and location, and much more.

APPENDIX A
Getting Around in AutoCAD

This appendix explains how to get around in AutoCAD. It describes the main menu, the drawing editor, the keyboard and digitizing tablet, and the Setup option on the root menu. If you are new to AutoCAD, you should read this appendix to familiarize yourself with the screen layout and with techniques for cursor movement and point selection.

Before starting AutoCAD, check that it has been installed properly. Also, either a path should have been set to the AutoCAD directory, or the DOS environment should have been set properly so that AutoCAD can find its configuration files. See Appendix B for details on AutoCAD installation and setup.

The Main Menu

At the DOS prompt, enter **ACAD**. You will get the AutoCAD main menu (see Figure A.1). From this menu, you can open a new or existing file, plot or print a drawing, configure AutoCAD for your hardware, or perform file management functions. This menu always appears before you open a file and when you exit a file. To issue an option, enter its number at the *Enter selection* prompt.

```
          A U T O C A D
Copyright (C) 1982,83,84,85,86,87,88 Autodesk, Inc.
Release 10 (10/7/88) IBM PC
Advanced Drafting Extensions 3
Serial Number:  79-213123

Main Menu

  0.  Exit AutoCAD
  1.  Begin a NEW drawing
  2.  Edit an EXISTING drawing
  3.  Plot a drawing
  4.  Printer Plot a drawing

  5.  Configure AutoCAD
  6.  File Utilities
  7.  Compile shape/font description file
  8.  Convert old drawing file

Enter selection:
```

Figure A.1: The main menu

Opening Files

To open a new file, enter **1** at the *Enter selection* prompt. You will get the prompt:

Enter name of drawing:

You can enter any name eight characters long or less. Do not include the .DWG AutoCAD drawing file extension. If you wish to use an existing drawing as a template for a new drawing, enter the name of the new file followed by an equal sign and the name of the existing file. For example,

Enter name of drawing: *<new=existing>*

The existing file will be untouched and a copy will be loaded into AutoCAD with the new name.

To open an existing drawing, enter **2** at the *Enter selection* prompt. Then, at the *Enter name of drawing* prompt, enter the name of the file to be edited.

Plotting and Printing

You can plot or print a drawing from the main menu by entering **3** or **4** at the *Enter selection* prompt. See Chapter 9 for a complete description of the plotting and printing process.

Configuring AutoCAD

You can set up AutoCAD's hardware options by entering **5** at the *Enter selection* prompt. This option allows you to select a plotter, printer, pointing device, and monitor, and to specify certain aspects of the way they will operate with AutoCAD. See Appendix B for details on the configuration process.

File Utilities

You can perform basic DOS file maintenance by entering **6** at the *Enter selection* prompt. You can rename files, copy and erase files, and display lists of files through this option. See **Files** in Chapter 11 for details.

Compile Shape/Font Description File

If you have created a shape or font description file, you can use the Shape, Text, or Dtext commands to compile it into an AutoCAD SHX file for easy access from AutoCAD. To do this, enter **7** at the *Enter selection* prompt. Then enter the name of the Shape file with the .SHP extension. AutoCAD uses the SHX files to store compiled text fonts and drawing shapes. See **Shape**, **Dtext**, and **Text** in Chapter 4 for more details. You can create custom shapes and fonts by writing a description file using special codes; however, description files are beyond the scope of this book. You may want to refer to *Advanced Techniques in AutoCAD* by Robert M. Thomas (SYBEX, 2nd edition 1989) for details on this subject.

Convert Old Drawing File

If you created drawings on versions 2.0 or earlier of AutoCAD, use option 8 on the main menu to convert them to an updated format. This is especially important if you plan to import older drawings using the **Insert** command. Option 8 will rename your old drawing file, giving it the extension .OLD and creating a new drawing file. Also, you can convert multiple files at once by using DOS wildcard characters when specifying file names.

Normally, old files are converted automatically when they are opened. However, where the old file contains objects edited using the Repeat/Endrep command, files cannot be converted automatically. Use option 8 to convert these difficult files.

The Drawing Editor Screen

Once you have entered the name of a file, you will get the drawing editor screen (see Figure A.2). This is where you draw and edit. The following paragraphs discuss the various parts of this screen.

The Drawing Area

The center portion of the screen is devoted to drawing. This is where you select objects and pick points with your cursor. For version 10 users, the lower-left corner displays the UCS icon (see **Ucsicon** in Chapter 3), which tells you at a glance the positive X and Y directions of the current UCS. It can also show you the location of the current UCS's origin. If you see a W in the UCS icon, you are in the World Coordinate System. For more information about the **UCS** Icon, consult Chapter 8.

Using the Cursor Once in the drawing editor, you will see two crossed lines as you move your pointing device. These lines are your drawing editor cursor, with which you select positions on the screen when you create objects. When a command prompts you to select objects, the cursor will change in shape to a small square (see **Point Selection** later in this appendix). When you use the Osnap functions, a square appears overlayed on the intersection of the cursor (see **Osnap** in Chapter 8 for details).

Take a moment to look at the keyboard cursor keys. There are four keys with arrows on them. Each key moves the cursor in the direction indicated by the arrow. The cursor continues to move as long as you hold down the key. The Home key makes the cursor appear on the screen if it is not already there. The End key deletes the cursor from the screen.

The Page Up and Page Down keys allow you to control the distance of cursor movement. If you press **Page Up**, the cursor takes larger steps as you press the arrow keys. Pressing **Page Up** again increases the step distance of the cursor by a factor of 10. There are two step increments, after which pressing **Page Up** won't do anything. To reduce the step distance, press **Page Down**.

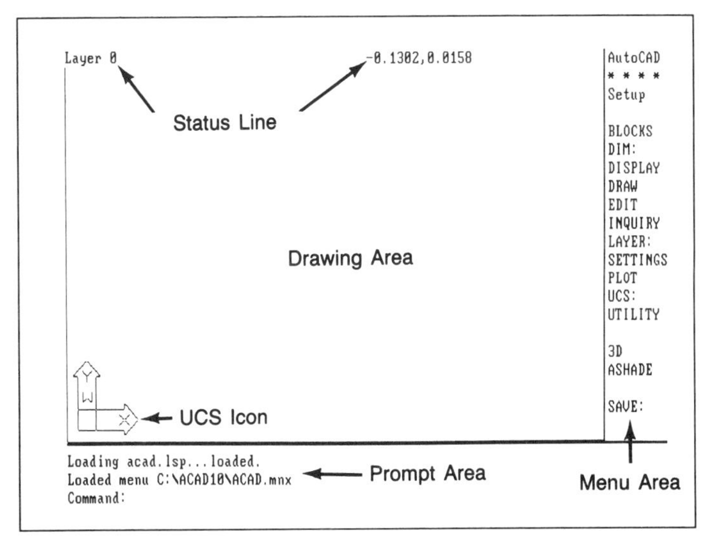

Figure A.2: The AutoCAD drawing editor screen

If you are using a mouse, you won't often use the arrow keys. You should know how, however, in case you work on a system without a pointing device. You can also use the cursor keys in conjunction with your mouse and the Snap mode and the Dynamic coordinate readout to accurately select points and distances. See **Placing the Cursor Accurately** later in this appendix for further information.

If you need to draw exactly vertical or horizontal lines, you can use the Ortho mode, which you toggle by pressing the **F8** key or the **Ctrl-O** keys. When Ortho mode is on, lines will be forced in a horizontal or vertical direction. Ortho mode will also force the line being edited by the Change command to a vertical or horizontal orientation. To draw lines at 30 or 45 degrees, it is probably easiest to specify a distance and angle through the keyboard using relative polar coordinates (described later in this chapter). If you need to draw a large portion of a drawing at 45 degrees, you can use the Snap command to rotate the cursor to 45 degrees and then use Ortho mode to force lines to be drawn at that angle. You can rotate the cursor to any angle you like. For more information on rotating the cursor, see Chapter 8.

The Menu Area

As shown in Figure A.2, the menu area is the right-hand portion of the screen. It contains in an easily accessible form nearly all of the available commands. When you first open a file, the root menu is displayed. Most of the options in the root menu are not actual AutoCAD commands but are the names of submenus within which you can find commands. This menu acts like the table of contents in a book, giving you access to specific types of commands grouped by function. When you pick an option from the root menu, another menu is displayed, showing you the commands that fall under the category of the selected option. For example, when you pick **Draw** from the root menu, a menu will display commands that relate to drawing. The Setup option on the root menu allows you to set up the working area of your drawing based on scale and final plot size. It is actually an AutoLISP program and not an AutoCAD command. See the

Setup section at the end of this appendix. The Dim, Layer, UCS, and Save options on the root menu are actual AutoCAD commands. Save will save the current file to disk (see **Save** later in this appendix). Dim, Layer, and UCS are described in chapters 2, 7, and 10, respectively.

Actual AutoCAD commands are denoted in the menu system by the colon. Whenever you see a menu option followed by a colon, the option is an AutoCAD command, though the spelling of the command on the menu may be abbreviated. In this book, each chapter reflects the contents of a root menu option.

Virtually every menu has the word "AutoCAD" and a row of asterisks at the top of the menu, and the options Last, Draw, and Edit at the bottom of the menu. Picking **AutoCAD** returns you to the root menu. Picking the row of asterisks displays the Osnap overrides, which allow you to select exact positions on objects (see Chapter 8 for details on **Osnap overrides**). The Last option returns you to the last menu used. The Draw and Edit options bring up the Draw and Edit menus, respectively.

Selecting Items from the Menu To pick an option from the root menu (or any of its submenus), move the cursor to the menu and highlight the desired option. Press the pick button on your pointing device to issue the option. As mentioned, picking options from the root menu displays other menus related to those options.

To pick a menu option without a mouse, type the first one, two, or three letters of the option. If two or more options have the same first letter, just type more letters in the name of the desired option until it is highlighted. Press the **Backspace** key after entering a few letters and the cursor will back up to previously highlighted options. To issue a highlighted option, press the **Ins** key at the bottom of the cursor keys. You can also get the cursor to move from the drawing area to the menu by pressing the **Ins** key. Once the highlight bar appears in the menu area, you can also use the ↑ and ↓ keys to highlight a menu option.

The Prompt Area

The bottom portion of the screen shown in Figure A.2 is devoted to the command prompts and your input. This is where you communicate with AutoCAD. Your keyboard entry as well as AutoCAD's response to your input will appear in this area.

At times, you may want to view information that has scrolled off the prompt area. If you press **F1**, you will see a text-only screen that displays the most recent 25 lines of command entries and prompts. Some commands that display textual information automatically switch the screen to text mode. If this occurs, you can press **F1** to return to the graphic screen. If you are viewing a text screen that is larger than 25 lines, you can press **Ctrl-S** to stop and start the scrolling of the text display.

The Status Line

At the top of the screen shown in Figure A.2, you will see the status line. At the left are the names of any active modes plus the current active layer (see **Keyboard Access to Modes** later in this appendix). Toward the center is the location of the cursor in absolute X,Y or relative polar coordinates. You can use the **F6** function key to toggle between three coordinate readout modes. The Static coordinate readout mode displays the absolute coordinate of points as you pick them. This mode is the default when you open a file. Dynamic X,Y readout mode displays the absolute X,Y coordinate of the cursor as it moves. Relative polar readout mode displays the cursor location in the relative polar format as it moves. In this mode, whenever you are prompted to select a point, the readout displays a coordinate relative to the last point picked.

The Pull-Down Menu Bar

If you are using a display device that supports the Advanced User Interface (AUI), you can use the pull-down menus, icon menus, and dialog boxes. The IBM CGA, EGA, VGA, or 8514 display or compatible or a Hercules display or compatible all support the AUI. Also supported is the Compaq Portable III Plasma Display. For support of other display devices, consult the manufacturer.

To activate the pull-down menus, move the cursor to the top of the screen. The pull-down menu bar appears. To "pull down" a menu, highlight the desired category on the menu bar and press your pointing device's pick button. The pull-down menu you've chosen will appear. Figure A.3 shows the screen with the Tools pull-down menu selected.

Some of the options on both the pull-down menus and the screen menu activate *dialog boxes* (see Figure A.4). These are like checklists that temporarily overlay the drawing editor and provide an alternative method for entering command options.

Some of the options on the pull-down menu activate *icon menus* (see Figure A.5). These are menus that display command options in a graphic form, such as hatch patterns and text fonts. You can also create custom icon menus for symbols libraries.

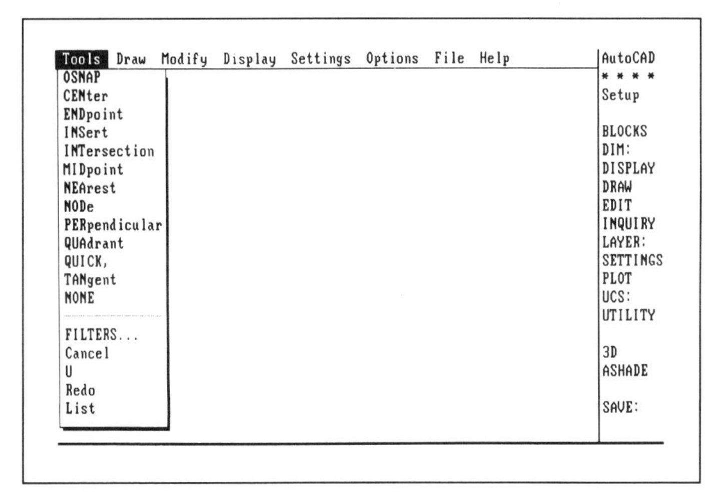

Figure A.3: The drawing editor with a pull-down menu (Tools) selected

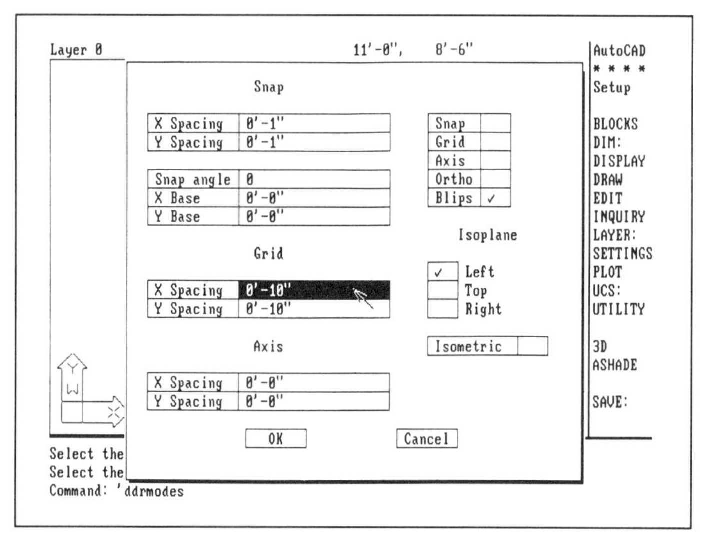

Figure A.4: The Drawing Aids dialog box

The Multiple Command Modifier When using AutoCAD's Draw, Edit, or Modify pull-down menus, you may notice that commands act differently when picked from any of these pull-down menus than they act when picked from other menus. At the end of the command sequence, instead of returning to the *Command* prompt, AutoCAD reissues the command last used. You can use the same feature while entering commands from the keyboard by preceding the command with the word "Multiple," as in the following example:

Command: **Multiple Copy**(↵)

Select objects:

If you enter this example at the *Command* prompt, the Copy command will operate in the usual way, displaying a *Select objects* prompt. But once you complete the command, instead of getting the *Command* prompt, you will get the *Select*

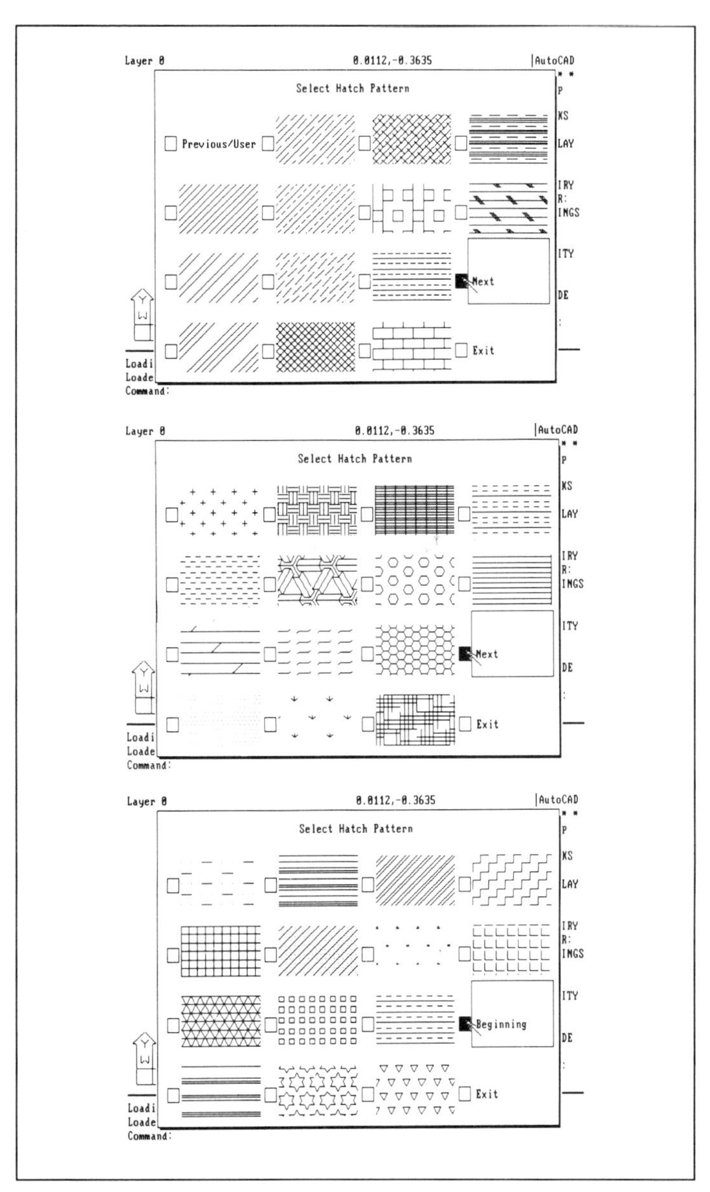

Figure A.5: The three hatch pattern icon menus

objects prompt again, allowing you to copy more objects. To exit the command and return to the *Command* prompt, enter **Ctrl-C**. The Multiple command modifier is handy when you are using the same command repeatedly.

The Tablet Menu

If you have a digitizing tablet, you can use AutoCAD's tablet menu (see Figure A.6). See Appendix B for details on how to

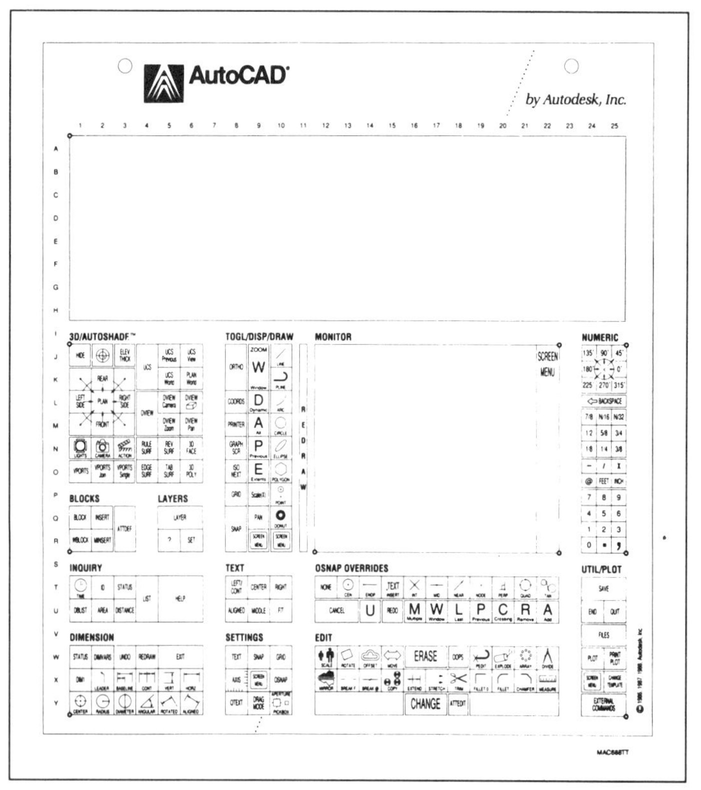

Figure A.6: The AutoCAD tablet menu courtesy of Autodesk Inc.

configure the tablet options for use with the tablet menu. Both the command name and an icon representing the command are displayed in boxes. These boxes are grouped into categories similar to those on the root menu. To activate a command from the tablet, move your pointing device to the box representing the desired command and press the pick button. Commands you pick from the tablet menu will often display a corresponding screen menu to allow you to pick the command options. The blank area at the top of the tablet menu is reserved for additional custom menu options.

Keyboard Access to Modes

AutoCAD offers several drawing modes. You can toggle on or off most of these modes via the keyboard. Table A.1 lists the drawing modes and their keys. Some of these modes are displayed on the status line in the upper-left corner of the screen when they are on.

Drawing Setup

AutoCAD provides a Setup program that establishes a drawing area based on your drawing scale and sheet size. The Setup program also automatically selects a unit style, such as architectural or decimal, based on the unit type you select during the setup process (see **Units** in Chapter 8 for details on unit types).

SEQUENCE OF STEPS

Command: **Setup**(↵)

Loading setup...

Select the units from the screen menu: [*The menu will display a list of unit types available. Pick one.*]

MODE	FUNCTION KEY	CONTROL KEY	COMMENTS
Flip screen	F1	n/a	Flips from graphics screen to text screen on single screen systems.
Snap	F9	Ctrl-B	Displayed on status line when on. See **Snap** in Chapter 8.
Coord	F6	Ctrl-D	Toggles Dynamic coordinate readout.
Isoplane	n/a	Ctrl-E	Only applicable when Snap style is set to Isometric. See **Snap** in Chapter 8.
Grid	F7	Ctrl-G	Displays grid when on. See **Grid** in Chapter 8.
Ortho	F8	Ctrl-O	Forces lines to be drawn at 0 or 90 degrees. Displayed on status line when on.
Echo text screen	n/a	Ctrl-Q	Sends all information displayed on text screen to printer. You can also use Shift-Prt-Scr to print current text screen.
Tablet	F10	Ctrl-T	Only applicable when tracing with digitizing tablet. See **Tablet** in Chapter 8.

Table A.1: AutoCAD Drawing Modes

Select a scale from the screen menu: [*The menu will display a list of scales available. Pick one.*]

Select the paper size from the screen menu: [*The menu will display a list of paper sizes available. Pick one or pick **VERTCAL>** if you want to the sheet to be oriented vertically.*]

USAGE

At the *Select a scale* prompt, you are presented with a set of predefined scales. You can also pick **Other** from the menu to enter a scale not shown on the menu. You then get the prompt

Enter the scale:

You must enter a single numeric value representing the desired scale. For example, if you want a scale of 1" equals 35′, enter the value of 12" × 35′ or 420.

At the *Select the paper size* prompt, you are presented with a set of predefined paper sizes. You can also pick **Other** from the menu to enter a paper size not shown on the menu. You will get the prompts

Enter the Horizontal Dimension of the paper:

Enter the Vertical Dimension of the paper:

Enter the desired paper size at each prompt.

When the setup is complete, a border is drawn indicating the edges of the drawing sheet. This border represents the drawing limits (see **Limits** in Chapter 8). Since this border represents the drawing sheet edge, its top and right sides will not be plotted. This is due to the margin of approximately 3/8" that most plotters leave around the drawing sheet. Plotters usually place the drawing origin in the lower-left corner of the sheet offset by the amount of the margin. You should draw another border inside the one provided by the Setup program and delete the original border.

Point Selection

AutoCAD commands that prompt you for point selection allow you to enter points by picking a point with your cursor, entering an absolute or relative coordinate value, or entering a relative polar coordinate. This section describes these methods of point selection and the filters you use to select three-dimensional points.

Entering Absolute Coordinates

You enter an absolute coordinate location by giving the X, Y, and Z coordinate values separated by commas, as in the following example:

Select point: **6,3,1**

This sample shows how to enter an absolute coordinate location of 6 in the X axis, 3 in the Y axis, and 1 in the Z axis. If you omit the Z value, AutoCAD assumes the current default Z value (see the **Elev** command for setting the current Z default value). Absolute coordinates use the current UCS's origin for the point of reference.

Entering Relative Coordinates

You enter relative coordinates as you enter absolute coordinates, but you precede them by an at sign (@), as in the following example:

Select point: **@6,3,1**

This example shows how to enter a relative distance of 6 units in the X axis, 3 in the Y axis, and 1 in the Z axis. If you omit the Z value, AutoCAD assumes the current default Z value (see the **Elev** command for setting the Z default value). Relative coordinates use the last point entered as the point of reference. To tell AutoCAD to use the last point selected, simply enter the at sign by itself at a point selection prompt.

Entering Relative Polar Coordinates

You enter relative polar coordinates by giving the distance preceded by an at sign and followed by a less-than sign and the angle, as in the following example:

Select point: **@6<45**

This example shows what to enter for a relative distance of 6 units at a 45-degree angle from the last point entered.

XYZ Point Filters

AutoCAD offers a method for three-dimensional point selection called *filtering*. Filtering allows you to enter an X, Y, or Z value by telling AutoCAD to use only the X, Y, or Z value of a selected point and then entering that point's remaining coordinate values. The following sequence of steps picks a point with a Z value of 4 while using the 3dface command:

Command: **3dface(↵)**

First point: **.xy(↵)**

[*Or pick* ***.xy*** *from the 3dface menu or from the Filters menu on the Tools pull-down menu.*]

of: *<start point>*

(need Z): [*Enter* ***4*** *for the Z coordinate value for point selected.*]

Next point: [*Continue to pick points using point filters if desired.*]

By entering **.xy** at the *First point* prompt, you tell AutoCAD to use only the X and Y components of the points selected to locate the point. After you pick a point, you are prompted for the Z value, which you can enter through the keyboard. You can continue to enter points using the .xy filter, thereby controlling the Z value of each point you enter.

Selecting Points Using the Cursor

Most of the time, you will use the cursor to input points. This section describes some of the methods and tools you can use to accurately place your cursor where you need it.

Using the Osnap Overrides The Osnap overrides allow you to select specific points on an object such as the end point or midpoint of a line. They are on the menu that appears when you pick the row of asterisks near the top of any menu or on the Tools pull-down menu.

To use these overrides, pick the desired override from the menu or enter its name at any point selection prompt, as in the following example:

Command: **Move**(↵)

Select objects: *<objects to move>*

Base point or displacement: **Endpoint**(↵) [*Or pick end point from the Asterisks menu or the Tools pull-down menu. A square will appear superimposed on the cursor intersection.*]

ENDPOINT of *<line end point>*

Second point of displacement: [*Pick another Osnap override, pick a point, or enter a distance.*]

This example uses the end point override to select the end point of a line as the base point for a move.

You can use the Osnap command to make one or several of the Osnap options active at all times. See **Osnap** in Chapter 8 for setting default Osnap modes and for more detailed information on all of the Osnap override options.

Drawing Orthogonal Lines You will often want to draw lines orthogonally—that is, in an exact horizontal and vertical direction. In hand drafting, you would use a T-square and triangle to do so. In AutoCAD, you use the Ortho mode. When Ortho mode is toggled on, all lines are drawn in an exact horizontal or vertical direction. You can toggle the Ortho mode by pressing the **F8** key or the **Ctrl-O** keys. When this mode is on, the word "Ortho" is displayed in the status line toward the top of the drawing editor screen.

At times, you will want to rotate your cursor to draw orthogonal lines at an angle other than 0 and 90 degrees. You can rotate the cursor by using the Rotate option under the Snap command. Then, using the Ortho mode, you can draw orthogonal lines at the angle of the cursor. See **Snap** in Chapter 8 for details on how to rotate the cursor.

Placing the Cursor Accurately

Normally, you specify exact distances by entering them at the keyboard, as described earlier in this appendix. However, you can also use your pointing device along with the Snap command, the dynamic coordinate readout, and the cursor keys to pick points and distances accurately.

The Snap function forces the cursor to move in exact increments that you specify. For example, you can set Snap for a distance of 0.125 or 1/8". Once this is done, your cursor will move in exact 0.125" increments. You can then turn the Snap mode on or off by pressing the **F9** key or the **Ctrl-B** keys (see **Snap** in Chapter 8 for details on how to set the snap distance).

The coordinate readout on the status line toward the top of the drawing editor displays the location of the cursor. You can use the F6 function key to toggle to the Relative polar readout mode while picking a string of points during a command. This mode dynamically displays the cursor location in the relative polar format as it moves. In this mode, the readout displays a coordinate relative to the last point picked whenever you are prompted to select a point.

By combining these two functions, Snap and the dynamic coordinate readout, you can select distances accurately by reading them from the coordinate readout as you move the cursor. If you try picking distances using the dynamic coordinate readout alone, without the aid of Snap, you cannot get an accurate distance reading. With Snap on, your cursor must move in fixed increments and the coordinate readout displays distances in the increments set by Snap.

Sometimes, even when Snap and the dynamic coordinate readout are turned on, you cannot read small distances from the readout. This often occurs when you have reduced your view to display a larger area of your drawing. Your display is not accurate enough to register cursor motion small enough to match the Snap distance. As you move your cursor, the coordinate readout value jumps by multiples of the snap distance instead of the actual snap distance. If this occurs, you can first get an approximate distance by using your pointing device and reading the coordinate readout. Then you can switch to the cursor keys to zero in on an exact distance. Unlike a mouse or digitizer, the cursor keys will move the cursor incrementally at the snap setting regardless of the extent of your view.

Since the Page Up key increases the cursor key step distance by a factor of 10, you can increase the distance the cursor moves to 10 times the Snap setting just by pressing the **Page Up** key. For example, suppose Snap is set to 0.125" and you are moving the cursor using the cursor keys. If you press the **Page Up** key, the cursor will move in increments of 1.25". The Page Dn key will bring the step distance back down to the snap value.

Saving Your Work on Disk

As you work in AutoCAD, it is a good idea to save your file to disk at 15 minute intervals, to protect your work against power outages or computer failures. The Save command allows you to store your file on disk without closing the file and leaving the drawing editor.

SEQUENCE OF STEPS

Command: **Save**(↵)

To issue Save from the menu system: **Save** *or* **File** pull-down | **Save**

File name <*Current file name*>: [*Enter file name or press ↵ to accept the default current file name.*]

USAGE

Save stores your currently open file to disk. When AutoCAD opens a file, it places the file in random access memory (RAM) where all of your drawing and editing takes place. This memory is quite volatile; you can lose any information in RAM if power to your computer is cut off or if your computer encounters other problems. The Save command will copy the drawing information in RAM to a more permanent form as a file on your disk. Information kept on your disk does not depend on continuous electrical power to be maintained.

APPENDIX B
Installing AutoCAD

This appendix shows how to install, configure, and allocate memory for AutoCAD. If your AutoCAD system is set up and working now, these essential preparatory steps have already been taken, either by the dealer or by someone in your workplace. If that is not the case, you'll find the necessary instructions here. You may also need to reconfigure your system if you add or change peripheral devices, and you may want to use the configuration process to "fine-tune" your system to optimize its performance.

To follow these instructions, you need to use some DOS commands. If you need more help with DOS than is provided here, consult your DOS manual or one of the many excellent books available, such as Judd Robbins' *Mastering DOS* (SYBEX, 2nd edition 1988).

Backing Up the Original Disks

The program disks that came with your system are the most important part of your AutoCAD package. Without them, you have no AutoCAD program. It is therefore important to make backup copies of them and use the copies to install your program. If you make any fatal errors during the installation, such as accidentally erasing files, you will still have the original disks to work with.

To back up your original disks, use the DOS DISKCOPY command. You should have ready for copying as many blank disks as there are disks in the original program. Start your computer. Be sure that the DOS file Diskcopy.COM is in the current directory. If not, go to the directory that contains this file and enter

DISKCOPY A: A:

at the DOS prompt. For a system with two floppy disk drives of the same type, enter

DISKCOPY A: B:

This copies the entire contents of one disk onto another. You will get the message

Insert source diskette in drive A:

Press Return when ready.

This tells you to place the original disk in drive A and press ↵ when it is ready to copy. The exact message depends on the version of DOS you are using. Some versions tell you to press any key, rather than the ↵ key, when ready.

Insert disk 1 in drive A and press ↵. You will get a message similar to the following:

Copying 9 sectors per track, 2 side(s)

The number of sectors depends on the type of disk you are using. When the computer is done reading the original disk, you get the message

Insert target diskette in drive A:

Press Return when ready

Remove the original disk and place a blank disk in drive A. Be sure you place a new blank disk in the drive and not one of the program disks. Press ↵. You will get the following message when the computer is done copying:

Copy complete

Copy another (Y/N)?

Press **Y** for yes. Repeat the procedure for the remaining disks.

Be sure to label your copies exactly as the originals are labeled, including the serial number from disk 1, and place a write-protect tab on them once you are done. Put your originals in a safe place away from any magnetic sources. If you have a digitizing tablet, do not put disks on top of it because the tablet uses a small electrical field, which can destroy data on a disk.

Placing AutoCAD Program Files on Your Hard Disk

To install AutoCAD, you will use the DOS commands MD and COPY. MD creates a directory on your hard disk; COPY moves files from one disk to another.

Once your computer is on and you see the DOS C> prompt, check that you are in the DOS root directory by entering **CD**. If you are in the root directory, you will get the message C:\. If you don't get this message, enter **CD** to change your current directory to the DOS root directory. Next enter

MD ACAD

to create the AutoCAD directory. The light indicating hard disk activity will come on for a second. Place disk 1 in drive A and enter

COPY A:*.* C:\ACAD

This will place the entire contents of disk 1 in the Acad directory on drive C. Do this for all the disks except the ones containing the drivers and the sample files.

When you are done, place the support files disk in drive A and enter the following at the DOS prompt:

COPY A:\SOURCE*.* C:\ACAD

If you have 720K or 360K disks, do this with the last one. It contains a directory called Source that holds other files used by AutoCAD. This command copies those files onto the Acad directory, where AutoCAD will have access to them.

While still in the root directory, enter

MD \DRV

This creates a directory where you will place the AutoCAD drivers. Next, place the driver disk in drive A. Enter

COPY A:*.* C:\DRV

If you have more than one driver disk, repeat the COPY command for the other driver disk. This will place the AutoCAD drivers in a separate directory where you can erase them easily. AutoCAD uses these driver files to control the various hardware options when it configures your system. These files do not have to be on your hard disk for AutoCAD to run, but it would be a good idea to load them whenever you configure AutoCAD. Once you have finished configuration, you can remove the files from the hard disk and free up some disk space.

When you are done copying the driver files, enter

COPY \DRV*.OVL \ACAD

An overlay file is included among the driver files. This overlay must be present in the Acad directory for AutoCAD to run. Since you copied the driver files onto the Drv directory, the overlay is present in that directory. By doing the above, you ensure that all of the overlay files are together on the Acad directory. If you have 1.2 megabyte disks, enter the following:

COPY \DRV*.EXE \ACAD

Because the main program file is on the driver disk, you must also copy it to the Acad directory. If you have 720K or 360K disks, this step is not necessary because the main program is on an overlay disk or on a disk by itself. Once this is done, you can proceed with the AutoCAD configuration.

Configuring AutoCAD

In this section, you will learn how to *configure* AutoCAD. Configuring means setting up AutoCAD to work with the particular hardware connected to your computer. Programs often rely on their own drivers to operate specialized equipment. By configuring AutoCAD, you tell it exactly what equipment it will be working with.

The Basic Configuration

Change the current directory to Acad by entering

CD \ACAD

Next enter

ACAD

You will get the introductory message. Press ↵ and the screen shown in Figure B.1 will tell you that AutoCAD needs to be configured. You will also get the prompt

Enter drive or directory containing the display device drivers:

This prompt is asking for the location of the drivers AutoCAD uses to operate the equipment it supports. Enter

C:\DRV

at this prompt.

You will get the first of two screens combined in Figure B.2 (lines 1–20). The first item to configure is the display system. This is a partial list of the display systems AutoCAD supports directly. Below number 20 you will see the message to press ↵ for more. Before you do so, see if you can find your display system on the list. If you do, note its number. If not, press ↵ and display options 21–33 will appear. If you still cannot find your monitor, check its documentation to see if it is compatible with one of the types listed.

```
          A U T O C A D
Copyright (C) 1982,83,84,85,86,87,88 Autodesk, Inc.
Release 10 (10/7/88) IBM PC
Advanced Drafting Extensions 3
Serial Number:  79-213123
NOT FOR RESALE

AutoCAD is not yet configured.
You must specify the devices to which AutoCAD will interface.

In order to interface to a device, AutoCAD needs the
control program for that device, called a device driver.
The device drivers are files with a type of .DRV.

You must tell AutoCAD the disk drive or directory in
which the device drivers are located.  If you specify a
disk drive, you must include the colon, as in A:

Enter drive or directory containing the Display device drivers:
```

Figure B.1: Screen shown when AutoCAD is not configured

Enter the number of your display system at the prompt

Select device number or ? to repeat list <10>:

Next, you will be prompted by a series of questions similar to the ones shown in Figure B.3. These options vary somewhat among display devices, so the instructions here are not very specific. However, the following sections describe some of the more common prompts.

Adjusting the Graphics Screen The first prompt usually asks if you have previously measured the height and width of a square on your screen. At this point, you haven't been able to see what a square looks like in AutoCAD; you should skip this prompt during the initial configuration. Press ↵ to accept the default, N for no. Later, if you notice that circles and squares appear stretched in one direction or another, you can compensate for that stretch by reconfiguring your display and answering yes to this prompt. You will be prompted for

```
Available video displays:

   1.  ADI display v4.0
   2.  Bell & Howell CDI IV
   3.  Cambridge Micro-1024
   4.  Compaq Portable III Plasma Display
   5.  Control Systems Artist I & II
   6.  Control Systems Transformer
   7.  Cordata 400 Line graphics
   8.  Cordata Fast Draft 480
   9.  GraphAx 20/20 display
  10.  Hercules Graphics Card
  11.  Hercules InColor
  12.  Hewlett-Packard 82960 Graphics Controller
  13.  Hewlett-Packard Enhanced Graphics Adapter
  14.  IBM Color/Graphics
  15.  IBM Enhanced Graphics Adapter
  16.  IBM Multi-Color Graphics Array
  17.  IBM Personal System/2 8514/A Display
  18.  IBM Professional Graphics Controller
  19.  IBM Video Graphics Array
  20.  Matrox PG-640 (obsolete)

 -- Press RETURN for more --
  21.  Micro-Display GENIUS
  22.  Number Nine NNIOS Graphics Display
  23.  Number Nine Revolution Board
  24.  Persyst BOB-16 Color/Graphics
  25.  Quintar
  26.  STB Chauffeur Monochrome
  27.  Sigma Designs Color 400
  28.  Tecmar Graphics Master
  29.  VMI Image Manager 1024
  30.  Vectrix PEPE Graphics Controller
  31.  Verticom H-series Graphics Controller
  32.  Verticom M-series Graphics Controller
  33.  Wyse Technology WY700

 Select device number or ? to repeat list <1>:
```

Figure B.2: List of display options

```
If you have previously measured the height and width of
a "square" on your graphics screen, you may use these
measurements to correct the aspect ratio.

Would you like to do so? <N>

Do you want a status line? <Y>

Do you want a command prompt area? <Y>

Do you want a screen menu area? <Y>

Do you want dark vectors on a light background? <Y>

Do you have the Sun-Flex Touchpen? <N>
```

Figure B.3: Typical display option questions

the current width and height of the square, and AutoCAD will set up the display to make circles and squares appear correctly. However, this procedure is seldom required.

You will also be asked if you want a status line, a prompt area, and a menu area. These things are part of AutoCAD's normal operation. Press ↵ at each of these prompts to accept the default, Y for yes.

If you are using version 9 or 10, you will also be asked if you want to display dark vectors (lines) on a light background. Accept the default, Y, so that AutoCAD will display your drawings like plots or printouts, with black lines on a white medium. Earlier versions of AutoCAD offer white or colored lines on a black background as the default, and no other options are available unless you have a color display.

There may be options specific to your display device. For example, the prompts shown in Figure B.3 are for a Hercules display adapter. The last prompt asks if you have the Sun-Flex Touch Pen. This option is specific to the Hercules display, and you won't see it while configuring any other display device. Check your AutoCAD installation guide for detailed instructions on your display device. As a rule, you can accept the defaults (shown in parentheses) provided by AutoCAD. You can always change them later if you like.

Selecting Input Devices Once you are done configuring your display, you will get a list of input device options. Again, check the list for the number of your device and enter that number at the prompt at the bottom of the list. If you have no input device other than the keyboard, choose option **1**, None. Answer any questions regarding your input device. Again, since different input devices offer different options, this chapter cannot provide details. However, the prompts are usually quite clear. You will also be asked to select an adapter port for your input device with the following prompt:

```
Connects to Asynchronous Communications Adapter port.
Standard ports are:
COM1
COM2

Enter port name, or address in hexadecimal <COM1>:
```

If you have two asynchronous communications ports, or *serial ports*, you use this opportunity to tell AutoCAD that you want to connect your input device to a port other than COM1. This allows you to use two serial devices, such as a tablet and a plotter, without having to switch cables.

To connect your plotter to the COM2 port, enter **2F8** at the *port name* prompt. This is the address of the port within the computer's memory, expressed as a hexadecimal number. The prompt says you can also enter the port's name, **COM2**, but in my experience the name doesn't always work, while the address always does.

Be sure you plug your input device into the proper serial port. If you don't know which port is COM2, you may have to switch ports to see which one works. If you are using version 9 or earlier, the port assignment prompt does not appear. Instead, select the serial port by using the **Allow**

detailed configuration or **Allow I/O port configuration** option on the Configuration menu.

If you have a digitizing tablet, you will also want to configure the tablet menu provided by Autodesk when you send in your registration card. Since this is done outside the system Configuration menu, it is explained a little later.

Selecting Output Devices Printer and plotter configuration works like display and input device configuration. You are shown a numbered list, at the bottom of which a prompt asks you to enter the number of the device you wish to connect to. Enter the number corresponding to your printer or plotter. As with the input device, you are prompted for a serial port assignment. You are also prompted for the printer and plotter default options that are displayed during AutoCAD's Prplot and Plot commands.

Once you are done with the configuration, you will get a list of the devices you selected (see Figure B.4). Press ↵ and you will get the Configuration menu and a prompt asking for

```
Copyright (C) 1982,83,84,85,86,87,88 Autodesk, Inc.
Release 10 (10/7/88) IBM PC
Advanced Drafting Extensions 3
Serial Number:  79-213123
NOT FOR RESALE

Configure AutoCAD.


Current AutoCAD configuration

  Video display:       Hercules Graphics Card

  Digitizer:           Mouse Systems Mouse
    Port: Asynchronous Communications Adapter COM1 at address 3F8 (hex)

  Plotter:             Hewlett-Packard 7475
    Port: Asynchronous Communications Adapter COM2 at address 2F8 (hex)

  Printer plotter:     IBM Graphics Printer  narrow carriage

Press RETURN to continue:
```

Figure B.4: Screen showing configured hardware options

a selection (see Figure B.5). Press ↵ to accept the default, 0, to exit to the main menu. The following message will appear:

If you answer N to the following question, all configuration changes you have just made will be discarded.

Keep configuration changes? <Y>

If you wish to save your current configuration, press ↵ to accept the default, Y. You will return to the main menu. Now you can begin drawing.

Changing Plotter Pen Selection Modes

If you have a multipen plotter, you can control the pen selection sequence AutoCAD uses to draw your drawings. The default setting causes the plotter to plot each color completely before selecting the next pen. This works fine if your plotter has a self-capping pen holder. If not, you can set AutoCAD to alternate between pens more frequently so wet-ink pens are less likely to dry out.

```
         A U T O C A D
Copyright (C) 1982,83,84,85,86,87,88 Autodesk, Inc.
Release 10 (10/7/88) IBM PC
Advanced Drafting Extensions 3
Serial Number:  79-213123
NOT FOR RESALE

Configuration menu

   0.  Exit to Main Menu
   1.  Show current configuration
   2.  Allow detailed configuration

   3.  Configure video display
   4.  Configure digitizer
   5.  Configure plotter
   6.  Configure printer plotter
   7.  Configure system console
   8.  Configure operating parameters

Enter selection <0>:
```

Figure B.5: The Configuration menu

After you have configured your system as described in the preceding sections and are in the main menu, select item 5, Configure AutoCAD, by entering **5** at the option-selection prompt. If you are currently in DOS, start AutoCAD to bring up the main menu and then enter **5**. You will get a list of your devices and a prompt to press ↵ to continue (see Figure B.4). Once you press ↵, you will get the Configuration menu (see Figure B.5).

Pick item 2, Allow Detailed Configuration, by entering **2** at the option-selection prompt. Item 2 is labeled Allow I/O Port Configuration on versions 9 and earlier. This option offers a few more configuration choices. In versions 9 and earlier, it also allows you to determine the serial ports to which your input and output devices are connected (see **Selecting Input Devices** in this appendix). In this case, you are accessing plotter pen-selection options not normally shown during the plotter configuration.

You get the prompt

```
Do you want to do detailed device configuration? <N>
```

Versions 9 and earlier will display the prompt

```
It is possible to configure the I/O ports to which some
AutoCAD devices are connected, but doing so may require
technical knowledge and is normally unnecessary.
Do you really wish to do I/O port configuration? <N>
```

Enter **Y**. You will get a display showing your devices, plus the *port address* to which the devices are connected (see Figure B.4). Versions 9 and earlier will display a screen similar to the one shown in Figure B.6. As discussed under **Selecting Input Devices**, the port address is the memory location assigned to the port, expressed as a hexadecimal number. The addresses of COM1 and COM2 are 3F8 and 2F8, respectively, but you can also enter the names.

Press ↵ to continue. You will again get the Configuration menu. Enter **5**, Configure Plotter, at the option-selection prompt. A prompt will ask if you wish to select a different plotter. Press ↵ to accept the default, N for no. Answer the prompts as you did when you first configured your plotter. Usually the defaults will reflect your current configuration, so you only need to press ↵ at each prompt. If you are using version 9 or earlier, this is where you can give a port assignment to your plotter.

Next, you will be asked if you wish to *calibrate* your plotter. Calibration allows you to adjust the plotter for accuracy in plotting to scale; it is seldom required. Press ↵ to accept the default, N.

When a plotter plots a drawing, it will often plot objects in the same order as they were created. This can lead to lengthy plot times since the pen may frequently travel across the entire drawing just to draw a single short line segment. Also, frequent pen changes due to changes in layers will slow the plotting process. Pen motion optimization will reorganize the way objects are drawn so the plotter doesn't spend a lot of time moving and changing the pen unnecessarily.

Next you will see the prompt

> The pen motion optimization can be selected from the following list. Higher numbers represent more optimization.

```
Copyright (C) 1982,83,84,85,86,87 Autodesk, Inc.
Release 9.0 (9/17/87) IBM PC
Advanced Drafting Extensions 3
Serial Number:  10-113610

Current AutoCAD configuration

  Video display:       Hercules Graphics Card

  Digitizer:           Mouse Systems Mouse [IBM]
    Port: Asynchronous Communications Adapter COM1 at address 3F8 (hex)
    Interrupt: 4

  Plotter:             Hewlett-Packard 7475
    Port: Asynchronous Communications Adapter COM1 at address 3F8 (hex)

  Printer plotter:     IBM Proprinter model


Port configuration questions will be asked during device configuration.

Press RETURN to continue:
```

Figure B.6: An AutoCAD version 9 configuration with I/O port listed

0. None
1. Endpoint swap only.
2. Pen sorting + endpoint swap.
3. Pen sorting + endpoint swap + limited motion optimization.
4. Pen sorting + endpoint swap + full motion optimization.

Select degree of pen motion optimization, 0 to 4 <4>:

At this prompt, you can select from four options that control pen selection and plotting optimization. The default setting is 4, the highest optimization level.

Endpoint swap means that if lines are parallel the plotter will draw one line and then start the next line from the nearest end point. Without this option, the plotter will plot lines in whatever direction they were entered.

Pen sorting sorts pens so that all of one color is plotted at once. This is fine if your plotter has a self-capping pen holder, or if it is a single-pen plotter. You do not want this option active, however, if you have a multipen plotter that does not cap the pens. If this is the case, you should enter option 1. This will increase your plotting time, but you will save time by not having to fix dry pens.

Motion optimization causes the plotter to plot objects that are close together before plotting objects in another area of the drawing. If this option is not used, as in option 2, the plotter will plot your drawing in the order the objects were added, regardless of their proximity to other objects. In some drawings, the time required for the extra pen motion may be significant.

Once you have selected an option for this setting, you will be prompted for your plotter default settings, as before. Refer to Chapter 9 for the meanings of these settings.

After you finish selecting the plotter settings, you are returned to the Configuration menu. Enter **0** at the option-selection prompt to return to the main menu. You are asked if you want to save the current settings. Press ↵ to accept the default, Y for yes. You are returned to the main menu. You can now start a new drawing, plot an existing drawing, or exit from AutoCAD. You may want to plot a drawing to test your current plotter configuration.

Clearing Your Hard Disk of Unused Drivers

Once you configure your system, enter DOS and go to the Drv directory by entering

CD \DRV

at the DOS prompt. Next enter

DEL C:\DRV*.*

Be sure you enter this command exactly as shown here. You will see the prompt

Are you sure (Y/N)?

Enter **Y**. If you later change any device, you must reload the drivers onto the hard disk, enter the Configuration menu, and reconfigure your system to use the new device.

Configuring Your Digitizing Tablet Menu

If you own a digitizing tablet that you want to use with the AutoCAD tablet menu template, you must configure your tablet menu. First, fasten your tablet menu template securely to the tablet using the plastic registration pins provided with the template. Be sure the area covered by the template is completely within the tablet's active drawing area.

Next, start AutoCAD by changing directories to Acad and then entering **acad**. Because you must be in a drawing file to configure the tablet, open a file called Temp (actually, any drawing file will do). Select option **1** from the main menu and then enter the word **Temp** at the prompt

```
Enter NAME of drawing:
```

Once the drawing editor is ready for your input, move your pointing device to the menu area to the right of the screen. Highlight the word "Settings" on the root menu and press your pick button. Next, pick **Tablet** from the Settings menu. Then pick **Config** from the tablet menu (if your tablet has already been configured, pick **Reconfig**). You will get the prompt

```
Digitize upper left corner of menu area 1:
```

For the next series of prompts, you will be locating the four tablet menu areas, starting with menu area 1 (see Figure B.7). Locate the position indicated in Figure B.7 as the upper-left corner of menu area 1. Place your puck or stylus to pick that point. The prompt will change to

```
Digitize lower left corner of menu area 1:
```

Again, locate the position indicated in Figure B.7 as the lower-left corner of menu area 1. Continue this process until you have selected three corners for four menu areas.

Next you will get the prompt

```
Digitize lower left corner of screen pointing area:
```

Pick the position indicated in Figure B.7. Finally, you get the prompt

```
Digitize upper right corner of screen pointing area:
```

Pick the position indicated in Figure B.7. Now you are done.

AutoCAD will remember this configuration until you change it again. Quit this file by entering **quit** at the keyboard.

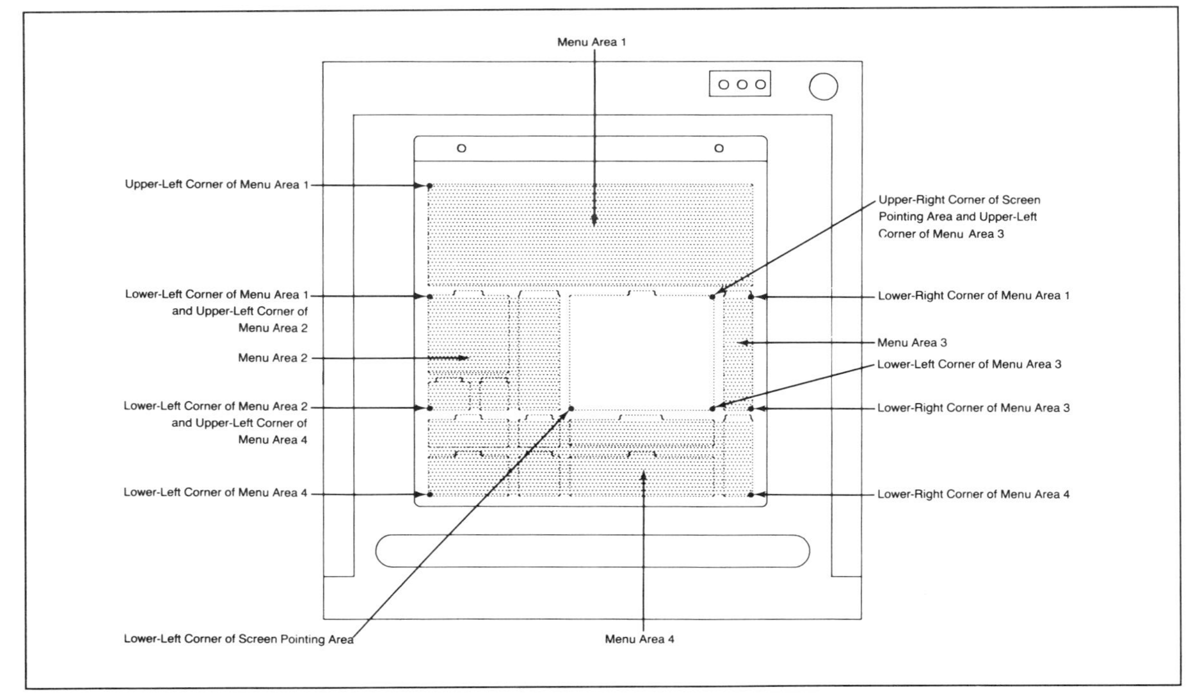

Figure B.7: How to locate the tablet menu areas

Or quit by picking **Autocad** from the top of the tablet menu, **Utility** from the root menu, **Quit** from the Utility menu, and then **Yes**. You will exit the drawing editor. Enter **0** to exit AutoCAD.

Solving Hardware Problems

The most common problem when connecting devices to serial ports is improper cabling and switch settings. Usually, proper cabling is supplied with the device, but sometimes it is not. The wires connecting the various pins on your cable must be arranged a certain way. If your plotter or other serial device does not work, be sure the cabling on your plotter conforms to the cabling diagram shown in your AutoCAD installation guide. Also be sure that the switches are properly set on your plotter or other serial device to receive and send data to AutoCAD. Again, you can find these settings in the installation guide.

Some devices require special setting up even after you have configured AutoCAD. These usually come with setup instructions. Check the manual that came with the device to be sure you haven't missed its setup options. When all else fails, call your vendor or the manufacturer.

Keeping Multiple Configurations

There may be times when you want AutoCAD configured in more than one way. For example, you may want one configuration, for presentations, in which the drawing editor's status line, prompt area, and menu area are not shown so that a drawing fills the entire screen. At the same time, you will want to use the standard screen configuration when you create and edit drawings. Normally, you would have to reconfigure AutoCAD every time you wanted to switch between these two configurations. However, you can use DOS to maintain several configurations that you select by entering different words to start AutoCAD.

The DOS features that allow you to maintain several configurations are batch files and the SET command. You will find it easier to apply the following instructions to your own AutoCAD setup if you are already familiar with these features. If you are not, you should first consult your DOS manual or one of the many excellent independent guides to the operating system.

As mentioned, when you configure AutoCAD, it stores the configuration information on files in the Acad directory. However, you can tell AutoCAD to store those configuration files in a specific place by using the SET command in DOS.

First you establish locations for these configuration files. The simplest way to do this is to add subdirectories under the Acad directory, each one being the location for a different set of configuration files. For example, you could create two subdirectories, one called Acad\Standard for a standard configuration, and the other called Acad\Clrscrn for a clear-screen configuration. You create these directories by entering

```
MD \ACAD\STANDARD
MD \ACAD\CLRSCRN
```

at the DOS prompt.

Once this is done, you need to create a batch file that allows you to specify which directory AutoCAD should look in for the desired configuration. This batch file could be named Gocad.BAT and be written as follows

```
SET ACADCFG=C:\ACAD\%1
CD \ACAD
ACAD
CD \
```

The first line in this batch file uses the SET command in conjunction with ACADCFG to tell AutoCAD to look in a specific directory for the configuration files. The %1 means that any word you enter after GOCAD will be placed where the %1 appears. For example, if you enter

GOCAD STANDARD

at the DOS prompt, DOS will place the word "standard" in the first line in the batch and will read it as

SET ACADCFG=C:\ACAD\STANDARD

Then when AutoCAD starts, it will look in the Acad\Standard directory for the configuration files.

After you set up the directories and create the batch file, you can start AutoCAD by entering

GOCAD STANDARD

You will be told that AutoCAD is not yet configured because there are actually no configuration files present in those directories. Configure AutoCAD as described earlier. Then exit it. Start AutoCAD again but this time enter

GOCAD CLRSCRN

Once again, you will be told that AutoCAD is not yet configured. Configure AutoCAD a different way by setting up the display to not show the menu, command prompt, and status lines. Do this by entering **N** at the prompts

Do you want a status line? <Y>

Do you want a command prompt area? <Y>

Do you want a screen menu area? <Y>

during the display configuration. You can then enter either **GOCAD STANDARD** or **GOCAD CLRSCRN** to get the desired drawing editor screen.

Allocating Memory for AutoCAD

Another way AutoCAD can make use of the DOS environment is to set up its own work space. Using the DOS SET command, you can adjust the total amount of RAM AutoCAD allocates for its work space and the amount of memory allocated to AutoLISP functions. You can also control the amount and location of extended or expanded memory AutoCAD uses for temporary files. The following sections discuss how to set these parameters. Once again, familiarity with DOS features such as the Autoexec.BAT file and the SET command will be helpful in following these instructions. Consult your DOS manual or an independent guide, for more information.

Adjusting the Free RAM

You can control the amount of RAM available to AutoCAD for calculations. The RAM work space, or *free RAM,* is normally about 24K (14K for versions 2.6 and 9). This is the default value when you do not use the SET command to adjust it. Complex drawings, combined with certain commands such as the 3D Hide command, will exceed the free RAM work space. When this happens, AutoCAD displays the message *Out of RAM,* closes the file, and returns you to the DOS prompt. You can use the SET command to adjust AutoCAD's free RAM by entering

SET ACADFREERAM = 25

at the DOS prompt. This will increase the amount of RAM work space to 25K. You must enter this value every time you start your computer, as it is lost whenever you turn your computer off or reset it. If the *Out of RAM* message persists, raise the value by 1 again. Keep raising the value until AutoCAD stops giving you the message. The maximum value for Acadfreeram is 30 (20 to 24 for versions 2.6 and 9). This fine tuning may take some time and experimentation, but it can save you from being dumped out of a file unexpectedly.

You can also lower the default to give AutoCAD more I/O page space for storing unused parts of files. This will increase AutoCAD's speed by allowing it to store more of the drawing in RAM before it must start paging to your hard disk. Follow the outlined procedure, but instead of raising the value by 1, lower it by 1 to 23. Open your most complex file and try editing it. Copy or move large parts of your drawing or import or explode large blocks. If it is a three-dimensional drawing, try removing hidden lines. If everything works, lower the value by 1 and test the file again. Keep doing this until you get the *Out of RAM* message. Then raise the value by 1. This will be the optimum Acadfreeram value for your work. The minimum value for Acadfreeram is 5.

Once you have established an Acadfreeram value you feel comfortable with, you can have it set automatically every time you start your computer by including it in the Autoexec.BAT file on your DOS root directory. This is an ASCII file that contains a series of commands for DOS to execute when you first start your computer; any instructions in this file will be executed.

If a dealer installed your software, the Autoexec.BAT file probably exists on your hard disk. The Acadfreeram setting may even be present in this file. If so, you can use your word processor to either modify the existing SET command or add it to the Autoexec.BAT file. If you don't have an Autoexec.BAT file, you can create one using your word processor, COPY CON, or Edlin.

Adjusting the Memory Available for LISP Functions

You can also use the SET command to set the amount of RAM AutoCAD allocates for your LISP functions. AutoCAD allocates two types of memory where AutoLISP is concerned: *heap* and *stack*. In very general terms, heap is memory used to store your functions and variables. This is also called *node space*. The stack holds arguments and partial results during the evaluation of expressions; it is critical when you have complex expressions. The default values for these types of memory are 40,000 for Lispheap and 3000 for Lispstack (or 5000 each in version 9 and earlier). This is usually adequate. However, if you get the message

```
insufficient node space
```

while attempting to run an AutoLISP program, you can increase these values. In most cases, the heap is the limiting space. If you get the preceding message, exit from AutoCAD and enter the following while in DOS:

set lispheap = 42000

set lispstack = 3000

In this example, you increase the heap space while keeping the stack space the same. If your expressions become very complex, you may want to increase the stack, but the total amount of heap and stack space cannot exceed 45,000 bytes. If you need to increase the amount of heap and stack space permanently, include these lines in your Autoexec.BAT file. If your system has a software add-on such as AutoCAD AEC, these values are probably already set in an Autoexec.BAT file that exists on your system. If they aren't set, follow the instructions that came with your add-on.

Using Extended Memory for AutoLISP

If you use an MS-DOS computer with an 80286 or 80386 processor and version 10 of AutoCAD, you can use extended memory for larger and more complex AutoLISP programs. Extended memory is memory above the 640K limit of DOS, addressable by the processor. It should not be confused with expanded memory, which you must purchase separately as a plug-in circuit board (otherwise known as Lotus/Intel/Microsoft expanded memory). You must have version 2.0 or greater of MS or PC DOS and at least 640K RAM for DOS and 512K RAM of unused extended memory.

To use Extended AutoLISP, you must have the following files in your AutoCAD directory:

Acadlx.OVL

Extlisp.EXE

Remlisp.EXE

Acadlx.OVL is a special overlay file that AutoCAD uses for Extended AutoLISP. Extlisp.EXE is a resident program that you must load before you start AutoCAD. Remlisp.EXE is a program that allows you to unload Extlisp.EXE to free DOS memory for other applications. Once you have these files on your hard disk and you are in the AutoCAD directory, enter **Extlisp** at the DOS prompt and then start AutoCAD. Go to the Configuration menu by selecting option **5** from the main menu. You will get a listing of your current AutoCAD configuration. Press ↵ and go to the Configure Operating Parameters menu by entering **8**. Enter **7** to select the AutoLISP features option. You are first asked if you want AutoLISP enabled. Answer Yes. Next, you are asked if you want to use Extended AutoLISP. Answer Yes and then exit to the main menu. AutoCAD is now set to use extended memory for AutoLISP. From now on, you must remember to load Extlisp.EXE before you start AutoCAD.

You can control the amount and location of extended memory used by Extlisp.EXE by setting the DOS environment. See the next section for details.

Adjusting Extended and Expanded Memory Use

Extended memory found on 286-based MS-DOS computers and expanded memory implemented by most memory expansion boards can be used by AutoCAD to store temporary files. These temporary files are created when AutoCAD runs out of room in RAM to store a drawing as it is being edited. Normally, temporary files are stored on the current default disk. Since AutoCAD must frequently access these temporary files, it will slow down considerably. When you store temporary files in expanded or extended memory, this slowdown is virtually eliminated. If either type of memory is present in your computer, AutoCAD will automatically use it. Expanded memory will be used first. However, you may want to control the amount and location of the memory AutoCAD uses. This is of special concern when you are using other programs that also use expanded or extended memory, such as the larger database managers, spreadsheets, and word processors.

Setting Extended Memory for Temporary Files and Extlisp To set the amount of extended memory used for temporary files, use the DOS SET command and enter the following at the DOS prompt before starting AutoCAD:

SET ACADXMEM=<*start location,size*>

The start location value can be anything between 1024K and 16384K, 1024K being the beginning of extended memory. Be sure you include the letter "K" after the memory location. The size can be any number but it must be followed by the letter "K." The following example shows what to enter if you have 512K of extended memory, the upper 256K of which you wish to allocate to AutoCAD:

SET ACADXMEM=1280k,256k

Note that there are no spaces in the ACADXMEM specification. The start location in this example is 1280K, which is 1024K + 256K. You can leave off the size value if you want to allocate all of the remaining extended memory to AutoCAD. Likewise, you can leave off the start location value if you want AutoCAD to select its own starting location. If you use only the size value, you must still precede the value with a comma. Finally, you can force AutoCAD to ignore extended memory by entering **none** in place of the start location and size value.

Allocating memory for Extlisp works in the same way as for temporary files. Instead of using Acadxmem, however, you use Lispxmem. As with Lispheap and Lispstack, you can include the Acadxmem and Lispxmem settings in your Autoexec.BAT file.

Setting Expanded Memory for Temporary Files To set the amount of expanded memory used by AutoCAD, use the DOS SET command and enter the following at the DOS prompt before starting AutoCAD:

SET ACADLIMEM=<*size*>

The size can be specified in 16K increments or in exact amounts. For example, if you enter **20** for the size, AutoCAD will allocate 20 × 16K, or 320K, of expanded memory for its use. You can also enter **320K** for the size to achieve the same result. Negative numbers will cause AutoCAD to allocate all but the amount entered for its use. You can also force AutoCAD to ignore expanded memory by entering **none** for the size value. You can include the Acadlimem setting in your Autoexec.BAT file to avoid having to set it each time you open AutoCAD.

Allocating Memory for the DOS Environment

For versions 3.2 and 3.3 of DOS, you may run out of environment space in which to store all the preceding AutoCAD settings. If so, you usually get the following message:

Out of environment space.

You can increase the DOS environment size with the DOS Shell function. Place the following line in your Config.SYS file in the root directory of your hard disk drive:

SHELL=C:\COMMAND.COM /E:512 /P

The DOS environment is usually given 128 bytes. The preceding example increases that size to 512 bytes—usually enough to store your AutoCAD settings and any other settings you may need for DOS and other programs. You can specify a larger or smaller size by replacing the 512 in the example with an alternate setting.

If you do not have a Config.SYS file, use DOS's COPY CON command or the Edlin line editor and create an ASCII file containing the following lines:

```
SHELL=C:\COMMAND.COM /E:512 /P
FILES=20
BUFFERS=32
```

The FILES=20 statement tells DOS to allow up to 20 open files at once. AutoCAD will open many temporary files in the course of its operation. Setting Files to 20 will improve AutoCAD's performace. The Buffers=32 statement tells DOS to store in RAM the information most recently read from the hard disk. Buffers improves overall disk access speed and therefore AutoCAD performance.

Improving Disk Performance

AutoCAD accesses the hard disk frequently to read its own system files and to read and write temporary working files. If your system has a hard disk with a slow access time, you may want to invest in a disk caching utility program. Disk caching improves the access time of your hard disk by storing the most frequently read portions of your disk in RAM. Since RAM access is much faster than hard disk access, you can gain an appreciable improvement in AutoCAD's overall speed by using disk caching. Most disk caching programs allow you to use expanded or extended memory for cache space. By using these types of memory, you can have a very large cache space without using up much of your regular system memory.

If you are using Microsoft Windows, you can use the Smartdrv.SYS program to set up a disk cache. This program is also provided with MS-DOS versions 3.3 and higher. Consult your Windows or MS-DOS manual for installation of Smartdrv.SYS.

APPENDIX C

Using AutoLISP Programs

To get the most from any CAD/CAM software, you will want to create some applications programs. No matter what software you use, you will probably find it lacking in some feature you need. This is why nearly every advanced CAD/CAM software package provides some programming capabilities.

The language you use to create AutoCAD applications is AutoLISP. AutoLISP is a form of Common LISP, the newest dialect of the oldest artificial-intelligence programming language: LISP. *Advanced Techniques in AutoCAD,* by Robert M. Thomas (SYBEX, 2nd edition 1989), has a good introduction to programming in AutoLISP. There are also numerous third-party AutoLISP add-ons to AutoCAD that provide specialized functions for architecture, piping, and landscape drawings, to name a few.

Programming in AutoLISP is beyond the scope of this book. However, this appendix explains how to load AutoLISP programs and briefly describes the programs supplied on the support disks. Some programs will simply show you AutoLISP's potential for enhancing your use of AutoCAD, others may prove to be useful in your daily applications.

Loading AutoLISP Programs

AutoLISP programs are usually ASCII text files with the .LSP extension. Before you can use these programs, you must load them while in the drawing editor. The files must be in the current directory or you must specify the drive and directory name in the following manner at the time of loading:

Command: **(load** "*drive*:/directory/filename"**)(↵)**

You don't have to include the .LSP extension in the file name. All AutoLISP functions are enclosed in parentheses. The load function in this example is no exception. Also, note that the forward slash is used, rather than the backslash normally used to designate directories. This often confuses first-time AutoLISP users. If the file to be loaded is in the current directory, you need not enter the drive and directory name. Once the file is loaded, the name of the program or a function within the program appears and you are returned to the *Command* prompt. You can then issue the AutoLISP program from the *Command* prompt, as you would any other AutoCAD command. However, you must enclose some AutoLISP functions within parentheses, as in the Fcopy sample shown later.

Loading AutoLisp Programs Automatically

If you find some of the following AutoLISP programs useful, you can combine them into a single file called Acad.LSP. Place Acad.LSP in your Autocad directory and they will be loaded automatically every time you open a drawing file.

You can use a simple word processor such as DOS Edlin to combine the files or you can enter the following at the DOS prompt:

type [*autolisp file name including extension*] **>>** **acad.lsp**

The file Acad.LSP will be created and the contents of the selected AutoLISP file will be copied into it. Be that sure the AutoLISP files you want are in the current directory and that you use a double greater-than sign. Do this for each AutoLISP program you wish to use regularly and then copy the Acad.LSP file to you AutoCAD directory.

Sample AutoLISP Programs from the Support Disk

The following sections briefly describe the sample AutoLISP programs supplied with your version 10 support disk. Some of these programs were also included in the support and bonus disks supplied with earlier versions of AutoCAD. Before you can use them, you must load them individually, as described earlier in this appendix. You can also combine these programs into a single file called Acad.LSP for automatic loading.

Edge.LSP

Changes visible edges of 3dfaces

SEQUENCE OF STEPS

Command: **Edge**(↵)

Display/<Select edge>: [*Pick edge to change visible/invisible mode or enter* ***D*** *to display invisible edges.*]

If you enter **D** at the previous prompt, the following prompt appears:

> Select/<All>: [*Press ↵ to display all invisible edges or* ***S*** *to select the edge of a specific 3dface.*]

USAGE

Edge allows you to easily change the visibility of edges on a 3dface. You may want to use this function instead of trying to control the visibility of edges while they are drawn (see **3dface** in Chapter 12).

3darray.LSP

Copies an array in 3D

SEQUENCE OF STEPS

> Command: **3darray**(↵)
>
> Select objects: [*Select objects to be arranged.*]
>
> Rectangular or Polar array (R/P): [*Enter* ***R*** *for rectangular array or* ***P*** *for polar or circular array.*]

If you enter **R** at the *Rectangular or Polar* prompt, you get the following series of prompts:

> number of rows (---) <1>:
>
> number of columns (|||)<1>:
>
> number of levels (...) <1>:

If you enter **P** at the *Rectangular or Polar* prompt, you get the following prompts:

> Number of items: [*Enter number of items in array, including originally selected objects.*]
>
> Angle to fill <360>: [*Enter angle array is to occupy.*]

Rotate objects as they are copied? <Y>: [*Enter* ***N*** *if arrayed objects are to maintain their current orientation.*]

Center point of array: [*Pick first point of axis of rotation.*]

Second point of axis of rotation: [*Pick other end of axis of rotation.*]

USAGE

3darray works like the Array command, except that it also allows you to copy or create the array in three dimensions. In both rectangular and polar arrays, a prompt is added that enables you to use three-dimensional space for the array.

Chgtext

Edits selected strings in text

SEQUENCE OF STEPS

Command: **Chgtext**(↵)

Select objects: *<text to be edited>*

Old string: *<character string to be changed>*

New string: *<new character string>*

USAGE

Chgtext allows you to edit a line of text without retyping the entire line. Normally, you use the Change command to change a word in a line of text, which requires that you retype the entire line. Chgtext allows you to specify a specific string of characters to be changed within a line, saving you from retyping the whole line.

You can also use Chgtext to change the same string of characters in a set of text lines. For example, if you have several notes in a drawing that read "1-1/2 inch pipe" and you want to change "1-1/2" to "1-3/4," you can use Chgtext to change all of the notes automatically. At the *Select objects* prompt, pick each note you want to edit. At the *Old string* prompt, enter **1/2**. At the *New string* prompt, enter **3/4**.

Dellayer.LSP

Deletes contents of a layer

SEQUENCE OF STEPS

Command: **Dellayer**(↵)

Layer to delete: *<name of layer to delete>*

USAGE

Dellayer will erase the entire contents of a layer.

Ssx

Allows selection based on properties

SEQUENCE OF STEPS

Command: (**ssx**)(↵)

or

Select objects: (**ssx**)(↵)

Block name/Color/Entity/LAyer/LType/Style/Thickness: [*Enter category by which objects are to be selected.*]

OPTIONS

Block name	Selects blocks by their name. You are prompted for a block name.

Color	Selects objects by their color. You are prompted for a color.
Entity	Selects objects by their type (for example, line, arc, circle, 3dface, and so on). You are prompted for an entity type.
LAyer	Selects objects by their layer. You are prompted for a layer name.
LType	Selects objects by their line type. You are prompted for a line type.
Style	Selects text by style. You are prompted for a text style.
Thickness	Selects objects by their thickness. You are prompted for a thickness.

USAGE

Ssx allows you to select objects by their properties in addition to the usual selection options (see the **Select** command for standard selection options). If you use Ssx at the *Command* prompt, the objects selected will become the most recent selection set, which you can act upon by using the Previous option from the *Select objects* prompt. Otherwise, you can use Ssx directly from the *Select objects* prompt to add objects to the current selection set.

Lexplode

Maintains layer of exploded objects

SEQUENCE OF STEPS

Command: **Lexplode**(↵)

Select block reference, polyline, dimension, or mesh: [*Pick object to be exploded.*]

USAGE

Lexplode performs the same function as the Explode command. However, instead of placing exploded objects on layer 0, it places them on the same layer as the original unexploded object.

Asctext

Inserts contents of ASCII file

SEQUENCE OF STEPS

Command: **Asctext**(↵)

File to read (including extension): *<name of ASCII file>*

Start point or Center/Middle/Right: [*Pick start point or enter **C**, **M**, or **R** for desired option.*]

Height: <default>: *<height>*

Rotation angle: *<angle>*

Change text options? <N>: [*Enter **Y** to specify text insertion options or press ↵ to import text.*]

If you enter **Y** at the *Change text options* prompt, you will get the following series of prompts:

Distance between lines/<Auto>: [*Enter distance or press ↵ to accept default.*]

First line to read/<1>: [*Enter number of the first line to be read from the ASCII file.*]

Number of lines to read/<All>: [*Enter number of lines to read from ASCII file.*]

Underscore each line? <N>: [*Enter **Y** to underscore each line.*]

Overscore each line? <N>: [*Enter **Y** to overscore each line.*]

Change text case? Upper/Lower/<N>: [*Enter **U** to change all text read from ASCII file to uppercase, **L** to change to lowercase, or ↵ for no change.*]

Set up columns? <N>: [*Enter **Y** to set up multiple columns of text or ↵ to begin importing file.*]

If you enter **Y** at the *Set up columns* prompt, the following prompts appear:

Distance between columns: *<distance>*

Number of lines per column: *<number of lines>*

USAGE

You can use Asctext.LSP to import ASCII text files into your drawing. This can be useful for general notes or large sections of text that are more easily handled in a word processor before you enter them into AutoCAD. Asctext has a variety of options with which you can control the text's appearance, such as underlining, line spacing, and columns.

When you answer the *File to read* prompt, use the forward slash (/) rather than the backslash (\) when specifying directories. You can also use the double backslash (\\).

Attredef.LSP

Updates and redefines attributes

SEQUENCE OF STEPS

Command: **Attredef**(↵)

Name of block you wish to redefine: *<name of existing block>*

Select new block...

Select objects: [*Select objects that are to comprise new block.*]

Insertion base point of new Block: *<base point for new block>*

USAGE

Attredef redefines attributes contained in a block. Normally, to change an attribute's location, orientation, size, or text style, you have to create a new block with new attributes, erase the old attribute blocks, and then reinsert the new blocks and reenter the attribute values. This is a time-consuming and difficult process. In contrast, Attredef automatically replaces all existing attributes with new attributes while still maintaining the existing attribute values. The attribute location, size, and orientation are all updated. Additional attributes in the new block are added and attributes not used in the new block are discarded. If the Handles mode is on, the replaced attributes are given new handles.

To use Attredef, you must first create the elements of the replacement block, including the attribute information, by using the Attdef command. Be sure the new attribute tags are the same as the old tags that you wish to maintain.

Ref.LSP

Reference point selection

SEQUENCE OF STEPS

[*at any point selection prompt*]: (**Ref**)(↵)

Reference point: *<reference point>*

Enter relative/polar coordinate (with @): [*Enter distance from reference point to desired point location using @.*]

USAGE

Ref allows you to pick a point in relation to another known point. For example, if you know you want to start a circle with its center at a distance of four units in the X axis and five units in the Y axis from the corner of a box, execute the following sequence:

Command: **Circle**(↵)

3P/2P/TTR/<Center point>: (**Ref**)(↵)

Reference point: [*Pick corner of box using the Endpoint Osnap override.*]

Enter relative/polar coordinate (with @): **@4,5**(↵)

The center of the circle will be placed at a distance of four units in the X direction and five units in the Y direction from the selected corner of the box.

APPENDIX D

Commands for Customizing AutoCAD

A few commands, used to customize AutoCAD, are not on the menu system. This appendix describes the Graphscr, Textscr, Redefine, and Undefine commands, which you can use to develop custom applications.

Graphscr and Textscr

Displays graphics/text screen

SEQUENCE OF STEPS

<any prompt>: **'Graphscr**(↵)

<any prompt>: **'Textscr**(↵)

USAGE

You can flip between graphics and text screens with the F1 function key. However, you cannot access this key from a

Script file or from a custom menu option. With Graphscr and Textscr, you can place instructions in a Script file or a menu option to flip the screen to text or graphics. If you have a dual-screen system, these commands are ignored.

Redefine and Undefine

Undefines/redefines AutoCAD commands

SEQUENCE OF STEPS

Command: **Undefine**(↵)

Command name: *<command name>*

Command: **Redefine**(↵)

Command name: *<command name>*

USAGE

The Undefine command allows you to suppress any standard AutoCAD command in favor of an AutoLISP program of the same name. For example, you may want to replace the AutoCAD Copy command with an AutoLISP program also called Copy. If you load this AutoLISP Copy command and enter **Copy** at the *Command* prompt, you get the standard Copy command. However, if you use Undefine to suppress the standard Copy command, you can use the AutoLISP Copy program.

If you need to enter the standard AutoCAD Copy command, you can precede the command with a period at the *Command* prompt, as follows:

Command: **.Copy**(↵)

Select objects:

You can also use the Redefine command to reinstate a command you suppressed with Undefine. You cannot issue an undefined command with the AutoLISP Command function unless you precede the command name with a period.

INDEX